Break-Out from the Crystal Palace

International Library of Sociology

Founded by Karl Mannheim
Editor: John Rex, University of Warwick

Arbor Scientiae
Arbor Vitiae

A catalogue of the books available in the **International Library of
Sociology** and other series of Social Science books published by Routledge &
Kegan Paul will be found at the end of this volume.

Break-Out from the Crystal Palace

The anarcho-psychological critique: Stirner, Nietzsche, Dostoevsky

John Carroll
Department of Sociology, La Trobe University, Australia

Routledge and Kegan Paul
London and Boston

First published in 1974
by Routledge & Kegan Paul Ltd
Broadway House, 68–74 Carter Lane,
London EC4V 5EL and
9 Park Street,
Boston, Mass. 02108, U.S.A.
Printed in Great Britain by
Unwin Brothers Limited,
The Gresham Press,
Old Woking, Surrey

ISBN 0 7100 7750 5

Library of Congress Catalog Card No. 73–89193

For my parents

Contents

Acknowledgments

I am indebted to Nigel Eastman, Anthony Giddens, Robert Marks, Peter Steele, Werner Pelz, Rainer Ruge, and John Hooper for various suggestions. This work was written as a doctoral dissertation for the University of Cambridge; it would not have been possible without the support of the Faculty of Economics and Politics. I owe my deepest gratitude, however, to George Steiner, who was much more than an academic supervisor for me. The entire project, from its initial formulation to its final detail, bears the stamp of his patient criticism and encouragement, applied with a rare sensitivity to the vicissitudes which beset the life and work of a research student.

1 Introduction: liberal-rationalism and the progress model

1

This study stands primarily as an essay in morals. It is governed by Nietzsche's contention that the moral intentions of every philosophy constitute the real germ of life from which the whole plant has grown. Hence, although the investigation broaches psychological, social, political, and economic, as well as philosophical, problems, its driving thrust is towards the question of ultimate values. At stake throughout the discussion is the question of how men conceive of whether what they do is good or evil, and what this means. Attention is focussed on the psychological role that their action, and in turn their evaluation of it, plays for them personally. An essay in morals concerns itself with the quality of what men do, with the metaphysical essence of human theories and practices. This study is at the same time an excursion in intellectual or cultural history.

Three different intellectual traditions, each of which developed fundamentally during the nineteenth century, have supplied contemporary Western civilization with its key social images of man. These traditions have exerted in their different ways a decisive and enduring influence on patterns of behaviour and social structure. First, there is the British, liberal, utilitarian, rationalist social philosophy which sprouted from the roots of the school of Political Economy, and provided the emerging industrial society with its guiding ideology. Second, there is the Marxist socialist tradition. Third, there is the tradition with which this study is centrally concerned, one whose principal interests are psychological and whose political orientation is anarchist. The first two traditions are well known; the third has been completely neglected by modern philosophers and intellectual historians alike.

This study will defend the proposition that what is referred to here as the 'anarcho-psychological tradition' developed in Europe between 1840 and 1890 as an original and coherent theory of human action. It

1

prepared the way for Freud's work, and for the subsequent modern interest in inner 'psychological man'. It also provided a theoretical representation of the habits and values, although often unstated, of individualist types such as the artist, the bohemian, *l'homme de lettres*, and the student. Finally, it played a crucial role in the emergence of the existentialist tradition.[1]

We are faced from the outset with the methodological problem of what constitutes an intellectual 'tradition'. No problem would arise if it were possible to set down clearly and distinctly a list of characteristics which define anarcho-psychology. Cultural history, however, is amenable to such a strategy only at a futilely superficial level, an assertion which this study as a whole will substantiate. What has been called 'tradition' is more accurately termed 'perspective'. The initial proposition states that a group of individual thinkers developed a new perspective on man's estate; they posed, largely independently of each other, a series of questions which had not hitherto been considered; it is the radical nature of anarcho-psychological questions which stakes out the ground common to its theorists, and makes it worthy of investigation. These thinkers do not found a tradition in the sense of an elaborated canon of principles which is then handed down and developed by the next in line. (Moreover, this study is not especially concerned with questions of direct influence of one theorist on another, or with the particular social or economic background from which any of them came.)

A metaphor, allowing for generous poetic licence, illustrates the methodological strategy to be followed. It is as if there were three dominant mountains in a perpetually cloud-covered range. The task is to map one of them by climbing it, and hopefully thereby get a clearer impression of the range as a whole. In order to fix bearings it becomes necessary to take sightings of the other two mountains from different perspectives during the ascent. Most of the time, however, is absorbed in close examination of the terrain which is covered, aided by comparisons with corresponding areas which become visible on the slopes of the two alternative mountains.

Three organizing principles are employed in reconstructing the genesis and some of the consequences of the anarcho-psychological perspective. First, the claim is made that before Freud this perspective had three outstanding exponents: Max Stirner, Friedrich Nietzsche, and Fyodor Dostoevsky, whose written works form the

---

[1] The claims of fascism and conservatism to be political philosophies significant in such a schematization are rejected on the grounds, firstly, that fascism in its full ramifications is no longer of central social concern, and secondly, that conservatism too, for better or worse, plays at most a marginal role in the political imagination of our time. Moreover, neither has been connected with the growth of intellectual disciplines like sociology and psychology which cannot today be excluded from any discussion of political ideas.

primary data of this study. Second, as mentioned, anarcho-psychology is treated as one of three competing world-views. The latter section of this first chapter is devoted to sketching the leading characteristics of the first body of social theory, that which is termed 'liberal-rationalism' and identified with an assumption of linear social progress and the utilitarian model of *homo economicus*. This tradition has been referred to popularly in so many vague and indiscriminate ways that it was felt necessary to spell out with some precision how it is understood here. Discussion of the aspects of the Marxist socialist tradition which are germane to anarcho-psychology fits naturally into the second chapter on ideology, where one section treats Marx's lengthy critique of Stirner. This section aims to clarify the issues which separate a radical anarchist psychology from a radical socialist sociology.

Third, the study is divided into three main chapters, reflecting the distinctive lines of critical anarcho-psychological argument which are levelled against existing patterns of social and economic morality and behaviour. The three organizing principles conjoin. The first anarcho-psychological argument, its critique of ideology, has as particular components a critique of liberalism and a critique of socialism. The second argument, the critique of knowledge, directs itself specifically against rationalist and empiricist assumptions. It also traces the nature and plausibility of an irrationalist epistemology. The third argument, the critique of *homo economicus*, sets itself in opposition to the materialism at the root of both utilitarian and Marxist traditions.

Although this work bears the formal structure of an historical investigation, it is not essentially concerned with the past for its own sake, for what really happened. It is history only in the sense of Hegel's reflection: 'We have, in traversing the past—however extensive its periods—only to do with what is *present*.'[1] What must be stressed is that the work that follows is the issue of a need to illuminate the present, to penetrate, and thereby gain some understanding of, a complex of social problems that are vitally contemporary. Although there will be little overt reference to the present, the argument is loosed from its primary context if one forgets that ultimately its thread unravels in an attempt, by the author, to clarify his own image of redemption. Implicit here is the contention of Walter Benjamin, in his theses on the philosophy of history, that our view of the past, which is the concern of history, is indissolubly bound up with our image of redemption, and thereby our personal image of happiness.[2]

[1] Hegel: *The Philosophy of History* (from students' lecture notes), trans. J. Sibree, 1956, p. 79.
[2] Walter Benjamin: *Illuminationen*, 1961, pp. 268–9.

There is no contradiction in writing an essay in morals in the form of an intellectual history. The past is the only terrain open to us when we are in search of clues to our present, for we are usually lost in our own time, being too absorbed in its infinite detail to gain much perspective. The more we understand about the aspects of the past which interest us the more adequately will they map the complexities of our own condition. Moreover, investigating the past is a means of discovering the path along which we have travelled, as a culture, as a society, and finally as individuals; this may help us to understand a little better where we have arrived, that is, where we are now.

This account of the investigation that follows raises at once the problem of objectivity, of what scientific status the work may claim. No historian can faithfully recreate the past. Every attempt at writing history is conditioned by what Max Weber called 'value-relevance': it cannot claim objectivity outside the bounds of the author's specific cultural orientations and some of his specific psychic dispositions.[1] What this means is that the range of objectivity is governed by the degree of truth contained in the assumption that I, an intellectual historian, am forced to make, the assumption that I myself am so thoroughly coloured, in my interests and perceptions, both by problems common to all men and by my own time, that my driving concerns will be communicable and of general interest.

The investigation proceeds necessarily by simplifying and stylizing 'reality'. Following Kant and later Weber, the human scientist selects out of an infinity of possible perceptions what is significant to him in a reality which is the effect of an infinity of determinant causes. He accepts that description can never be exhaustive. And, while there is an objective reality of verbally transmissible ideas, entities, and events, no study can be free of subjective factors. It would not be possible in 1973 to present the thought, for example, of Max Stirner with the precise inflexions that he intended in 1844. Indeed, what is presented is not Stirner himself, but my reading of Stirner, with its own coherencies and its own stresses.

Nevertheless, historical propositions do provide objective orientations in a sense other than that they are communicable at a certain time within a certain culture. For the historian of ideas, original

---

1 Max Weber: *The Methodology of the Social Sciences*, ed., 1949, pp. 76–85. These essays are taken as read. It is not within the ambit of this study to take up the question of hermeneutics as it was posed by Dilthey, nor to enter the debate on methodology which has been at the core of German philosophy and sociology since his time, and has continued into our own with the work of Habermas. Let it suffice to add that this study is conceived of as belonging to the *Geisteswissenschaften*, as Dilthey defined the human or cultural sciences.

texts and information about the situation in which they were written and received constitute a framework within which the propositions can be discussed. Some of the propositions tendered here are open to falsification by empirical historical evidence.

The study as a whole claims objectivity also in respecting the logical criteria of clarity, consistency, and coherency within its own terms of reference. The difficult question is what precisely are these terms of reference. The most an intellectual historian can achieve at this point, once he has stated what seem to him to be his goals and his method of approaching them, is to proceed self-critically, examining the presuppositions of his work as it evolves. To facilitate this operation one chapter is devoted here to the anarcho-psychological critique of knowledge; it attempts to clarify the terms of reference.

2

The progressive secularization of the religious quest for truth forms the mainstream which governs the flow of all intellectual currents in Europe over the last three centuries. The image of human redemption is recast so that traditional routes for spiritual pilgrimage are transformed into a single path leading towards the goal of rationality. Rationality in its most general terms simply signifies order, in the sense either of cognitive meaning or of technical control over the human and the natural environment. Reason is many-sided: the concept at the centre of Hegel's philosophical system has little ostensibly in common with the rationality presupposed by the hypothetico-deductive scientific model, and neither may be relevant to the practical activities of a group of people trying to rationalize a social structure in which they can live in tolerable harmony. But, in spite of the many-sided nature of Reason, one only of its ministering traditions has held sway over the development of modern Europe.

The intellectual achievements of the eighteenth century reflected an increasingly pervasive concentration on the rationalistic model which gained its paradigmatic statement, and celebrated its greatest triumph, in the field of Newtonian physics. In particular, the Enlightenment movement in both France and Scotland sought to take the model outside the bounds of the natural sciences and apply it to the general study of the human condition.

However, it was only late in the eighteenth century that the endeavour to embed social theory in hypothetico-deductive methods became more than the enthusiastic gesture typical of the French *philosophes*. It is significant that systematic social theory should have first appeared in Britain, where the advanced state of both governmental and industrial institutions provided an empirical basis for an economic theory incorporating progress assumptions. Moreover, Adam Smith's *The Wealth of Nations* (1775) not only founded economics as a science (the significance of the Physiocrats is slight, beside that of Smith), but provided the example which inspired Bentham to extrapolate Newtonian methods into other spheres of social investigation. This section is devoted to outlining the principal ideas founding the world-view, here named 'liberal-rationalism', which grew out of the application of the rational-empirical techniques of the natural sciences to the analysis of man in society. Thereafter, the central concern of this study will be to examine a competing social theory, one drawing on an alternative notion of rationality, one which, moreover, at times repudiates Reason altogether.

The liberal-rationalist thesis finds its apogee in the works of Jeremy Bentham. Although many of its prominent themes are traceable back to other eighteenth-century philosophers such as Hume, Condillac, Helvétius, Priestley, Smith, and Condorcet, it was Bentham who organized them and built them into a coherent, systematic body of theory—the utilitarian ideology. The principal texts for the following summary of the tenets of liberal-rationalism are Bentham's *An Introduction to the Principles of Morals and Legislation* (1789) and Elie Halévy's study of the corpus of his work, its origins, and some of its influences—*The Growth of Philosophic Radicalism*.

Virtually all of the implications of liberal-rationalism which will be examined in the following chapters have their source in the type of *rationalism* which was fundamental to Bentham's purpose. His ambition, one which has infected all but few subsequent social scientists, was to become the Newton of society and its problems—economic, social, political, and legal. He wanted to establish morals as an exact science,[1] to withdraw it from the control of feeling and subject it to the rule of reason. The fantasy articulating this ambition was that of man as *l'homme machine*, La Mettrie's image (1748) of man reducible through scientific investigation to determined conditions. By projecting this image as an ideal into the future Bentham created the inspiration for economic planning, for 'social engineering' as we know it today.

Care is necessary in elucidating Bentham's principles so as to distinguish what he discusses with the individual and what with society as the frame of reference. For Bentham the individual is wholly egoistic, he seeks pleasure and he seeks to avoid pain.[2] There

---

[1] Elie Halévy: *The Growth of Philosophic Radicalism*, trans. Mary Morris, 1934, p. 12.

[2] Jeremy Bentham: *An Introduction to the Principles of Morals and Legislation*, 1907, ch. 2.

is no human morality except the one which identifies good with pleasure and evil with pain;[1] morality is the act of being happy.[2] Hence we arrive at the fulcrum of the system, the principle of utility:[3]

That principle which approves or disapproves of every action whatsoever, according to the tendency which it appears to have to augment or diminish the happiness of the party whose interest is in question. ['Benefit', 'advantage', 'pleasure', 'good', and 'happiness' are synonyms.]

To this point we have précis'd a simple and unambiguous, individualist philosophy of hedonism or eudaemonism.

Bentham's first intention in discussing the social body is his ubiquitous Newtonian one, to quantify and to sum. Thus:[4]

The interest of the community is . . . the sum of the interests of the several members who compose it.

For Halévy herein lies Bentham's *individualistic* postulate; it complements his *rationalistic* postulate.[5] The basic unit of analysis is the individual; society is atomized, it is an aggregate of individual members having no ontological reality of its own. Bentham would face no problem here, where he moves from the *one* to the *many*, if he held to a 'principle of fusion of interests' in community, whereby each individual feels sympathy for his neighbour's interest, or alternatively a 'principle of natural identity of interests', which postulates that somehow individual egoisms harmonize and automatically bring out the common social good.[6] However, holding to more Hobbesean beliefs he rejects these utopian assumptions in favour of a 'principle of the artificial identification of interests', under which it becomes necessary to have a legislator, and a means of sanctioning his laws, in order to enforce a harmony of egoisms. Hence, through law, the private interest is brought into coincidence with the public one. The legislator, whose sole function is to maximize the pleasure of the society as a whole, applies the 'pleasure-pain calculus', a matrix into which are fed numerical indices of the emotional significance of the individual's response to any event or series of events.[7]

A number of assumptions are necessary if pleasure and pain are to be quantified. The first case of the rationalistic postulate is that each portion of wealth is connected with a corresponding portion of

[1] Bentham, op. cit., ch. 2, XIV–XIX. [2] Halévy, op. cit., p. 477.
[3] Bentham, op. cit., ch. 1, II–III.   [4] Ibid., ch. 1, IV.
[5] Halévy, op. cit., p. 500.   [6] Ibid., pp. 13–15.
[7] Bentham, op. cit., ch. 4.

happiness. This can be appropriately termed the *economic* assumption: it is an axiom, if usually unstated, of economic theory since Adam Smith. The second case of the postulate asserts that the individual is the best judge of his own interest; in other words, in the sphere of the socio-economic he acts 'rationally'—in his own 'real' interest.[1] This rationality in terms of the *one* self does not necessarily coincide with societary rationality—the maximizing of pleasure for the *many*. Hence, the social reformer, cognizant of both systems of rationality, draws them into harmony by means of rational laws—rational again in the utilitarian sense, this time of minimizing pain.

In the specific area of economic behaviour Bentham avoids the problem of generalizing from the *one* to the *many* by assuming, like Adam Smith, a principle of the natural identity of interests.[2] This principle, taken with the postulate of the self-determining individual, establishes the philosophical basis for *laissez-faire* economics: when the individual is aware of his own interest, which in turn harmonizes with the general social interest, then the system is self-operating and needs no external control.

Although Bentham himself should not be placed too specifically within the *laissez-faire* framework, for he knew that it is rarely that egoisms will naturally harmonize, his predominant ambition did remain to turn society by means of legislation into a predictable, well-ordered economic system; he did, moreover, find the paradigm for legal and social science in Adam Smith's system of Political Economy. As a consequence we can pertinently signify the object of his researches, the idealized goal of his reforms, as *homo economicus*. The pleasure-pain principle founds a materialist doctrine; fulfilment is conceived of in terms of economic sufficiency for all. It was inherent in the frame of mind which produced the utility calculus, and in the working structure of that calculus itself, that the only parameter on which it would operate was money.

In 1787, two years before the publication of Bentham's principles, James Watt perfected his steam engine. As the first man to apply technological principles concerning heat and mechanical energy to large-scale work problems he effectively bridged the gap between Newtonian models and man's practical struggle to control his environment. Although Bentham may have seen the outlines of his social theory in Smith's economic model, it was the self-regulating

---

1 Halévy, op. cit., p. 99. This postulate is allied to the more practicable formulation of the utility principle, in terms of which pleasure and pain do not have to be strictly quantified: 'Act so as to ensure, as far as you can, that people get what they want, according to their own preferences' (John Plamenatz: *Man and Society*, 1963, vol. 2, p. 12).

2 Halévy, op. cit., p. 149.

machine, as it was being constructed and used for the first time, which more closely embodied the image of his ideal society—one which would 'work like clockwork'. The hope that society, even man, would one day run like a well-lubricated machine was to receive repeated analogical reinforcement from nineteenth-century technological innovation. Technology did more than provide symbols for some of the prominent intellectual concerns of the age, it invested them with added vigour and the uniquely inspiring sense of pioneering a revolution of a significance unprecedented in history. Thus the thermostat, patented in 1831, the invention which made possible the control of temperature in now completely self-regulating processes, revealed symbolically the 'cybernetic' role that legislation was intended to play in Bentham's social system—a pressure valve to be used as a last resort when the mechanism becomes overheated.[1] The patterns of contemporary ideology could not remain immune to the urgent, turbulent forward-thrust engendered by technological, industrial progress.

If Bentham's system could operate ideally there would be no ethical problem; through legislation what *ought* to be the case would become what *is* the case, with both defined by the principle of utility. However, this could not be, even in a rational-utilitarian universe, as Bentham himself realized; it would be logically possible for the calculus, in being applied to choose between alternative courses of action, to accord them equal quanta of happiness.[2] Bentham supplies the 'happiness enumeration principle' for this eventuality, according to which the happiness of the greater number of people is preferred to that of the lesser.[3] But utility theory cannot arbitrate in this manner; it cannot affirm or deny such a principle. Bentham has been forced to introduce an extraneous moral judgment.

There is a second problem to which he also admits. Many situations in which Benthamite legislation will be necessary are not amenable to pleasure and pain being quantified in money terms—for example, aspects of crime and punishment. Bentham assumes that value can somehow still be assessed, and indeed he devoted much of his energy to establishing precise categories for this process of measurement. Nevertheless, he writes:[4]

---

[1] The tendency, growing through the nineteenth century, for the social sciences to adopt the language of the mechanical sciences finally infected even such a 'non-economic' discipline as psychoanalysis.

[2] It is worth noting a striking technological analogue for the 'utility calculus'. During the 1820s Charles Babbage was developing the calculator/tabulator which would eventually make Bentham's calculus a real possibility; in 1834 he invented the principle of the analytical engine, the prototype for the automatic computer of the twentieth century.

[3] Halévy, op. cit., p. 501.

[4] Bentham, op. cit., ch. 4, VI.

It is not to be expected that this process should be strictly pursued previously to every moral judgment, or to every legislative or juridical operation. It may, however, be always kept in view.

Nothing characterizes the movement Bentham started, or the nature of the influence it was to exert in other intellectual spheres, in politics, or in the development of economic theory, more than the sheer optimism with which the principles of science (here the definition of precise categories within which to assess behaviour quantitatively) were applied to social life. At its root this optimism was founded on an unassailable faith in the possibility of human *melioration* and *progress*. The seminal statement of the progress thesis was Condorcet's *L'Esquisse d'un tableau historique des progrès de l'esprit humain* (1795). Condorcet, influenced by earlier, more crude progress ideas such as those of Turgot, developed Enlightenment optimism into a linear model of history. In his view barbaric, savage, primitive society through the application of human reason over many centuries had finally attained a state of civilization which was enlightened, free, and little burdened by prejudice;[1] civilization, moreover, would continue to be infinitely perfectible. Bentham's progress assumption is more specific; he believes that an expansion in knowledge, and a greater sophistication in the tools for analysing social action, prepare the way for a realizable increase in human happiness.[2]

Bentham's utilitarianism was not explicitly a form of liberalism. Indeed his philosophy, as Halévy has pointed out, is written for the restrictors of man's liberty, for the legislators and politicians.[3] He did not seem convinced that liberty, as John Stuart Mill was to conceive of it, represents a goal of human activity; if it is, then it is one very much secondary to that of security.[4] Liberty and happiness were not coextensive for Bentham. Nevertheless, Mill's treatise *On Liberty* (1859) articulated themes which had been implicit in the utilitarian tradition from the beginning. Bentham had emphasized that laws reduce liberty; moreover, while still pinning his argument to the framework of utility theory (in this case with the implication that constraint immediately effects an increase of pain), he deduced

[1] Condorcet: *The Progress of the Human Mind*, trans. June Barraclough, 1955, p. 173.
[2] A view popularly held in English art circles in the first half of the nineteenth century (for example by Charles Eastlake) was that the example of scientific progress could be carried into painting; a new age in which paintings would not merely be different but would be *greater* than all their predecessors had opened. (Even Hegel, in his lectures on aesthetics, denies the validity of such comparative value judgments.)
[3] Halévy, op. cit., p. 74.
[4] Ibid., p. 84, and Gertrude Himmelfarb: *Victorian Minds*, 1968, p. 77.

that legislation should be kept to a minimum.[1] Implicit here is Mill's assertion that community encroachment in the sphere of action of the individual is warranted only when that individual acts contrary to the interest of the community; liberty is thus characterized as 'freedom from'. Bentham is a liberal in principle in that he accepts man as he is, and wants to help him be his *own* best judge; in practice he is far less liberal, for his calculus and his social plans imply a paternalism antithetical to any libertarian ethic. Mill was more sceptical than Bentham about the universal application of the utility principle, but not on the grounds of its inbuilt authoritarianism. Happiness for him was 'much too complex and indefinite an end to be sought except through the medium of various secondary ends'.[2] But, as we noted, Bentham also had been forced to introduce 'secondary ends', or, more correctly, extraneous moral laws, values set up in their own right.[3] Mill's principle of liberty has this status: while it is reducible to the utility ethic, such reductionism undervalues the moral force invested in it.[4]

Bentham believed that all social phenomena are reducible to laws: the laws of the social world are explicable in terms of the 'laws of

[1] Bentham's model prison, the Panopticon, was an authoritarian, hideously mechanical institution, allowing no regard for the emotional—in particular, pleasure—needs of the prisoners; it clearly contravened his principles. His personal ambitions have been shown to be incompatible with the circumspect application of the pleasure-pain calculus (Himmelfarb, op. cit., ch. 2: 'The Haunted House of Jeremy Bentham'). In defining the liberal-rationalist tradition of ideas we are interested only in its strongest formulation, and consequently bypass whatever aberrations it may have sustained, reserving judgment as to whether they are its necessary effects.

[2] *Mill on Bentham and Coleridge*, ed. and intro. F. R. Leavis, 1967, p. 90.

[3] Running parallel to the difficulties which the utilitarian tradition was finding over the ethical question of ultimate ends—in essence, whether the utility principle was adequate to generate a total theory of social action—was the thermodynamic debate. In 1874 Carnot had enunciated the principle of the reversible cycle of heat flow which was eventually to make possible the internal combustion engine; but, at the same time, he had laid the way for the second law of thermodynamics—the concept of entropy. The old principle, that of the conservation of energy, had in effect answered the question of whether human life would maintain itself, by postulating an equilibrating tendency in heat and energy flow; it was now complemented by the gravely pessimistic view that heat is constantly dissipated, that the universe is running down—the antithesis to the Darwinian optimism that the human race becomes stronger through natural selection. This scientific pessimism was later to be mirrored in the social philosophy of Nietzsche, Pareto, and Freud, in their profound doubts about the possibility of human progress.

[4] Mill records in his *Autobiography* how he moved away from the purely rationalistic utilitarianism of his upbringing after his mental breakdown; he stresses the influence of his wife in his later writings, especially *On Liberty*, an influence which brought with it the balance of humanity and feeling rather than reason.

11

human nature'.[1] Here, particularly, the English tradition of Philosophic Radicalism was echoed in the work of Auguste Comte. *Positivism* also was established as the science of society, whose problems were seen as being amenable to solution by Newtonian methods. Comte also drew on Condorcet's 'progress' assumption, believing that his sociology, by comprehending society as a totality, could be used to accelerate its progress. While the positivist criticized the utilitarian for applying the deductive method to study something which was so complex that it could be adequately grasped only by statistical techniques,[2] his empiricism was rationalist in our sense (that is, not strictly limiting the definition to analysis by means of the deductive method). The positivist placed ultimate faith in man's power of reason, and in the existence of an underlying order in nature and society, which could be revealed by means of this greatest of human faculties and its inductive applications.

One last important element was added to this tradition in 1859, the year of Mill's *On Liberty* and Darwin's *Origin of Species*, in a book which at once encompassed the themes of Philosophic Radicalism and summed them up—Samuel Smiles's *Self-Help*. Smiles reinforced Mill's emphasis on individuality and self-culture, and developed the *laissez-faire* ethic by recounting the lives of men who through the virtues of perseverance, energy, thoroughness, honesty, thrift, self-reliance, and common sense—in short self-help—achieved the economic and status goals they set themselves. Utilitarianism had found its portrait gallery of heroes, inscribed with a vigorous exhortation to all men to strive in their image; this philistine romanticism established the bourgeois hero-prototype—the penniless office-boy who works his way to economic fortune and thus wins his way into the mercantile plutocracy. Smiles's pragmatic individualism, which is utilitarian in its ethos (even culture must be useful),[3] is balanced by an altruistic devotion to society, its welfare and its progress.

E. P. Thompson writes: 'Methodism and Utilitarianism, taken together, make up the dominant ideology of the Industrial Revolution'.[4] Smiles's book is a definitive example of the fusion of utilitarian philosophy and the Protestant ethic. Puritan strains underpin *Self-Help*: man must find his lawful calling and work at it industriously,[5] abiding in his leisure time by the laws of thrift and self-restraint;[6] *time*, in anticipation of F. W. Taylor's 'scientific manage-

---

1
2 Halévy, op. cit., p. 433.
3 Ibid., p. 496.
4 Samuel Smiles: *Self-Help*, 1968, p. 212.
 E. P. Thompson: *The Making of the English Working Class*, 1968, p. 441.
5 Smiles, op. cit., p. 200.
6 Ibid., pp. 189–91.

ment', must never be wasted.[1] Although Smiles criticizes miserliness and praises cheerfulness,[2] he places such emphasis on perseverance as to devalue natural ability and unmoralized passion; he is suspicious of genius and goes so far as to say with approval of Joshua Reynolds: 'He would not believe in what is called inspiration, but only in study and labour'.[3] *Self-Help* is a pungent exhortation to be moderate in all spheres but one, and there to dedicate one's energy wholesale to one's chosen life-task or vocation.

Asa Briggs notes that few books have reflected the spirit of their age more faithfully and successfully than *Self-Help*; it sold 20,000 copies in its first year, and about a quarter of a million by the end of the century.[4] Like Dr Andrew Ure's advocatory philosophy of the machine, the manufactured good, and the factory in his *Philosophy of Manufactures* (1835), it is one of the key handbooks of industrial Britain on the rise.

I have chosen the appellation 'liberal-rationalism' for the complex of beliefs which have been grouped together here. Whereas the 'rationalist' part is clearly justified, the objection might be raised that 'liberalism', especially with regard to Bentham, is only a derivative aspect of Philosophic Radicalism. However, individualism and *laissez-faire* (the latter at least in economics) are foundation stones of utilitarian philosophy, and are as seminal to Bentham as to the more pragmatically oriented Samuel Smiles. No single term encapsulates these themes as neatly as Mill's 'liberalism'. Finally, the belief in progress depended not only on the rationalistic assumption that socio-economic behaviour is amenable to the scientific method, but also on a confidence in the resources of the individual, on the assumption that he would flourish in a 'liberal' society in which there was a minimum of legislative constraint—that *he* would progress and take the society as a whole with him. To delimit this ideological tradition strictly according to the principle of utility would be to blunt its philosophical significance; accordingly, the term 'utilitarian' is unstressed in our derivation. Liberal-rationalism did attempt to cope with the problem created by the clash of interests which occurs when the individual *enters* society; it did so by introducing a second moral principle, one which in its most influential form was subsumed under Mill's concept of 'liberty'.

Liberal-rationalism is a world-view founded on beliefs in rationality, utility, self-help, and progress. It was the world-view that cradled nineteenth-century industrialization, certainly in Britain; out of it came the dynamic concepts through which the ambitions of the age were focussed—productive force and efficiency, *rendement* and

[1] Smiles, op. cit., p. 26.   [2] Ibid., pp. 201, 241.   [3] Ibid., p. 208.
[4] Asa Briggs's introduction to the 1959, centenary edition.

Triebkraft.[1] It converted undirected, polymorphous activity into purposive action, and thereby invested the utilization of physical and human resources in industry with new energy. In retrospect, moreover, it rationalized this transformation as a realization of progress for the whole of mankind.

Although the anarcho-psychologists developed as individuals and philosophers in cultures essentially different from Britain in its early stages of industrialization, they all abstracted virtually the same ideology as the primary target for their attack on the consciousness of their own time. This ideology, in its most coherent and trenchant form, was the one pieced together here as liberal-rationalism: it summed up what, in addition to socialist tenets, was crucially anathema to their multiplex vision of human dignity. The anarcho-psychologists were not closely acquainted with many of its founding statements (Stirner, the only one to read English, knew the work of Adam Smith; Nietzsche refers to Comte and Mill about a dozen times each in his writings, but never at length,[2] and he mentions Bentham once; both Nietzsche and Dostoevsky refer briefly to Herbert Spencer). Nevertheless, they gleaned its substance from their diverse reading, from what was commonly 'in the air' at the time, from similar standpoints and attitudes held within their own cultural traditions, and, most significantly, from what they observed as the advance of industrial civilization and its root idiom. Dostoevsky, for example, was probably not acquainted directly with the work of anyone specifically mentioned in this section apart from John Stuart Mill and yet he singled out utilitarianism, scientific determinism, rationalism, and the progress thesis with devastating insight. Finally, liberal-rationalism became for the anarcho-psychologists the ominous scaffolding of the establishing order in European society. One of the tasks of this study is to demonstrate how they used this theoretical tradition as a dialectical opposite against which to develop their own ideas.

In spite of many necessary parallels, the industrialization of France and Germany took place under significantly different socio-political conditions.

2 Nietzsche did, however, possess five volumes from Mill's *Werke*, which he heavily pencil-marked with comments (Max Oehler: *Nietzsches Bibliothek*, 1942, p. 41).

2 The critique of ideology

The origins of anarcho-psychology

The intellectual historian must set buoys to mark the flood and ebb of particular tides which run in the ocean of human history. He contributes to man's understanding of himself and his social experience by paying the high price of having to accept an intrusive degree of simplification, even arbitrariness, in his work. Noting that October 1844 stands out as the inaugural month for anarcho-psychology provides us with a convenient point of orientation.

It was in this month of 1844 that the first copies of *Der Einzige und sein Eigentum* were, most probably, distributed in Berlin. Even the Young Hegelian friends of its 38-year-old schoolmaster author, the shy, retiring Max Stirner, were staggered by what had been clandestinely written within their midst.[1] In the same month, about one hundred miles to the south, in a small village not far from Leipzig, Friedrich Nietzsche was born.

Anarcho-psychology necessarily had progenitors. Key passages in the work of both Stirner and Dostoevsky echo Christ's parables. All of the anarcho-psychologists were to share the debt that Freud confessed, to the poets of many ages and many cultures. Stirner and Nietzsche, in this regard, owe much to Goethe. There is a debt to thinkers of quite different intellectual dispositions; in the case of Stirner, to Hegel and Feuerbach, in the case of Nietzsche, to Schopenhauer. Strains of a sometimes similar type of psychological anar-

---

1 A biography of Max Stirner, an account of the influence that his work has had since 1844, and a brief assessment of its importance are included in my introduction to Max Stirner: The *Ego and His Own* (sel. and intro. John Carroll, 1971). References to Stirner will be either to this edition, denoted henceforth as *Ego*, or, in a few cases, to the complete 1912 edition (trans. S. T. Byington), *Ego* (1912); See note on p. 178, below.

chism are to be found in the writings of Charles Fourier. Finally, there is one case of remarkable anticipation. The placing of William Blake as an *Einzelgänger*, a man apart from his time, is supported by the fact of his wide-ranging and intimate kinship with the figures central to this study, none of whom were acquainted with his work.[1]

It has been orthodox among intellectual historians, and indeed among a number of anarchist theoreticians themselves, to regard Stirner as one of the seminal writers in what is conceived of as the anarchist tradition. He is credited as the father of 'individualist anarchism', as distinct from the 'mutualism' of Proudhon, Bakunin's 'anarcho-communism', or the 'anarcho-syndicalism' which has been attributed to Tolstoy and Gandhi.[2] His unrelenting attacks on the structures of social authority, on the State, on political parties, on educational institutions, place him, as a theorist, unambiguously with the anarchists on the political spectrum.

What has not been recognized is that Stirner initiates the method of *psychological* thinking which has usually been attributed to Nietzsche, the method to be developed most fully and systematically by Freud. His work has retained its freshness and trenchancy through time primarily because its radical political analysis is grounded in psychology. His best aphorisms bear that pungency which Nietzsche was to make his signature, an incisiveness which marks the accuracy of their probe into the sensitive tissue at the nucleus of human motivation. The locus of Stirner's interest is the individual psyche; he investigates the effects on this psyche of some of the ways men choose in their social context to pattern their behaviour, and of the manner in which they then conceive of themselves. *Der Einzige* is a psychological philosophy of the growth of *ego*, of self-realization, and as such shares features with the *Bildungsroman*. Through its sustained, cyclically progressing monologue, meditating the vicissitudes of the unique individual, it develops an inner logic akin to that which endows the novels of character individuation with their fundamental coherence.

Stirner's psychological anarchism suggests that attachment to ideological and institutional structures of political authority reflects attachment to deeper and more general frames of authority. There is implicit anticipation of the notion of the 'authoritarian personality'.

---

1 Nietzsche would have had to qualify his acerbic, dismissive comments on the English and their psychological obtuseness if he had known Blake's work. It is André Gide who will establish a Blake-Dostoevsky-Nietzsche tradition.

2 George Woodcock: *Anarchism*, 1963, pp. 17–19. These brief general remarks on Stirner's anarchism are elaborated in the Introduction to *Ego*; important texts are referenced in its bibliography.

This perspective indicts as merely ideological those branches of anarchism, and indeed of all political theory, which fail to take account of the psychology of the need for authority—its unconscious origins, the nature of the individual's relationship to particular orders of dominance. These ideologies operate exclusively in an abstract realm of ideas; they do not come to grips with social and psychological reality. Stirner's pursuit of psychological explanation provides anarchism with a wider rubric.

The deeper and more general frames of authority which constitute the focus of Stirner's social critique can be meaningfully collected under the heading of ideology. We define *ideology* as any system of ideas about human behaviour and social life, containing its own moral imperatives, and held in some sense to communicate absolute truth. Throughout our discussion the term will be used pejoratively: ideology bears, finally, the characteristic of abstraction, of masking rather than illuminating reality. Marx viewed ideology as philosophy failed, philosophy detached from the concrete material relationships of society: political ideas not grounded historio-sociologically. The anarcho-psychologists select ideology for critique for the contrasting reason that it fails to mediate the domain of the individual's self-enjoyment and his self-realization. The first standpoint explicates ideology as socially determined, the second as psychologically determined: both accuse it of remaining oblivious to its own determinations. We devote a section later in this chapter to the conflicting attitudes of Stirner and Marx to ideology.

The works of both Stirner and Nietzsche develop as a critique of existing patterns of human thought and behaviour; their driving ambition is to provide the key to a revalued world. The critique operates on the ideological veneers which distort human communication, which inhibit individual fulfilment and enjoyment, and thereby preclude self-realization. It is directed at the unconscious causes of the attachment to religious, moral, and political ideologies, and the effects of the resulting self-deceptions. In its own way, taking ideology as the primal and generative structure of authority, it is profoundly anarchist; it sets itself the task of demolishing what it sees as the most powerful ideologies of its own period in history.

The first distinctive anarcho-psychological argument, the critique of ideology, is developed by Stirner and re-echoed, in part amplified, by Nietzsche. This study concentrates on Stirner on the grounds that his work precedes that of Nietzsche and has been curiously neglected in the subsequent history of European thought. Some sense of the remarkable degree to which there is anticipation will be conveyed by footnoting passages from Nietzsche germane to the text proper. A concluding section discusses the advances Nietzsche makes on the critique he takes up.

17

The antichrist

Both Stirner and Nietzsche chose Christianity as the first specific target in their critique of ideology. They represented the Christian religion and its moral imperatives as the ideology which had exerted the dominant influence over the long cultural development of Western society, and even over their own time. There was no more vivid example of the power that a body of ideas could generate and command.

We introduce the general critique of ideology through the specific case of Christianity, and Stirner's analysis of its psychological origins in the individual personality. Nietzsche's assault on Christianity is at most of its key points identical. To play the opening moves of one's philosophy as a gambit against Christianity in the 1840s was to follow the tradition of the radical neo-Hegelians of the period.[1] For that matter Hegel, who left his views on religion in a highly ambiguous state, had oriented much of his early writing around reinterpreting the Gospels.[2] David Friedrich Strauss took the initiative in the secular critique of the New Testament with his *Das Leben Jesu*, a book appearing in 1835, which is best described as humanizing Christ.[3] Strauss developed two major themes: that myth played a significant role in the Gospels, and that not only Jesus but all mankind embodies the union of human and divine nature. Bruno Bauer followed with his *Posaune des jüngsten Gerichts über Hegel den Atheisten und Antichristen. Ein Ultimatum* (1841) and, most influentially, his three-volume *Kritik der evangelischen Geschichte der Synoptiker* (1841–2). Bauer, with painstaking and often pedantic logic, denied the historicity as well as the divinity of Christ, and ascribed to the Gospels the status of any other mythology—philosophy rather than history.[4]

The rising wave of speculative impiety was not to go unchecked for long. In February 1841, the king called the aged Schelling to Berlin to rout out, in his own words, 'the dragon-seed of Hegelianism', and to restore the intellectual authority of the church[5] (it was a shrewd choice, for Schelling had borne no little rancour against the Hegelian tradition ever since its ideas had eclipsed the popularity of

[1] E.g., William J. Brazill: *The Young Hegelians*, 1970, ch. 1.
[2] Walter Kaufmann: *Hegel*, 1966, ss. 8–10.
[3] Sidney Hook: *From Hegel to Marx*, 1950, pp. 82–7.
David McLellan: *The Young Hegelians and Karl Marx*, 1969, pp. 1–4, and Brazill, op. cit., ch. 3.
[4] Hook, op. cit., pp. 89–97; Brazill, op. cit., pp. 186–92. The prolific Bauer published a spate of books in the next two years on associated themes: *Die gute Sache der Freiheit* (1842), *Die Judenfrage* (1843), and *Das entdeckte Christentum* (1843), the last of which McLellan refers to as 'probably the most violent attack ever launched on Christianity' (McLellan, op. cit., p. 33).
[5] McLellan, op. cit., p. 27.

18

his own philosophical system, many years earlier). The first lectures were given in November on 'The Philosophy of Revelation', and an enthusiastic audience included Engels, Bakunin, Turgenev, and Kierkegaard. But in spite of the king's efforts an event of great importance not only for radical theology, but for the future of all critical social thought, had occurred in April of the same year, 1841: Ludwig Feuerbach had published his *Das Wesen des Christentums*. It is necessary to give a brief sketch of his breakthrough as his ideas form the most significant post-Hegel influence on Stirner.[1]

Feuerbach follows Hegel in reinterpreting Rousseau's notion of *aliénation*. He applies it to the sphere of religion, in which he sees man abdicating his own powers and qualities, and transposing or displacing them, and thus his essential self, on to an independent, ineffable god beyond the world of the human. Religion, like speculative philosophy, he argues, makes the divinity primary—the subject—and predicates the qualities of man as its attributes.[2] It makes 'real beings and things into arbitrary signs, vehicles, symbols, or predicates of a distinct, transcendent, absolute, i.e. abstract being'.[3] Thus 'God is love' is a theology in which man, an insignificant particular, face to face with the universe, is attached to the abstract predicate, love, and is impoverished and limited before the absolute, God. In Feuerbach's words:[4]

> Man—this is the mystery of religion—projects his being into objectivity, and then again makes himself an object to this projected image of himself thus converted into a subject.

Thus, in a crisis (in fact vacuum) of identity man seeks an invincible *alter ego* in God. Man himself, Feuerbach continues, should be the criterion of truth; but this man cannot be known through the intellect, for empirical existence is proved by the senses alone.[5] Here are the first soundings for the subsequent turn against idealism; Feuerbach hints, in his references to the senses and to *a posteriori* understanding, at an inadequacy in the hegemony of Reason. However, he failed to pursue this line, and in the main his attack on

---

[1] It is not our intention to pursue in any detail Stirner's intellectual roots, except where evaluation of *major* strands of his thought might gain thereby. The only important study of the development of Stirner's philosophy, Henri Arvon's *Aux Sources de l'existentialisme: Max Stirner*, 1954, gives a thorough account of his indebtedness to his German contemporaries, the Young Hegelians (earlier studies suffer from lack of available information about the period). Brazill, also, in his detailed study of the development of Young Hegelian thought, gives a clear impression of how much Stirner borrowed. Moreover, much has been written in recent years about this group, from the point of view of its influence on Marx.

[2] Ludwig Feuerbach: *The Essence of Christianity*, trans. George Eliot, 1957, p. 21.

[3] Ibid., p. xi.   [4] Ibid., p. 29.   [5] Ibid., pp. xiii, 201.

religion is conducted on an idealist level—shuffling concepts. It is the idealist Feuerbach, who simply swaps religion into another part of the equation, whom Stirner is to reject—Stirner denies the equation in itself.

The highest essence of man is found in the three qualities, will, love, and thought, all of which can suffuse him with their infinitude, and produce the state of total awe of which Feuerbach approves as the real religious experience. God is now the divineness of the attribute. Thus the subject, God, is determined by the predicate— justice, love, or whichever quality is the essence of the moment—and its rank must be accorded to this predicate and not to the subject; subject and predicate are *transformed* into each other. Feuerbach transforms man into the subject of all equations and appropriates the concept 'God' to describe the feeling of infinite freedom sparked by the union of subject and predicate; when man is in love, love becomes man. The subject has become the 'personified existing predicate, the predicate conceived as existing. Subject and predicate are distinguished only as existence and essence.'[1] Feuerbach makes man the centre of his universe and he makes his divine experiences, especially those located in interpersonal relationships, the centre of his humanity. In his work theology becomes anthropology, a secularization of thought which prepares the way for Marx's materialist and Stirner and Nietzsche's psychological attack on metaphysics.

Stirner develops Feuerbach's theological framework into a general theory of alienation. He paraphrases the argument he takes up with the assertion that was later to be widely attributed to Nietzsche: God is dead.[2] It was God not only in the specifically religious sense, but as a metaphor for any value existing beyond the power of the individual, who had become obsolete. In particular, Stirner singles out the liberal humanist ideal, the universal human essence, 'Man', as the increasingly dominant substitute for the Christian illusion. Feuerbach, the philosopher of the new humanism, had not progressed beyond religious thinking: for Stirner he was the last prophet working within the crumbling Christian tradition. Stirner himself claims to face forward at the frontier of the post-Christian world.

We consider first the stage of Stirner's critique of Christianity which he derives from Feuerbach. At the core of religion is a divided self, longing for what is conceived of as the 'ideal life',[3] but forced to live in a present which provides inadequate satisfactions. The Christian chases after an image of himself which is invariably elsewhere,

[1] Feuerbach, op. cit., p. 19.
[2] *Ego*, p. 109. In fact, both Jean Paul and Hegel had already used the expression.
[3] Ibid., pp. 224–6.

and which, he is convinced, would be the incarnation of the true and the good life if he could realize it. He exists at a distance from engaged living, hoping that in death he might, in Stirner's words, 'rise again'.[1] The consequence is that the religious person, whom Stirner rarely distinguishes from the Christian, devotes himself to spiritual affairs, and chooses an ethereal vocation ratified by the supreme 'fixed idea', God. The more he does this the more he finds his other self, his concrete self here-and-now, confronted with narrowed horizons.

Stirner passes beyond Feuerbach in his insistence that not only is the God of religion a projection of man's alienated self, but so is every ideal, every cause, every 'fixed idea', for they all entice men into following a *spook* which is neither of their creation nor within their power. Occupying the central place in this 'realm of essences, spooks, and ghosts'[2] are the moral principles which have derived from Christianity, in particular their guiding axis—*love*. The equation 'God is love' expresses concern only for the general essence of humanity; it is another abstraction which devalues the uniqueness of the individual by matching him against an ideal. Stirner responds: 'He who is infatuated with *Man* leaves persons out of account'.[3] Love has become a force superseding the individual's desires; Feuerbach's conception of love abstracts, and hence alienates, the individual from the loved object.[4]

Stirner has turned Feuerbach's argument back against itself. He expands the domain of the *religious* to include abstract idealism of the type represented by Feuerbach's humanism. Whether the ideal is specifically Christian or not it serves the same psychological function for the individual. Stirner continues his critique of Feuerbach by defining the religious man as he who puts his *essence* above himself.[5] In fact, and this has not been recognized, Stirner spells out in numerous examples the axiom which was to become the lynchpin of existentialist philosophy, epigrammed from Heidegger's work by Sartre: existence precedes essence.[6] Stirner illustrates how the individual ego, whose ontological ground is simply the self-reflection that it itself exists, is fettered as soon as it subordinates itself to qualities or essences. By conceiving of himself as a Christian, or a pious man, or a compassionate man, the individual forces himself into conformity with the socially determined image of what it

---

[1] *Ego*, p. 225.   [2] Ibid., p. 56.
[3] Ibid., p. 83. Cf. Nietzsche: 'The individual [*einzelne*] hides himself in the general concept "man" '. (*Morgenröte* 26—the system used in this study to reference the writings of Nietzsche, Dostoevsky, and Freud is explained in the opening section of the Bibliography, p. 178-9 below.)
[4] *Ego*, p. 203.   [5] Ibid., pp. 51–3.
[6] Jean-Paul Sartre: *Being and Nothingness*, 1969, p. 438.

means to be Christian, or a pious, compassionate man. An essence in this sense gains meaning only as a common characteristic within a social group; it is significant only as a social generality. That is, if an essence could be purely individual it could not at the same time be communicable. Here in the critique of religion are the roots of Stirner's notably existentialist subjectivism.

Some of the consequences of Christian 'love' are detailed in *Der Einzige*. He who is possessed by love 'persecutes with dull mercilessness the individual, the real man, under the phlegmatic title of measures against the "unman" '.[1] One of Stirner's implications is that it has not been the aggression of individuals that has been responsible for the great atrocities which have marked Western history. Rather it has been groups, moved to fervour by ideals, acting 'for God's sake' in the manner of the Spanish Inquisition, that have selected out other groups as being subhuman and persecuted them. Nietzsche puts the point more generally: 'Madness is rare in individuals—but in groups, parties, nations, and ages it is the rule'.[2]

Stirner is more concerned with the general question of the nature of idealism than the commonplace that any idealistic human group is prone to contradictions between the pledging of its ethical canon and its concrete actions. Similarly, a rationalist Voltairean critique of religion, such as Bertrand Russell mounts in *Why I am not a Christian*, and such as would have been consistent with Bentham's position, does not interest him. While agreeing that there is no 'reason' for believing in 'ghosts', he would add that this, rather than explaining much about the religious phenomenon, suggests that more penetrating questions should be directed at the notion of 'reason' and the role it plays in human consciousness and behaviour. His own interest is directed at the hitherto unapproached question of motivation: what is religion's psychological function? Stirner was puzzled by the fanaticism with which men embrace Christianity, the degree to which they could subjugate their own individualities to its tenets. He was convinced, moreover, that the Christian religion had become a sickness which, rather than helping man to live, had cut him off from the possibility of the 'good life'. Stirner's psychological approach takes the individual psyche as the only coherent and meaningful unit of analysis; economic and social action is significant only in terms of its interchange with this psyche, how it confirms or threatens it. Thus the external world is differentiated according to whether it generates ego-enhancing or ego-degrading forces. Stirner sets himself the task, convinced in this analytic context that human affection founded on

---

[1] *Ego*, p. 196. Cf. Nietzsche's extensive analysis of rancour and revenge; e.g. 'How much cruelty and animal torture has come out of *those religions which have invented sin*' (*Morgenröte* 53).

[2] *Jenseits* 156.

enjoyment is viable, of showing that to cast off the religious chains need not lead to a state of anxious anomie.

Stirner typifies the religious nature as residing in the 'cleric'. The cleric is afraid that the flesh and its worldly lusts might gain mastery over him, so he suppresses them, glorifies the spirit, and devotes himself to good causes.[1] His life is regulated and judged in terms of God, the idealist's projection of the sinless, perfectly selfless man. Like all great caricatures, Stirner's cleric becomes a universal character-type on closer acquaintance; Christianity, in this critique, is a paradigm for all moral and religious bodies of doctrine; the problems that confront its priests and the means they employ to cope with them are particular forms of the general problems which face men when they are orienting themselves to ideals and to values. Nietzsche was to choose the same character-type (*asketische Priester*) for the central role in his *Zur Genealogie der Moral*: he identified the development of contemporary decadence with the historical figure of the priest. Julien Benda was to title a highly influential book *La Trahison des clercs* (1927): he argued that the hitherto aristocratic, free-willed and strong-principled intellectual had degenerated into the clerk/cleric.

'Religion must be ethics, ethics alone is religion.'[2] From a net of moral sanctity all relationships bound by Christian love and friendship gain their sustenance. Stirner analyses the principle of love as a defence against the forbidding dominance of the world. A particular feeling is assumed, preconceived, very much in the style of a prejudice; experience, and tolerance, are cripplingly narrowed in the determination to follow that idea in all its purity, to posit the idealized feeling as a security against the hostile environment. And as life becomes less and less inherently enjoyable, as morality saps its spontaneity, as it succumbs to the sway of preconceived ideas, the flight to religion becomes the more necessary. Stirner describes the process, to borrow Freudian terms, of the *superego* replacing the *id* as the dominant psychic function. We note the key passage:[3]

> Henceforth man no longer, in typical cases, shudders at ghosts *outside* him, but at himself; he is terrified at himself. In the depth of his breast dwells the *spirit of sin*.

Here is an anticipation of what psychoanalysis was to detail as the combined process of identification and introjection. The association of Stirner's work with the Freudian theory of repression receives another one of many reinforcements in a characterization it makes of

---

[1] *Ego*, p. 80 among many references.
[2] *Ego* (1912), p. 74.
[3] *Ego*, p. 57. This, in embryo, is Nietzsche's derivation of the 'bad conscience' (*Genealogie* II:16).

the final victory of the religious mind. It has occurred when the subject can say:[1] 'The ugly—for example—makes a repulsive impression on me; but, determined to love, I master this impression as I do every antipathy.' Religion thus redefines love, originally a feeling state, as a moral concept. Spiritual life is sterilely intellectual; it no longer 'draws any nourishment from nature'.[2]

Stirner regards 'discontent with the present man' as the fertile breeding ground for religion.[3] This debilitated state of being, in which sensuality is inhibited by a strong-willed piety, is further consolidated by feelings of guilt:[4]

> But the habit of the religious way of thinking has biased our mind so grievously that we are—terrified at *ourselves* in our nakedness and naturalness; it has degraded us so that we dream ourselves depraved by nature, born devils . . . The Christian is nothing but a sensual man who, knowing of the sacred and being conscious that he violates it, sees in himself a poor sinner; sensuality, recognized as 'sinfulness', is Christian consciousness, is the Christian himself.

The religious vicious circle is constituted. Anxiety promotes self-abnegation, which, in turn, aggravates the comparison with the dogmatic ideal of man and God; this sustains deeper feelings of guilt and inadequacy and further intensifies the remoteness of the ideal. It is no coincidence, adds Stirner, that nearly all the great works of mind (*Geist*) were created by Protestants—the renunciators of the sensual.[5] Christianity has substituted ideals and concepts for sensual experience.

Stirner distinguishes between individual moral beliefs, which are relatively easy to overthrow, and the generalized force behind them — morality.[6] Morality is taken in two senses, as the bad conscience itself, the watchdog of mind, and as the energy, the fanatical zeal, which informs it.[7] Consciousness and conscience are closely related; the cleric is driven to believe in sacred things, to hold to religious concepts, because his conscience would be unbearable were there no

---

[1] *Ego*, p. 204.

[2] *Ego* (1912), p. 25.

[3] So did Nietzsche, in particular in his analysis of reactive emotion and the slave morality (e.g. *Genealogie* I:x).

[4] *Ego*, p. 116; *Ego* (1912), p. 417. These themes were to become essential to Nietzsche.

[5] *Ego*, p. 87. Cf. Nietzsche: 'If one tethers one's heart severely and imprisons it, one can give one's spirit many liberties' (*Jenseits* 87), and: 'The Protestant parson is the grandfather of German philosophy' (*Antichrist* 10).

[6] *Ego*, p. 85.

[7] He identifies bad conscience with the weapon of morality in his 1843 article, 'Einiges Vorläufige vom Liebesstaat' (republished in Max Stirner: *Kleinere Schriften*, 1914, p. 272).

positive goals for him to strive towards.[1] In the end the Christian love-morality produces the Christian proposition that the world is vacuous; the cleric's defence against incipient nihilism, against the 'Christian contempt of the world', is the 'sacred duty' he has created for himself and to which he has put himself in bondage.[2] Stirner here suggests a Nietzschean theme which we will later take up: that the last phase of intense religious moralizing is concomitant with the rise of nihilism, that both are symptoms of the same cultural malaise.

Stirner argues that the religious mind copes with anxiety by converting it into 'sacred dread' of the higher being. In effect original sin, the mythological cloak for anxiety, can thus be expiated in worship and self-abnegation. The vague fears which unbalance man are thereby explained away as the just punishment for his sinful nature; at the same time the floating energy which funds the anxiety linked with these fears is transformed into reverence and honour for the invulnerably divine arbiter, God. Thus anxiety is the catalyst in the growth of virtue and holiness.[3]

Stirner lampoons the Christian commandments: the 'heartlessness' of the adulterer, for example, is that he has no feeling for the sacred institution of marriage.[4] Christian enthusiasm and warm-heartedness are not for the person, but for the law and the institution.[5] The morality itself is loved, not the experience which it presupposed.

---

[1] *Ego*, p. 85.

[2] Ibid., pp. 86–8. For Nietzsche, one of the two worst contagions carried by the ascetic priest is his 'great nausea at man', his disgust and contempt for human life (*Genealogie* III:14); 'the will to self-maltreatment provided the conditions for the *value* of the unegoistic' (*Genealogie* II:18).

[3] *Ego*, pp. 77–8. Stirner's attack on Christianity reads as an uncannily accurate anticipation of Nietzsche, especially on considering the originality and sophistication of the psychology involved. The point is strikingly illustrated in Nietzsche's assessment of his own work in the last chapter of his last book, *Ecce Homo*:

> Have I been understood?—What defines me, what sets me apart from the whole rest of humanity is that I *uncovered* Christian morality . . . [On Christian morality] That one taught men to despise the very first instincts of life; that one mendaciously invented a 'soul', a 'spirit' to ruin the body; that one taught men to experience the presupposition of life, sexuality, as something unclean; that one looks for the evil principle in what is most profoundly necessary for growth, in *severe* self-love (this very word constitutes slander); that conversely one regards the typical signs of decline and contradiction of the instincts, the 'selfless', the loss of a centre of gravity, 'depersonalization' and 'neighbour love' (addiction to the neighbour) as the *higher* value—what am I saying?—the absolute value! . . . The only morality that has been taught so far, that of un-selfing, reveals a will to the end; fundamentally, it negates life.

[4] *Ego*, pp. 135–6.

[5] Like many of Christianity's critics, and in particular Nietzsche, Stirner does not attack the figure of Christ, but his Church, and its religiosity—see my footnote to p. 221 of *Ego*.

Friendship, marriage, property, indeed all relations between men, become sacred in and of themselves. He sums up his own disgust at Christianity's ubiquitous hold—while the whole world is still haunted, he affirms with a crafty pun: 'one free *grisette* against a housand virgins grown grey in virtue!'[1]

Stirner's critique of Christianity is, at one level, of keen contemporary interest; at another it is antiquated. In so far as Christianity does provide a prototype for ideology in general, the analysis endures, as it does in the particular case of humanist idealism. Later we shall support Nietzsche's contention that residues of Christian morality pervade socialist and positivist systems. Stirner and Nietzsche both locate the essence of Christianity in the clerical type: the cautious, calculating, rigid moralist who is devoted to ideals, principles, concepts, and numbers, but not to individual people. In our fourth chapter we will discuss anarcho-psychology's discovery of the secular embodiment of this type in Benthamite, utilitarian *homo economicus*.

What is most impressively radical about Stirner's method, given his time, is that he grounds his egoism psychologically. He inaugurates the reconstitution of philosophical debate as Nietzsche was to further it. He does not address himself to the religious question of how the divine reveals itself, nor to the philosophical questions of what is true and how is truth possible. He poses the psychological question: why does man need God, or surrogate gods such as History, Man and Truth? He does not enquire after the logic of ideology, its content, but after what it is in man that drives him to create cosmologies within which he then imprisons himself. He uses the Christian example to examine the deleterious effects of ideology on its individual adherents, and on the society in which they live.

It is this psychological perspective which distinguishes Stirner from the Hegelian tradition, and in particular from its all-important *method* of thinking. The psychology which Hegel introduced with the category of *Angst* into *Die Phänomenologie des Geistes* remains marginal, unsustained. Later in the same work he disparages psychology.[2] More significant are the psychological strains in Feuerbach's incorporation of Hegel's category of objectification into an analysis of religious alienation. Stirner extends this psychology into a methodology in its own right. Like Freud he sets out to piece together a theory of human behaviour, and a model for the whole individual personality, from a series of examples of highly charged types of action. General theory and particular case develop concurrently, reflecting and influencing each other. The crucial difference between Stirner and Freud is that the philosopher of individualist anarchism does not develop his theory systematically; theory often

---

[1] *Ego*, p. 72.
[2] *The Phenomenology of Mind*, trans. J. B. Baillie, 1949, pp. 331-3, 349-51.

remains an embryonic shadow behind concrete examples of such phenomena as evangelizing persecution. General themes and hypotheses are frequently left implicit. One consequence of this anarchist indifference towards systematic theory is that *Der Einzige* gains from a gaiety and buoyancy of style, which in itself adds a dimension to its thesis. However, there is also the negative consequence that the argument is often impressionistic, that it is not fully explored: implications which relate to the larger thesis are not spelt out. Freud's commitment to developing an explicit and consistent theory helped him to gain an unmatched degree of psychological purchase on the many-sided complex of human reality.

A critique of Christianity of the sustained intensity of that levelled by Stirner and Nietzsche, however insightful the psychology it generated, inevitably reads today as somehow dated. We cannot conceive of the social and psychological climate that provoked these fervid anti-Christian writings. This is particularly marked in the case of Nietzsche: so much of his work is acutely in phase with contemporary cultural problems that the passion, even fanaticism, of his *Der Antichrist* strikes a peculiarly alien key. (The historical significance of this critique is not in question. Indeed, it should not be forgotten that Freud, who played an instrumental role in the fracturing of the piously Christian superego in Europe, had been strongly influenced in the 1890s and thereafter by a pervasive climate of Nietzschean ideas. One of the largest reefs on which organized religion foundered was the psychology that Stirner helped to pioneer.)

The attack on Christianity has had an enduring impact; it has sustained its capacity to provoke and to shock, not because of its demolition of one specific example of organized religion, but because it represents the most incisive, comprehensive, and convincing argument for ethical relativism in the Western tradition. It will become clearer as we proceed further that Stirner and Nietzsche's 'God is dead!' condemns as futile what appears to be a universal human drive—that to discover a consistent, monistic hierarchy of values, or what Kant called the 'complete purposive unity', and identified with God. The demolition of theology ultimately places in question what may be civilized man's most fundamental quest for security.

The immoralist

An ideology is a moral system. It supplies a means of interpreting the social world, as a coherent assembly of good and evil hierarchies and tendencies. Every ideology is explicitly or implicitly grounded in a system of values. It thereby provides an ordering of the human environment which includes imperatives governing how to live and what to do. The critique of Christianity generalizes into a critique of morality.

We have found the rudiments of a new psychology of human motivation, anticipating Nietzsche and Freud, in Stirner's critique of Christianity. These are consolidated in his profoundly 'Nietzschean' attack on moralism. The egoist first as 'desecrator' (*Entheiliger*), then as 'immoralist' (*Unsittlicher*),[1] thus reads Stirner's formula for the revaluation of life. As the holy was incompatible with egoism, so is the moral. Before turning to the 'all things are possible' of the immoralist, it is necessary to understand why Stirner reacts so vehemently against *moral* action.

Stirner views 'good' and 'evil' as artificial indices taken up by individuals to save them making the difficult choices of life; they neatly divide the activities of man into the positive and the negative. But, from Stirner's perspective, which has a long history traceable back through Hobbes and Machiavelli, the moral law is neither natural nor necessary. The sceptic, Timon, is quoted in *Der Einzige*: 'in itself nothing is either good or bad, but man only thinks of it thus or thus'.[2] Stirner develops this insight in the philosophical framework created by Hegel and Feuerbach, then translates it into a vision of man who has transcended morality. He is in the strict sense an 'a-moralist'; he moves towards a position independent of, rather than in opposition to, social mores. He is an 'immoralist' in the sense that he identifies with those whom moralists call 'immoral', and in the sense in which Nietzsche introduced this term to describe himself— as an 'anti-moralist'.

Morality has essentially two undesirable effects. Firstly, it breeds hypocrisy. Man is entirely self-centred, believes Stirner, but for some reason he often is ridden with guilt, and seeks to deny his egoism: he achieves this denial through morality. There is the suggestion that guilt and lack of egoism are associates, and that moral systems are adopted by the unegoistic to satisfy their constant need to explain, to excuse, and to justify themselves and their guilt-tainted acts. Stirner prefigures Sartre's central notion of 'bad faith', of the individual living at a remove from his 'true self', in self-deceit. The retort of

---

1 Stirner follows Hegel in his choice of *Sittlichkeit*, rather than Kant's *Moralität*, to represent the substance of ethics. *Sittlichkeit* for Hegel was a total ethics, even ethos, which, although internalized in the individual, allowed him to relate beyond himself, and thus functioned as the blood of social interaction (Kaufman: *Hegel* 6 and 10). Stirner prefers the more *organic* Hegelian ethics to that of Kant. But, in essence, he lumps both together: the internalized morality of Hegel is but a later form, psychologically viewed, of *Moralität*. In order to refute Hegel, Stirner retains his language. (It is plain from the text that he intends *Sitten* in a much broader sense than its common English equivalent, *custom*—for example, *Ego*, p. 64, where derivatives from *sittlich* are employed throughout.)

2 *Ego* (1912), p. 28; we recall the almost identical sentiment of *Hamlet* II:ii:259.

Der Einzige is: 'Just recognize yourselves again, just recognize what you really are, and let go your hypocritical endeavours, your foolish mania to be something else than you are'.[1]

A man loves another person not, at the base, to make the other happy, but because he enjoys the state of loving. This harsh insight was anticipated, characteristically, in the libertine stoicism of La Rochefoucauld; Nietzsche made it more precise with his aphorism: 'In the end one loves one's desire and not what is desired'.[2] It becomes a cornerstone of the anarcho-psychological perspective, and Freud also will repeat it. Its full implication is that one man never loves another immediately. The person whom he claims to love the most is the one who elicits from him the deepest or the widest range of desires and passions. He uses the other as a complementary electrode: he needs him in order to express and realize himself, in order to experience his own passions. Similarly, when he remembers the past he does not recall events and individuals directly, but only the desires and hopes that he experienced through or with them. This is the *egoist axiom*: it dismisses as psychologically invalid any view of society which does not take the egoistic individual as the primary phenomenon, and every other social unit as subsidiary to his desires, however conditioned or repressed those desires may be.

The parable of the Good Samaritan illustrates a theme which is implicit in Stirner. A man is not loved by those who ought, by all accounts (racial tie, moral belief, and so on), to love him, but by those who *need* his love (the alien, the unloved, the Samaritan). Thus love comes very much by chance: who can predict whether a Samaritan—and why bother to call him 'good'? Stirner would ask—will happen along the road at the right time? Moreover, the attempt to make love certain, to institutionalize it by turning it into a moral *ought*, is self-defeating—the man who tells himself to love will never love spontaneously, the man who possessively demands love will surely lose it.

The cleric will always pass by the unholy stranger; and why not, says the immoralist (the cleric's hypocrisy is another question). No one has a *right* to another's love. 'The egoist's love rises in selfishness, flows in the bed of selfishness, and empties into selfishness again.'[3]

Stirner is not the prophet of callous isolation in spite of his caustic words; his intention is to put that focus of much of human hope and philosophy—love—on an honest, concrete footing. He wants to cut away the bigotry, the desire to appear unegoistic, and preserve the emotional base of the experience. It goes without saying that:[4]

If I see the loved one suffer, I suffer with him, and I know no rest until I have tried everything to comfort and cheer him; if

---

[1] *Ego*, p. 119.   [2] *Jenseits* 175.   [3] *Ego*, pp. 201–3.   [4] Ibid., p. 200.

I see him glad, I too become glad over his joy . . . because I cannot bear the troubled crease on the beloved forehead, for that reason, and therefore for my sake, I kiss it away.

The great Russian critic and socialist, Belinsky, offered some cautionary comments in 1848 after reading *Der Einzige* and taking its argument very much to heart:[1]

It would be juvenile to be frightened of the word 'egoism' itself. It has been proved that a man feels and thinks and acts invariably according to the law of egotistical urges, and indeed, he cannot have any others. The unfortunate thing is that mystical doctrines have brought the term into disgrace, giving it the meaning of the caterer to all the base passions and instincts in man, and we have already become accustomed to understand it in that sense. The word was dishonoured for no good reason, since it denotes a completely natural, essential, and, therefore, legitimate phenomenon, and, moreover, includes, as does all that is essential and natural, the possibility of moral inference.

Now, if it is accepted that all action is egoistic, the problem becomes to distinguish between different levels of satisfaction. Stirner does this, in effect, by developing a theory of repression. The important question, he claims, is not how egoistic a man is, but how much enjoyment he gets out of his life. The desire to appear selfless, the argument continues, restricts full and carefree satisfaction; the attempt to strike a moral pose subverts, as it inhibits, man's sensual resources. The half-hearted egoist is perpetually holding himself back. Dropping the hypocritical good reasons for behaviour, Stirner believes, will result in a great liberation of energy and the possibility of a full-blooded, joyful egoism. This is Stirner's optimism: it nourishes his hopes for individual, and subsequently social, melioration. But Nietzsche, who also emphasized a direct connection between, on the one hand, the rationalizing mind and its concern with the 'good', and on the other, flagging egoism, or, in his own words, a waning Will-to-Power, warned repeatedly that such optimism is naive and unfounded. As we shall examine, he doubted whether individuals, or even societies, could do much to reverse their heritage of accumulating guilt.

Morality's second undesirable effect, according to Stirner, is the repression of natural instincts. Nietzsche formulates the argument: 'morality is a way of turning one's back on the will to existence'.[2]

---

[1] P. V. Annenkov: *The Extraordinary Decade*, 1968, p. 407. Belinsky's point here stands as an anticipatory reply to the mystical critique of egoism which Dostoevsky will later develop.

[2] *Wille* 11.

Perhaps the severest debility the clerical type must overcome is the desire to be moderate in all things. Self-retention, half-heartedness, partial and premeditated involvement, are all subsumed under the word 'moderation'. But what is being saved, concealed from the world? Not a precious self, Stirner replies, for the rich ego freely expresses itself, 'gets the value out of itself'. It is the unrealized self, scared of how naked it will appear when exposed, which withdraws and protects itself by being 'in moderation'.[1] The selfless one is incapable of placing real value on property, for contact with object, thought, and feeling is only clinched in his enjoyment of them. Unable to find a means for self-expression in the concrete sensual world, he turns to the Church. Stirner regarded his own time as one of transition, 'no longer vigorous enough to serve *morality* without doubt or weakening, not yet reckless enough to live wholly to egoism . . .'[2] Such half-heartedness leads, on the one hand, to hedging spontaneous acts with moral justifications, and, on the other, to compensating for moral inhibitions by giving vocal approval to the spontaneous. The moderate man, in this sense, has no natural resources by which he can distinguish the self-enhancing from the self-destroying act; he is poor in the midst of his possessions.[3]

The scars of morality, like those of religion, are not all internal. Hypocrisy is the less distasteful effect of the rationalization of some types of human behaviour. As in the case of religious fanaticism, Stirner warns: 'love becomes crazy by a *must* taking it out of my power'.[4] Abstract generalities, such as 'justice', establish a means of discrimination; they rationalize aggression against certain groups or individuals. They both stimulate violent emotions and provide them with a target. Stirner anticipates Nietzsche's analysis of the reactive emotion, resentment: he argues that the immoralist individual who follows his own desires will suffer most at the hands of the envious moralists.[5] He states that he would prefer to be at the mercy of a man's selfishness than of his ideals about himself.[6]

Stirner and Nietzsche imply that there is a type of freedom

---

[1] *Ego*, p. 210. The most salient trait of Zarathustra's 'last man', the most degraded of modern society's offspring, is his moderation in all things.

[2] *Ego*, p. 67.

[3] In his comments on European nihilism Nietzsche associates the triumph of truth, love, and justice with the 'preeminence of what is un-egoistic, self-denial, negation of the will' (*Wille* 30).

[4] *Ego*, p. 201.

[5] Ibid., pp. 135–6. Nietzsche's summing up of the significance of his *Morgenröte* illustrates how close he is to Stirner: 'The decisive symptom that shows how the priest (including those *crypto*-priests, the philosophers) has become master quite generally . . . is the fact that what is unegoistic is met with hostility' (*Ecce Homo* III:iv:2).

[6] *Ego*, pp. 213–14. A theme to be re-echoed by D. H. Lawrence as well as Nietzsche.

available to man in which ideology is not dominant, in which morality is adaptable to the needs of the individual: a state beyond good
and evil. One counter-argument, which is stronger than they cater
for, runs to the effect that this assumption is psychologically unfounded, that it is utopian in the repressive sense of serving to
awaken unrealizable hopes. The case is put by the Grand Inquisitor
in Dostoevsky's *The Brothers Karamazov*. He argues against Christ,
who represents a position identical to that of Stirner, that men do
not want this freedom, that they do not seek to determine their own
values. He impeaches Christ for having too little compassion for
man, for failing to respect his choice, which will be for happiness,
given that happiness and freedom are incompatible. The Inquisitor
himself chooses to take on the responsibility of making decisions and
determining values; he provides the happier majority with bread to
eat, and miracles to save them from boredom. He would grant the
truth of Stirner's: 'You love man therefore you torture the individual
man'.[1] His defence is that the will of the majority urges that Christ be
killed. The Christ's response, to kiss the Grand Inquisitor, is baffling-
ly and assertively anarchic, in the characteristic sense that little more
can be said about it than that it expresses the individual. It is irrational in that it rejects the terms of the debate—the Inquisitor's case,
as stated, had been a persuasive one. The debate founders on the
dichotomy which has bedevilled political philosophy since Plato,
that between the *one* and the *many*. Christ's: 'learn by my example, if
you so choose!' and his offer of guidance to help others discover
their own ethical system, is plausibly realistic in the case of the one,
or the few. But, in the case of the many, the Grand Inquisitor has not
been answered; we postpone further discussion of this pragmatist
defence of ideology.

Stirner's highly flexible aphoristic style is a far cry from the stiff,
concept-strictured writing of Hegel, and even of Feuerbach; indeed,
Ruge wrote enthusiastically of *Der Einzige* as the 'first readable book
in philosophy that Germany has produced'.[2] Stirner's critique of
morality is at its best in incisive representations of the delusions of
the self-righteous, moral man; for example:[3]

> Show me a sinner in the world still, if no one any longer needs
> to do what suits a superior! . . . You brought the sinner with
> you in your head, therefore you found him, therefore you
> inserted him everywhere. Do not call men sinners, and they are
> not: you alone are the creator of sinners; you, who fancy that
> you love men, are the very one to throw them into the mire of

---

[1] *Ego*, p. 200.
[2] Brazill, op. cit., p. 215.
[3] *Ego* (1912), p. 479; *Ego*, p. 255. Nietzsche titles section 76 of his *Morgenröte:*
'Who thinks evil, makes evil'.

sin, the very one to divide them into vicious and virtuous, into human and inhuman; the very one to befoul them with the slaver of your possessedness; for you love not *men* but *man*. But I tell you, you have never seen a sinner, you have only— dreamed of him.

Such an exclusive concern for the moral well-being of others is one of the cardinal symptoms of self-estrangement. The cleric avoids too much introspection in his crusades in case his deeds fail to match up to his ideal. The egoist, lacking interest in the 'virtue' of other men, looms as a two-fold threat. He destroys the universal importance accorded to moral law by showing that life independent of it is possible. Secondly, and even more intolerably for the pious, he manages to do so with shameless enjoyment. The psychology of resentment points out that the clerical type will view anything egoistical with a peculiarly intense hostility.[1]

Where there is a moral mind there has been a moral education. Stirner develops the implication of his 1834 examination thesis— education should encourage the potential to become actual, and stimulate unique qualities to develop themselves.[2] Education ought to bring man to himself, not to society, it should teach him to explore his own feelings and not the imparted responses that someone else considers he ought to experience.[3] For this, the 1834 thesis argued, he needs a teacher, a 'higher man', to guide him and inspire him by his example, until the student gains the confidence in himself to reject the image of authority that is not of his own creation.[4] The basis for the true understanding of another person, for mature relationship, is learnt in the 'I–I' (*Ich zum Ich*) relationship that is possible between student and teacher. Stirner's case, one peculiarly relevant for modern 'progressive' movements in education, was extremely radical in pre-1848 Prussia where the austere paternalism of the school formed an unquestioned axiom of education. More-over, its anti-Benthamism is striking: Stirner's 'free pedagogy' finds its antithesis in the utilitarian school of Gradgrind, whose motto was 'fact not fancy', in Dickens's *Hard Times* (1854).

This hope for a sensitive and mature teacher, with whom the children can have personal relations in which they are treated as equals, is a far cry from the type of moralistic education in which the students are moulded to fit the bed of the ideal man and his social etiquette:[5]

Yes, yes, children must early be *made* to practise piety, godliness, and propriety; a person of good breeding is one in

[1] *Ego*, p. 69. [2] *Über Schulgesetze*, p. 15. [3] *Ego*, p. 75.
[4] *Über Schulgesetze*, pp. 15–16. [5] *Ego*, pp. 84, 75.

whom 'good maxims' have been *instilled* and *impressed*, poured
in through a funnel, thrashed in and preached in . . . The
young are of age when they twitter like the old.

Stirner believes that in so far as the intention of education is to train
the child for a vocation it is a millstone around his neck. This
utilitarian education which endeavours to produce set types is
geared to the belief that each individual has an ordained calling in
life, to be selected and shaped by the social system. Stirner responds:
'I live after a calling as little as the flower grows and gives fragrance
after a calling'.[1] The source of all power is within man; there is no
destiny, vocation, or calling to be realized from without; *impression*
is significant only when it helps to elucidate *expression*. Education
should be the catalyst for self-awareness, where 'self' is an active,
protrusive, 'in the process of becoming', phenomenon. Stirner
rephrases his existential ontology:[2]

My first babble is the token of the life of a 'true man', the
struggles of my life are the outpourings of his force, my last
breath is the last exhalation of the force of the 'man'.

Stirner's critique of vocation, of blueprinted action, of externally-
determined styles of life points to a view of progress characteristic
of the *Bildungsroman*, one specifically restricted to self-realization.
Stirner implies that attachment to a rationalistic, teleological
notion of progress indicates the absence of true progress; he whose
life does not unfold satisfyingly under its own momentum is driven
to moralize it, to set up goals and rationalize their achievement as
progress.

Education is the strongest weapon available for restricting the
questions people ask, controlling what they think, and ensuring that
they get their thoughts 'from above', as Stirner puts it.[3] Through
education the State has the supreme power of defining its subjects'
view of the world, for 'as a rule, people do not think farther than
their teachers have thought'.[4] Like the Church, the State fences off
certain realms of consciousness as 'evil', it selectively programmes the
mind by closing off the awareness of entire spheres of experience.[5]
(One corollary to this is that a teacher's freedom is realized simply by
making himself *audible*.[6])

A society invokes morality most vehemently in the sphere of crime
and punishment. Stirner's anarchic rejection of social definitions of
good and evil is a logical extension of his egoist thesis. What is
particularly striking is his opposition to petty theft. He does not

---

[1] *Ego*, p. 261.   [2] Ibid., p. 230.   [3] Ibid., p. 242.   [4] Ibid., p. 244.
[5] In general, ibid., pp. 242–4; in particular, my footnote to p. 244.
[6] Ibid., p. 245.

accept the liberal attitude that crime degrades the 'humanity' in man (again the meaningless abstraction). The petty thief is too little an egoist, for he values an object for its prestige in another's eyes, rather than for its direct utility to him. He is the most pathetic victim of society because he accepts its morality and its property valuations: they excite in him socially legitimized aspirations which he cannot satisfy without breaking other laws.[1]

There is a deeper psychological current running through Stirner's analysis of the cleric, to whose characteristics we can now add the revengeful desire to punish. 'The Christian is not owner of his "bad desires" so long as he has to combat them; for him who contends against vice, vice *exists*.'[2] Here in one short aphorism is the insight that was to form a cornerstone in the work of both Nietzsche and Freud. He who condemns vice in another is afraid that the very same vice exists repressed in himself; this fear supplies energy that can intensify revulsion to the pitch of frenzied persecution, or we might say, following Stirner's word-convoluting style, makes 'vic-ious' condemnation of the vice. By punishing the criminal the moral man hopes to dissuade the evil imprisoned in his own breast from escaping. Fear of self is projected in hatred of the immoral other. Again we have entered the realm of the *unconscious*.[3]

A strong hostility to vice indicates the presence of dangerous forces beneath the surface of the moralist's consciousness. Stirner does not take the one further step that Freud took, with his suggestion that 'the punishment will not infrequently give those who carry it out an opportunity of committing the same outrage under the colour of an act of expiation'.[4]

The ground is laid in Stirner's exploration of the ego for work on the unconscious. No longer is the attempt to identify motive with intention possible. The motive behind an action cannot necessarily

---

[1] Stirner's immoralism must be differentiated from that fêted as the first literary attempt to incarnate Nietzsche's ideas, André Gide's *L'Immoraliste* (1902). Gide was absorbed by a different problem. He sought to infuse behaviour at odds with the mores of his society (e.g. homosexuality) with a kind of moral respectability. There is nothing full-blooded about his *immoraliste*—he is tentative, somewhat ineffectual, and above all, the captive of the very guilt he seeks to overcome. Like Stirner, Gide searched for self-honesty, but his liberation became a compromise with the guilt that society heaped upon him. There was no scope for full transcendence, which is not to question his novel's psychological credentials.

[2] *Ego*, pp. 252–3.

[3] Eduard von Hartmann was one of the first philosophers to refer to Stirner, in his highly popular and influential book on the unconscious: *Philosophie des Unbewussten* (1869).

[4] Quoted by Paul Roazen (*Freud: Political and Social Thought*, 1969, p. 138). Nietzsche also analysed the pleasure men derive from punishing others (e.g. *Jenseits* 55).

be inferred from the actor's stated intention; except in the case of instrumental action, in which the goal is determined in advance, man tends to act first and then rationalize his action. Stirner goes further: action such as punishment, which is backed by strong moral legitimation, indicates that the actor, instead of embodying the virtue to which he ascribes his action, is the unconscious bearer of its complementary vice.[1] His comments on the motives of the punisher, and on the effects of his 'justice', completely undermine the Benthamite meliorist theory of punishment. His doubts about liberal-humanism stem from this same insight that an ideal often masks the absence of the very emotional quality (say, compassion) which it supposedly represents. Here also in the psychological analysis of morality are the roots of the later existentialist concern with self-honesty as a primary value.

The anxiety-producing schism between 'bad desires' and a pure ideal of self generates fanaticism. Stirner's choice of *fanaticism* (*Fanatismus*) to describe this moral intensity is deliberative. His constant concern with revitalizing language, repossessing it as a creative force, leads him in this case to an etymological derivative from *fanum* (sacred). He describes the 'moral shudder' which launches the fanatical punishment of incest and bigamy.[2]

In this outline of Stirner's thought we are more concerned with understanding the theoretical weapons he has designed than following in detail their particular applications (in general the application follows directly from the principle). It is worth noting, however, his attitude to those who love weighing the 'good' and 'evil' of every possible action. He closes a two-page discussion of the moral issues considered relevant to the question of suicide by stating: 'Such contradictions form the tragic conflict universally in the moral drama; and one must think and feel morally to be able to take an interest in it.'[3]

For Stirner, self-alienation springs from the dissociation of action, and a consciousness of action, from the basic instincts and feelings. In fact, he has turned Kant's rationalist moralism on its head: 'Either man is led by his sensuality, and is, following it,

---

[1] Cf. *King Lear:*
Thou rascal beadle hold thy bloody hand!
Why dost thou lash that whore? Strip thy own back.
Thou hotly lusts to use her in that kind
For which thou whip'st her.
(Act IV:vi:157–60)

[2] *Ego*, pp. 61–2. See my footnote 1 to p. 62, and the footnote to p. 222 which illustrates his further assault on accepted morality: 'I do not renounce from any access of humility, even the power over life and death.' Nietzsche also directed specific criticism at 'moral fanaticism' (e.g. *Morgenröte*, *Vorrede*, 3).

[3] *Ego* (1912), pp. 430–2.

immoral, or he is led by the good'.[1] He confronts the moral man, who obeys what he *thinks* he ought to do, in defiance of his more spontaneous feelings, with the vitalist figure of the egoist. Nietzsche puts it that weakness should not be fought 'with a kind of justification and moralization', but with a *système fortifiant*.[2]

Nietzsche's claim to immoralism was that he had gone 'beyond good and evil'. As a result of having shown that there is no absolute good, that morality reflects subjective psychological needs, he considered himself the first thinker not to be driven unselfcritically into value judgments. He sought simply to understand; the categories of good and evil were unnecessary for him. But he himself has taught more persuasively than anyone that to renounce God, to move beyond the threshold of moral systems, is to deny any means for ordering the world:

> Are we (who have killed God) not plunging continually?
> Backward, sideward, forward, in all directions? Is there any up and down left? Are we not straying through an infinite nothing?[3]

The act of understanding involves selection, the simplification through language of the infinitely complex chaos of unreflected reality. The drive to understand stems from a need to cope with experience, to reduce the levels of anxiety which it provokes, to find an order in it such that the individual can thenceforth better choose how to act. At this point the individual seeks an 'up and down', an ordering of perceptions and experiences in hierarchies of differing moral valencies.

As soon as he has recourse to knowledge, to help him make his choices, he has distanced himself from his immediate desires; he has entered the conceptual universe of *good* and *evil*. Only the mythical 'noble savage' lives outside morality: he has never experienced its categories. Nietzsche's ideal character type, the master, like Stirner's egoist, is purely impulsive and spontaneous, he neither experiences reactive emotion nor requires moral imperatives in order to act. But he is not incarnate in nineteenth-century Western society. Nietzsche's assertion that 'all that is good is instinct'[4] can only stand as a means of distinguishing enhancing from inhibiting forces in each person; it does not imply that there either is, or should be, the realized ideal of the completely instinctual individual. The tendency in Nietzsche's late work is for the 'beyond good and evil' formulation to give way to 'the revaluation of all values': here is implicit recognition that morality in the wider sense is endemic to the human condition, and

---

[1] *Ego*, p. 64. Cf. Nietzsche's attack on Kant as parson and decadent—*Antichrist* 10–11.
[2] *Wille* 47.   [3] *Wissenschaft* 125.   [4] *Götzen-Dämmerung* vi:2.

that the real task is not to rid life of ethics but rid ethics of its ideological content.

In what sense then does the description 'immoralist' retain significance? It does so in a number of circumscribed ways. Stirner and Nietzsche demonstrate the relativity of all moral judgments: there is no absolute *good*, there is no Kantian categorical imperative. They seek to defuse morality: to reduce obligations to preferences. They reveal how prone morality is to being used as a means of rationalization, a cloak for concealing violent and brutish passions, and making of their sadistic expression a virtue. They expose the repressive role that the drive to moralize plays within the individual character, the way in which it impedes self-understanding. The achievement of the anarcho-psychological perspective which they represent is, in this sphere, to go beyond the type of dogmatic, unselfreflective moralism which was dominant in middle and late nineteenth-century Europe. It sought to reconstitute moral classification as an aid to self-knowledge, a mediator between the conscious self and both the external world and the subconscious inner man.

Nietzsche urges that the old priest-type of morality be exposed and renounced. But he is reluctant to specify the nature of the new order of values to replace it, preferring to spell out the manner in which the individual should relate himself to them. Man needs to establish an 'up and down' in order to live; Nietzsche's point is that he should at least be conscious of what he does when he chooses values, of the degree of arbitrariness involved in his choice. Thus values are tools for exploration, they are probationary; they must constantly be put in question, kept under scrutiny, with the individual testing them out to see how hollow they ring. It is this *method* of using values which becomes the ultimate value.[1]

The immoralist inference is that man should judge as little as possible. Although Nietzsche grants morality, he found a method of thinking designed to undermine its particular manifestations. Nietzsche himself was a great moralist; his writings abound with value judgments about individuals, character types, modes of thinking, and national traits. It is as if he develops immoralist psychology in order to tame his own nature, to keep his own greatest vice in check. Adorno has put St Paul's reference to the thorn in his side more pointedly:[2] 'The splinter in your eye is the best magnifying glass'. The prodigious scope of Nietzsche's insight into the moralist psyche and the nature of reactive emotions stands as his greatest contribution to our knowledge.

---

[1] Nietzsche gives some support to this interpretation in a general aphorism: 'The most valuable insights are arrived at last; but the most valuable insights are *methods*' (*Wille* 469).

[2] T. W. Adorno: *Minima Moralia*, 1951, p. 57.

There is a strong strain of Protestant masochism in this assault on morality and ideology. What is set as the key value is the capacity itself for coping with uncertainty, for relishing the unknown, for proving able to progressively destroy the scaffolding for understanding and evaluating experience as it is being constructed. Framing this perspective is the Protestant image of the utterly self-reliant, responsible individual, and Ibsen's harsh dictum from *An Enemy of the People*: 'The strongest man in the world is he who stands most alone'.

The existentialist

At the base of the philosophical innovations of Stirner and Nietzsche is ontology: their radically new perspective on religion, on morals, on political and social life, stems from their attitude to *being*. Their entire work branches out from the stem conviction that there is a primary order of reality about which all that can be said is that the individual exists, that 'I am!' The individual first exists, and then begins to define himself. Essences, the communicable, socially mediated dimension of individual character, belong to the second order of reality. Behind them lies an unconscious, irreducible, never realizable or comprehensible force, an inviolable coherency: the individuum. This is the ground of *der Einzige*, the unique one, the realm of what Stirner calls his 'creative nothing'. Existentialism, whose primary philosophical concern has been with questions of *being*, of *das Wesen* or *l'être*, and in particular with the axiom that existence precedes essence, received its first well-developed modern statement in 1844. Heidegger and Sartre, like Nietzsche, neglect the man who, on a number of key issues, is their most significant precursor.

The political anarchism of Stirner and Nietzsche is a logical development of their ontological anarchism: their denigration of social authorities represents one dimension of their endeavour to displace the authority of essences and stress the primacy of the *I*. Both see the springs of the human condition as anarchic, wilful, problematical, a complex of forces with their deeply individual source beneath the superstructure of social mediation; both recognize what Plato referred to as the 'unutterable' in each individual, a noumenal core which makes of human thinking, by necessity, an isolated, introspective activity. The social or essentialist superstructure is by itself lifeless; its function is to provide the *I* with a means of expression.

The defining axiom of this ontologically grounded psychology is vividly represented by Freud's favourite metaphor for the psyche: the iceberg. But the most strikingly similar, and, at this point in our

D

argument, illuminating, psychoanalytical formulation is to be found in the work of the strangely neglected Georg Groddeck. Groddeck argues, principally in his *Das Buch des Es* (1921), that the individual is governed by an unconscious being, the *it*, which both funds his instincts, his desires, and his emotions, and patterns them. This *it*, or *id* as Freud's notion of *das Es* is translated into English, a notion incidentally which Freud credits to Groddeck, lies beneath the range of conscious control. The role of consciousness is to interpret the messages from the *it*, whether they be expressed in emotions, dreams, physical disorders, or mental stresses. Self-understanding is consequently defined as the process of coming to know the ways of the *it*. The 'I am' has its generative source in the 'it', not with the conscious ego.

The strong existentialist themes in Stirner's philosophy find their most complete expression in his reply to Feuerbach's critique of *Der Einzige*.[1] For Stirner identity or self-ness is not primarily a sum of qualities; rather it is that which the individual knows without having to predicate this knowledge; it is the precondition of all knowledge, 'the *who*, the *he* of the phrase'. Thus the ego is a sense (a feeling, an intuition, even a comprehension) of identity; it is the spine that supports and conditions the growth of personality. The 'I think, therefore I am' of Descartes, the 'I feel, therefore I am' of late eighteenth-century Romanticism, and the 'I possess, therefore I am' of bourgeois man are dogmas, partial at that, incorporated to define a being that is incapable of defining itself. Certainly the existentialist 'I am!' is also dogmatic, but for Stirner, the only dogma which is not *alienating*, the one which does not make being other than itself.

It might clarify Stirner's ontology to point out that the *who* of the phrase is structurally similar to Nietzsche's image of man as a bridge,[2] the carriageway that supports the process of 'becoming who one is'; being is thus the dynamic shell within which man realizes himself. Then the question 'Who am I?' is essentially unanswerable, for I, as a potentiality, am no more than a bridge whose traffic is always in motion, and carrying its supports on with it. Stirner exalts movement: the unique one is the statement that changes, that fades into silence every minute, the vehicle of a continually developing-in-dying *I*.[3]

The 'egoist' plays the same functional role in Stirner's philosophy as the *Übermensch* does in Nietzsche's.[4] It is an ideal-type, to which

1 'Recensenten Stirners' (1845); the relevant section is included in *Ego*, pp. 257–9.
2 E.g., *Zarathustra, Vorrede* 4.   3 *Ego*, pp. 257–9.
4 Following Danto's convention in retaining the original German *Übermensch* rather than substituting either of the unhappy English translations, 'superman' or 'overman' (Arthur C. Danto: *Nietzsche as Philosopher*, 1965, pp. 196–7).

man can at best approximate;[1] it is a supra-human end towards which all striving should aim, an intimation of the direction in which life is at its best. In this schema the process itself, the means not the end, is the goal of human action: not to arrive but to make the most of the journey. Rilke was to use the 'Angel' as a device equivalent to these ideal-types in his *Duinese Elegien*: the hint to, and the promise of, perfection in human life, the consummate imprint of the rare, fleeting moments when man transcends his mundane necessities.

Stirner's ontological first principle is not exactly the simple 'I am!'; he rather asserts that 'I am—present!'[2] All that the individual can say with certain knowledge is that he exists and is present, that he exists because he feels or senses the presence of himself. Memories of the past and hopes for the future are at one remove. Heidegger will make 'presence' one of his key categories: one of his ontological theorems states '*Sein heisst Anwesen*'. He develops Stirner's axiom by substituting *anwesend*, the alternative German for 'present', for Stirner's '*gegenwärtig*'.[3] The English loses the full meaning of *anwesend*, which translates literally as 'being-at': thus to be present is to have entered a state of *being*. The English has the virtue that *presence* is subsumed under *present*: temporal presence implies spatial presence. Stirner's axiom serves also as an ethical imperative, exhorting the individual to savour the here-and-now, to get the best out of it.

Stirner is the philosopher of the infinitely possible. The egoist is the limitless one; his freedom lies in his ability to create his own infinity. Stirner has in effect taken the omnipotence fantasy of the child, who believes that he has unlimited power in choice and action, and made it accessible to the adult, who is soberly conscious of the ideological traps inherent in ideals and fantasies. But whilst Stirner's 'I elect for myself what I have a fancy for, and in electing I show myself—arbitrary'[4] provides a salutary antidote to conformist religion and unreflected obedience to social conventions and values, it remains one-sided. It rings with the defiance which is blind to social necessity, which refuses to acknowledge what Freud will call the 'reality principle'. It represses the recognition that loss, despair, constraint, and frustration are inherent in the human condition. This philosophy does not take a full and balanced account of human passions.

[1] The ideal-type is closely analogous to the mathematical notion of the limit to which an infinite series converges, ever more closely, but without ever quite reaching. It is a convenient tool for locating the series, and the salient feature of each of its elements, without being able to define fully any element.

[2] *Ego*, pp. 117–18.

[3] Martin Heidegger: *Being and Time*, 1962.

[4] *Ego*, p. 241.

And yet, at another level, Stirner's affirmation of freedom rings true. It capitalizes the moments when life quickens and excites, moments of high intensity and absorption, the moments which will be remembered with nostalgia, and will almost invariably be the ones counted to have made life worthwhile. It passes all else by as relatively unimportant. Stirner has faith that experience is never irretrievably cut from these moments. He heads his preface with Goethe's 'I have founded my affair on nothing'. The next line of Goethe's poem, *Vanitas! Vanitatem Vanitas!* is equally central for him: 'And to me belongs the entire world'. There are moments when an individual becomes omnipotent.

We are confronted by a flaw in the orthodox structure of Western logic. One of the main roots of the anarcho-psychological perspective, and its opposition to rationalist-positivist thought and to progress models of society, is its disbelief in the law of non-contradiction. Implicit in the work of Stirner, Nietzsche, and Dostoevsky is the conviction that knowledge cannot be comprehensive, and consequently that there do not exist hypotheses which are both interesting and tell the whole truth. The reality of the human condition is far too complex to be encompassed by propositions: philosophy can proceed only part-way towards creating propositions, and then for only a few of the many facets of this reality.[1] In the specific case under discussion, it is true both that Stirner's work is one-sided, when viewed from the perspective of, say, Freud, and that it is adequately comprehensive, when viewed from a more romantic individualist perspective. The two perspectives do not mutually exclude each other; they could both be held by the same individual at different levels of his consciousness, or as applicable in different situations according to their nature or his own mood.

The laws of consistency on which positivism depends cannot accommodate such logic: any sense of knowledge steadily accumulating is undermined, as is belief in progress in any supra-individual sphere. What results is, as will be clarified in later discussion, an epistemology based on the partial truth, or, to be optimistic, the *half-truth*. Interesting insights must be qualified with a 'but', they never tell the whole truth; another proposition will emerge which contradicts them at some level, but which is also true. Finally, half-truths are the best truths we have.

Nietzsche's hostility to systematic thought derives from his overwhelming sense of the limitation of knowledge, his conviction that systems create the delusion of comprehensive understanding. His work articulates the belief that human knowledge, at its best,

---

[1] In recent years a neo-rationalist model of science has been constructed by Karl Popper which takes account of many of these limitations inherent in human understanding.

can provide no more than a series of aphoristic insights. These insights will not be systematic, they will not fit neatly together, but neither will they be completely random: they are communicable as the self-reflections of a coherent entity, the individual. Anarcho-psychology postulates a logic of the individual, of his impulses, moods, and thoughts, which supersedes all other logics, and in particular the logic of abstract thought which derives from Aristotle.

In spite of Stirner's existentialist leanings, his egoist critique of hypocrisy, or *mauvaise foi*, is not backed by any moral affirmation of truth or honesty. Personal integrity is a value for him only to the degree that it facilitates self-expression: Stirner does not hanker after the 'dignity of man'. He does place value on 'ownness' (*Eigenheit*), a concept of authenticity concretely bound to the individual self and its realization.[1] What he rejects in this context is the brand of nihilistic existentialism which when articulated states: 'in this meaningless world at least I must display before others my honesty in the face of despair, my integrity'. Like the atheism that Stirner rejects it has not shaken off the religious mentality—within the void of stifled egoism it still gropes for abstractions.

Stirner anticipates existentialist philosophy in the emphasis he places on concrete, lived and living, experience, in his sustained critique of religious, moral and metaphysical ideals, and above all in the stress he places upon the *self*. However, he is not unequivocally attached to the primacy of self or ego; indeed, ontology, as a focus on being, occupies a curious place within his philosophy, one which may be illustrated by referring to a modern debate within the psychoanalytic movement. Fairbairn, the pioneer of object-relations theory, places primary emphasis in his work on the individual's need to maintain contact with an object; his position contrasts with Freud's instinct theory, which centres around the need to find instinctual gratification. According to Fairbairn man is innately driven to seek objects and not primarily to seek pleasure.[2] Contemporary 'ego-psychology' has tended towards Fairbairn, as has the so-called 'existentialist psychoanalysis' of R. D. Laing. Stirner's orientation, however, in spite of his paeans to ego, is analogous to that of Freud: he portrays the ego as growing in a matrix of instinctual satisfactions. The central concern of this hedonism, as we

[1] Again he directly anticipates a central Heideggerian concept: *eigentlich*, usually translated as 'authentic'. Some sense of the measure of the debt to Stirner is conveyed by one of Heidegger's definitions, from an essay of 1943, of what it means 'to find': 'den Fund zu eigen bekommen, um in ihm als dem Eigentum zu wohnen' (*Erläuterungen zu Hölderlins Dichtung*, Frankfurt, Klosterman, 1971, p. 14). The centrality of Stirner's play on *eigen* (own) and *Eigentum* (property) will become apparent as we proceed.

[2] W. R. D. Fairbairn: *Psychoanalytic Studies of the Personality*, 1952.

have stressed, is the liberation of internal forces and desires. The drive to establish relationships is secondary, or merely instrumental.

We have noted that a total escape from ethics is not an option available to Western man. It is instructive to delineate the different ethical responses to a world in which the Christian God had been deposed, in which absolute morality in any guise was no longer credible. Apart from the idealization of History as a redemptive process, which sprang out of the Hegelian tradition, and the attachment to an unambivalent notion of sustained progress, both of which fall into the category of ideology attacked by Stirner and Nietzsche, there appear roughly seven meaningfully differentiable ethical systems. This classification is not intended to provide categories which are either very precise or strictly mutually exclusive. Its aim is merely to further discussion of the various ethical positions available within the vague rubric of existentialism.

First, there is the hedonist ethic. Stated in its extreme form, urging a return to the purely instinctual life of the apocryphal noble savage, it is facilely utopian. It is blind to the dependency of human society on some degree of instinctual renunciation if it is to function. But there is a more refined version of the hedonist ethic: it stresses self-enjoyment rather than animal pleasure, it values gaiety, exuberance, *joie de vivre*.

Second, there is the ethic of rebellion for its own sake. Put bluntly it holds that in an absurd world, where there is no 'up and down', there is at least some integrity in revolting against the false, illusory structures of meaning that men create around themselves. The explicit statement of this position is Camus' *L'Homme révolté*.

Third, there is the aestheticist ethic. It holds that what is distinctively and valuably human is what man does and creates with style, elegantly, movingly — aesthetically. Whatever man does is absurd; there is at least dignity in doing it well. Nietzsche is driven in part to this position; it is more obviously the preserve of 'art for art's sake' theorists such as Flaubert.

Fourth, there is the ethic of stoic pessimism. Schopenhauer gave theoretical expression to the view that life is ineluctably painful, dour, and unrewarding. Sartre's talk about the 'agony of responsibility' places itself here. Freud was probably the modern to give this ethic its most impressive incarnation. There was a strong Old Testament moralistic strain in his dedication to knowledge, a sense of duty and service. Characteristic of his conception of his own life and his vocation was his sardonic, yet pained: 'Much is won if we succeed in transforming hysterical misery into common unhappiness'.

Fifth, there is the ethic which places ultimate value in the mystical experience, or in noumenal connections between the individual and his external environment. As we shall later examine, this becomes significant to Dostoevsky. Rilke gives sublime poetic formulation to mystical, transcendental values and their presence in human experience: they are mediated in his vision through the figures of Orpheus and the Angel. The mystical ethic is central too to the late work of Heidegger, especially to his meditations on Hölderlin's poetry, and his *Vorträge und Aufsätze*.

Sixth, there is the individualist ethic. It holds that the only non-arbitrary, coherent phenomenon is the individual, bounded by his life and his death. There is no stronger statement of this position than that already discussed in the work of Stirner and Nietzsche. It is reflected also in the view held by Dilthey and Jaspers that the most meaningful task for the human sciences is biography: there at least the limits of the subject matter are defined, as is the locus of coherency underlying the study. According to this classification, an ethic of personal responsibility is conceived of as a fusion of individualist and stoicist ethics.

Seventh, there is the ethic of friendship. It has taken different forms. Schiller's idealist *Don Carlos* holds that only a man's relationship with his friend is sacred: all else can be sacrificed to preserve this union. Carl Zuckmayer concludes in his autobiography, *Als wär's ein Stück von mir*, that in the human dialectic between the will to live and despair there is one synthesis, and that is friendship. An attachment to the more general principles of mutual aid, comradeship, or *solidarité* is also representative of this ethic.

Stirner's emphasis on self-enjoyment associates him with the hedonist ethic as much as his emphasis on self-realization and egoism associates him with the individualist ethic. It will become clear later that traces of the rebel ethic also permeate his work. There are good reasons, additionally, for connecting him with the friendship ethic, but in a special sense. Neither Schiller's idealism, Kropotkin's principle of mutual aid, nor Sartre's advocacy of commitment and engagement find parallels in *Der Einzige*. But his 'I love men because love makes *me* happy', taken together with references to the comradeship of children in their play, and to other 'merry egoist unions',[1] suggests an embryonic notion of egoistic friendship. Nietzsche's more specific valuation of the friend amplified themes in Stirner which are only lightly voiced. Zarathustra comes to preach not the neighbour, but the friend.[2] This friendship is totally amoral; there is no Kantian 'ought' in the relationship, there is no Benthamite sense of calculated obligation. This is the warrior friendship of Achilles and Patroclus, it is the friendship of Gilgamesh which satisfies the need for a high-spirited comrade, his match, with whom to play out his almost superhuman store of energy. Nietzsche describes the friend as the one most capable of being an enemy, of taking the other seriously enough

1 *Ego*, p. 218.   2 *Zarathustra* I:14 and 16.

to confront him with his failings. This conception is deliberately anti-sentimental; it explicitly sets itself against a humanist idealization of 'love'.

Stirner's development of what are notably existentialist themes is inextricably bound to his critique of liberalism. It is therefore convenient at this point to introduce the attack on this specific political ideology. We have already treated the first half of the argument. Stirner in calling Feuerbach's work 'the last metamorphosis of the Christian religion'[1] identified him not only with humanism, but also with liberal political ideology. Stirner saw liberalism as having failed to emancipate itself from moralistic images of man: the liberation it offered was merely from one fixed standpoint to another.[2] Although the God outside had been forgotten, devotion to the ideals of 'man', 'truth', and 'freedom' had become all the more strict.

With Nietzsche the focus of the critique of liberal ideology switches to the English, and in particular John Stuart Mill, who is taken as the prototypal moralist. Mill is portrayed as the cleric perpetually waging war against evil. Nietzsche regards his ideals as obscuring psychological reality: egalitarian democracy is Christianity made natural, altruism in political dress.[3] Working from the egoist axiom, Nietzsche attacks utilitarianism as the most mendacious form of egoism, egoism moralized into the ethic of the 'greatest happiness of the greatest number'.[4] He affirms his favoured master morality as 'the antithesis of that low degree of warmth which any calculating prudence, any calculus of utility, presupposes'.[5]

From the anarcho-psychological perspective the English liberal, utilitarian, democratic achievement constituted the most powerfully dangerous embodiment of the moral mind, the most serious manifestation of political ideology. Nietzsche's repeated attacks on liberal-democratic ideals follow Stirner's analysis of clericalism: the liberal is the half-hearted one whose instincts have become ineffectual.[6] Liberal-rationalism moralizes pleasure: 'Man does *not* strive for pleasure; only the Englishman does'.[7] Nietzsche does not view socialism any more kindly, accusing it of perpetrating the same vices;

---

[1] *Ego*, p. 90.   [2] Ibid., p. 238.
[3] *Wille* 30, 215, and 925–6. It is worth noting that Nietzsche criticized George Eliot, and by implication the English in general, for imagining that she had done away with the Christian God, whereas, in fact, she clung all the more fiercely to its morality (*Götzen-Dämmerung* x:5). His attitude precisely mirrors that of Stirner to Feuerbach. Moreover, George Eliot was the first translator of Feuerbach into English, and even wrote in a letter dated 29/4/1854 to her friend and editor Sara Hennell: 'With the ideas of Feuerbach I everywhere agree'.
[4] *Wille* 62 and *Jenseits* 228.   [5] *Genealogie* I:2.   [6] *Wille* 864.
[7] *Götzen-Dämmerung* i:12.

he dubs it 'la religion de la souffrance humaine'.[1] Thomas Mann will transform these themes into a militant nationalistic defence of vital Teutonic culture against the encroachment of the effete, decadent, liberal-democracy of France and England.[2]

Feuerbachian liberalism was to pass in Germany, and more abruptly than Stirner would have imagined in 1844. Liberal-humanism disappeared with the failure of the revolutions of 1848; events did indeed suggest that its high-flown idealism had distanced it from the social and political reality. Its political eclipse thus followed quickly after its philosophical one. The real alternatives became Prussian autocracy à la Bismarck, Marxist socialism as yet still in its infancy, and for the individual—particularly the bohemian or the artist—in its peculiar inward-turned, self-contained style, Stirnerian anarchism.

Stirner viewed all the radical political philosophies of his time as forms of liberalism, with their common source in Feuerbach. We postpone to the later section on Marx his discussion of communism, which he associated with Weitling and referred to as 'social liberalism'. His critique of his friend Bruno Bauer's school of 'criticism', which he classed as 'humane liberalism', is neither of contemporary relevance nor of significance to our argument.[3] Finally, Proudhon is classed as a 'social liberal' because of his attachment to an image of the ideal society. For Stirner, Proudhon's plans for the social utopia precluded any real understanding of property, which he was forced to relate to an abstract concept of the just and beneficent society.[4] Stirner would have been equally hostile to Kropotkin, regarding his principle of 'mutual aid' as merely another misty liberal-humanist ideal. Anarcho-individualism, as it is conceived in *Der Einzige*, indicts other theories of anarchism for not taking their attack on authority far enough, for retaining a supra-individual social ideal.

The second part of Stirner's critique of liberalism centres on the notion of freedom. Liberalism is in effect defined as that political philosophy which follows the principle of 'freedom from': it directs itself to removing constraints, to reducing infringements on the individual's free choice. Stirner's argument is that this is a purely negative principle, that the passion to be 'rid of' heralds nihilism: when all constraint has been peeled away nothing but a void remains.[5] His point is that the successful application of liberal *means*

---

[1] *Jenseits* 21.

[2] Thomas Mann: *Betrachtungen eines Unpolitischen*, 1918.

[3] On Stirner's relationship to Bruno Bauer, see Brazill, op. cit., p. 213, and my first footnote to p. 90 of *Ego*. Bauer did clearly influence Stirner, but the quality of his written philosophy does not compare with that of his friend.

[4] Arvon (op. cit., pp. 85–7) suggests that Stirner borrowed this point from Edgar Bauer.

[5] *Ego*, pp. 111–13. Stirner's point can claim some sociological support from

does not ensure that where previously there was constraint there will be fulfilment, that where there was misery there will be enjoyment. He accuses a liberty principle such as Mill's of being irrelevant, of concealing the real issues. He counterposes the notion of 'ownness' to the ideal of 'freedom'. Real freedom is a positive movement towards taking possession and realizing one's own. It is to be assessed by a qualitative evaluation of the content of experience, not a description of its extrinsic form:[1]

> The man who is set free is nothing but a freedman, a *libertinus*, a dog dragging a piece of chain with him; he is an unfree man in the garment of freedom, like the ass in the lion's skin . . . all freedom is essentially—self-liberation . . . Of what use is it to the sheep that no one abridges their freedom of speech? They stick to bleating.

Stirner's intended task might be characterized as *freeing* the individual *from* ideology; similarly Freud set himself the task of freeing the individual from his neurotic fixations. But this is a freeing from *in order to* release that which lies within: 'ownness'. The endeavour depends for its success on the resources of the 'own', of what Stirner calls the 'creative nothing' at the core of being. The liberal-rationalist concept of 'freedom' is trivial from this perspective, for it misses the crucial point as to whether the individual is capable of coming into presence. Substantive freedom is this capability itself. The metaphor of peeling the onion layer by layer, of 'freeing from', has nothing fundamental in common with the metaphor of neutralizing the poisons in the soil in which the bulb is planted.

The anarcho-individualist and social action

Stirner applies his critique of ideology to social structure. He argues that the power of the State is essentially ideological, depending on the successful indoctrination of its subjects. He maintains that this Leviathan would become redundant if its citizens realized that it acts in opposition to their individual interests, and that they have the power to organize themselves. Thus, with other anarchist theorists, he holds that the State is both repressive and superfluous.

Erving Goffman's *Stigma* (1968), p. 21. Goffman quotes an example of people who become dependent on their stigma (e.g. a face without a nose) as the distinctive feature of their identity. When it is removed (made 'normal') they lose the scapegoat for their ills, their shield from social responsibility, and the anxiety which follows must be diagnosed as resulting from a loss of sense of identity.

[1] *Ego*, pp. 122–3, and, in particular, my footnote to p. 122—it is equally relevant to this passage. Nietzsche sets up the 'Will-to-Power', his equivalent to 'ownness', as the counter-principle to '*laisser-aller*' (*Wille* 122).

He differs from them in contending that any principle of social organization will provoke inherently repressive operations. Stirner's position compares instructively with that of Freud, who also believed that society with its arrangements is of its essence repressive of the individual and his 'polymorphous perversity'. But Freud added that society is nevertheless, even in these terms, necessary.

In this section we examine the last stage in Stirner's critique of ideology, in particular his belief that the way to neutralize the State is to lay bare the illusions legitimating its power. At the same time we consider some of his own recommendations for social action.

Stirner advocates ruthless realization of the right of the individual: this allows no compromise with social organization. 'Every State is a *despotism*';[1] every State needs a strict morality; every State depends on freezing the will of the individual; for the State 'might is right' and violence the means to legitimating this right.[2] 'The State has always the sole purpose to limit, tame, subordinate, the individual...[3] I am free in *no* State...[4] I am the deadly enemy of the State...[5] the egoist has nothing to say to the State except "Get out of my sunshine" '.[6]

Stirner follows the realist tradition in political theory, that of Machiavelli and Hobbes, in extracting one principle from politics — might is right.[7] However, instead of completing his social picture with a dour pessimistic view of man as a violent warmonger by nature, he shares with Rousseau a passionate optimism for the creative potentiality of life. The comparison stretches no further. Stirner accepts the responsibility for piecing together a basis for community within the limits set by his renunciation of all supra-individual authority. He can neither, with Hobbes, postulate the State as a necessary expedient, restraining the 'war of all against all', nor with Rousseau believe in the possibility of a 'social contract' that interprets the 'general will' of the people: both lead to despotism, both set limits. Stirner's anarchist solution to the problem, in the words of Georg Simmel, 'How is society possible?', and consequently the political dimension to the anarcho-psychological perspective, is inextricably bound to his sociology of the existing State. To this we now turn.

---

1 *Ego*, p. 132.   2 Ibid., p. 133.   3 Ibid., p. 150.   4 Ibid., p. 149.
5 Ibid., p. 165.
6 Ibid., p. 156. Cf. Nietzsche, whose attitude to the State matches Stirner's step by step: 'Wherever the State ceases, the man who is not superfluous really begins: there begins the song of the necessary one, the unique and irreplaceable melody'. For a paraphrasing of Nietzsche's attitude to politics see Karl Jaspers: *Nietzsche*, 1965, ch. 4; here p. 255.
7 Ralf Dahrendorf contrasts the two mainstreams of political thought — the Thrasymachus/Hobbes tradition and the Socrates/Rousseau tradition — in his article 'In Praise of Thrasymachus' (*Essays in the Theory of Society*, 1968).

The State represents for Stirner all organized authority above the influence of the individual. It is composed of the complex of government, its bureaucracies, and its instruments such as the educational system and the police force; but it is defined above all else by its *power*. The State is the predominant alienating force in modern life: it 'cannot endure that man stand in direct relation to man; it must step between as—*mediator*, must—*intervene*'.[1] Through creating order and stability it creates dependence.

Stirner now develops the dichotomy that he had suggested in 1843 between the principles of 'love' and 'will' in politics.[2] Dutiful *love*, as it can be manifested in the law-encompassed order established by the State, serves to obfuscate political reality. Politics is about power, not love, retorts Stirner. The State condones love only when it is within the ambit of its laws; it is love of the State which is tolerated. Stirner lays bare what he sees as the authoritarian reality: 'The common weal may cheer aloud while I must "come to heel"; the State may shine while I starve'.[3] As the Church plays upon guilt to reinforce the moral law, the State calls in its police to defend the civil law. Stirner realized that the distinction between the internal authority of conscience and external authority can be slight: he noted that 'Every Prussian carries his *gendarme* in his breast'.[4]

'*Right* is the *spirit* of *society*', begins the chapter headed 'My Power'.[5] Stirner points out that in common speech 'it served him right!' is generally the solemn judgment of justice, invoked in referring to failure. He suggests that it could be no less aptly used to applaud a successful enterprise;[6] as the situation is, however, this 'right' is introduced in order to give a fact, an *is*, a moral valence, and turn it into an *ought*. But a criminal is in the wrong only because the punishers gain the upper hand, and thus the might to assert their right.[7] His only sin is against a mundane authority more powerful than himself. The egoist, on the other hand, recognizes no moral right and no principle of justice; he knows that life is not *just*:[8]

[1] *Ego*, p. 164. Cf. Schiller's rejection of the will of the State, in *Don Carlos*, in favour of friendship.

[2] 'Einiges Vorläufige vom Liebesstaat', *Kleinere Schriften*, pp. 269–77. The crux of the argument is that: 'In the arms of love the will relaxes and sleeps, and only the wish, the petition wakes'. Stirner quotes the Governor of Berlin: 'Repose [*Ruhe*] is the first duty of the citizen!' (p. 277).

[3] *Ego*, p. 141. A sadly prophetic comment considering that Stirner's last years were lived in wretched poverty. Nietzsche makes the identical criticism of the State sacrificing the individual 'for the sake of the general interest' (*Morgenröte* 146; *Menschliches* II:ii:186).

[4] Ibid., pp. 153–4.   [5] *Ego* (1912), p. 242.   [6] *Ego*, p. 130.

[7] Nietzsche makes the identical point (*Morgenröte* 20), then later in his *Genealogie* develops it in a more complex and profound form.

[8] *Ego*, pp. 127–8. Nietzsche analyses the concepts 'right' and 'power' similarly (*Morgenröte* 112).

The tiger that assails me is in the right and I who strike him down am also in the right. I defend against him not my *right*, but *myself* . . . The only thing I am not entitled to do is what I do not do with a free cheer, that is, what I do not entitle myself to do.

When a man is coerced to tell the truth he can be under no personal obligation to obey, for he has given the State no right to his confidence. Truth has no value in itself; it is not sacred; one has the full 'right' to lie in order to protect a friend.[1] This is the first hint of an irrationalist idea important for all the anarcho-psychologists, that *truth*, however profound and well substantiated it is, which comes into conflict with the individual's self-interest, should be rejected.

Stirner asks why he should surrender to this 'wretched stability', why he should 'freeze his will', why he should be duty bound to a body which gives him no pleasure; his anarchism states ultimately that the privilege of equality before the law is meaningless to one who sees the reality underneath the ideology and who therefore does not respect that law. Anticipating Marcuse by a century and a quarter, he finds that the State by means of its repressive laws commits *violence* just as effectively as if its police struck physical blows; it calls the individual's counter-violence crime. The threat of violence is as coercive as its implementation; in the end the State tolerates only the 'harmless'.[2] Stirner, like Nietzsche, calls for a realistic assessment of politics and its rationalizing moralities; his attitudes directly oppose the optimism of Bentham and Mill, and their belief that society could be organized according to rational principles and a universally-accepted liberal-utilitarian ethic. To his view any social concept such as the 'happiness of the greatest number' is an illusion, mystifying reality. The liberal-rationalist morality is blind to the nature of the individual's ubiquitous egoism; its primary abstraction, 'liberty', has no correlate in the experience of the individual and thus serves but to distract him from himself.

In an important sense Stirner regards the covert violence of the State as more oppressive than a spontaneous outburst of aggression; for, hidden under the deceptive guise of social harmony and consideration, it is the more vicious and pitiless when it finally bursts forth. The institutions of the State in the modern world have incorporated the cleric's resentful righteousness. What has emerged is a form of utilitarianism in which the State and its needs are sovereign.[3]

Although Stirner holds no truck with the dictum that all men are equal, he is more of a democrat than Nietzsche with his élitist

---

[1] *Ego*, pp. 208–11.
[2] Ibid., pp. 133–5, 149; see, in particular, my note 3 to *Ego*, p. 133.
[3] Ibid., p. 142.

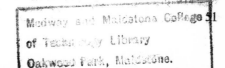

teleology: 'A people [*Volk*] is nature's detour to arrive at six or seven great men—and then to get around them'.[1] That is, unless for Nietzsche the 'great' are simply the egoists. Each man, for Stirner, has the unique resources to make himself great—at least in his own eyes. Stirner's utopianism may have been to value the potential of the majority of men too highly, at least given foreseeable socio-cultural conditions, and to fail to recognize that successful self-expression is often, if not always, directly connected to the presence of a dark, guilt- or shame-ridden side to the individual.

The State's most effective and most insidious form of violence is that perpetrated against children through their education. Stirner points out how this education stretches man to fit a Procrustean bed of ideology, how it applies the 'shears of civilization'.[2] This 'violence to thought' is even more repressive than the persecution of blasphemy, for the irreverent thought has not been granted consciousness.

Stirner's response to the State is *insurrection*. He looks back into history and finds that all Churches, all States, indeed all generalities, have at one stage fallen, and as a result of the 'secession of individuals'.[3] The reform of the State is futile, for authority itself is the issue at stake; it is vulnerable only to permanent insurrection, lasting until the egoist can joyfully exclaim: 'Mankind is buried, and I am my own, I am the laughing heir!'[4] Thus the task of the political philosopher is to make the people conscious of the degree to which the power of the State is a figment of their own imaginations.

Stirner concludes his 1843 attack on Eugène Sue, the moralizing novelist who never describes a character who could be called a 'self-created man', by asserting: 'Our time is not sick, in order to be cured, but it is old and its hour has struck'.[5] He chooses the metaphor of senility rather than sickness; society needs to be invigorated with new life, not to have the little energy that remains paralysed by moral condemnation of its outlets, or by the attempt to instate a new political morality. He takes the position that Georges Sorel was to popularize in his *Réflexions sur la violence* (1908), arguing that society, if it is not to decay, must be revitalized. With no presentiment of the reality of twentieth-century fascism he can enthusiastically argue that new sources of passion must be tapped.

Stirner, at the core of his anarchism, distinguishes between revolution and insurrection. The act of revolution is irrelevant, merely leading to new structures of organizational authority. It does not escape from the ideological cage: one spook is replaced by another. On the other hand, 'insurrection leads us no longer to *let* ourselves be arranged, but to arrange ourselves, and set no glittering

---

[1] *Jenseits* 126.   [2] *Ego*, p. 149.   [3] Ibid., p. 141.   [4] Ibid., p. 143.
[5] See my footnote 2 to *Ego*, p. 199; also *Kleinere Schriften*, pp. 289, 294.

hopes on "institutions" '.[1] The intentions of the insurgent are neither political nor social, but egoistic. Stirner accordingly views political parties with disfavour; even opposition parties, the havens of revolutionaries, are no more than States within the State.[2]

The act of greatest subversion, the case for insurrection maintains against the liberal and the socialist alike, is the one of indifference. A man, or a group, finds it unbearable that someone can be simply uninterested in his, or its, convictions. The enemies of Christ— Stirner's prototypal insurgent—could not bear his independence; his 'Give to the emperor that which is the emperor's'[3] showed a contempt for the affairs of State and its politics—for the moral order—that their self-respect would not let them tolerate. There is a degree of complicity, or mutual respect, between the believer and the man who attacks his beliefs (the revolutionary), for the latter takes them seriously. Nietzsche argues in parallel that one has to be capable of hating a person in order to love him.[4] Stirner has here anticipated one of Freud's most important discoveries, that in the unconscious opposites are often identical.[5]

Stirner clarifies the mechanics of insurrection, the politics of the 'secession of individuals', and at the same time shows the possibility of a theory of social action extrapolated from an ethics centred on the individual. We take as our point of entry his discussion of freedom of the press, an issue of crucial importance to him and his friends who were always potential targets for the Prussian censor.[6]

The two forms of freedom that we have noted are to be read in the specific case of censored journalism. Freedom in the first sense, as 'freedom from', as liberation from overt coercion, is contingent on the permission of the State, and hence the beneficent disposition of the people.[7] Stirner suggests that in England, where there was no press censorship, no problem arose because everyone believed in the State and so were incapable of writing against it. Hence the conception of 'responsible press'—responsible to the State.[8] Here the authenticity

---

[1] *Ego*, pp. 219–23; here p. 219.
[2] Ibid., pp. 157–60; see, in particular, my note to *Ego*, p. 158. Stirner's argument reappears as the central theme in Albert Camus' *L'Homme révolté*, 1951; Camus devotes one section of the book to Stirner.
[3] Ibid., p. 220. Cf. Philip in Schiller's *Don Carlos*:
    Happily might I hear
    That Carlos hates my advice, yet with
    Displeasure detect, that he disdains it.
[4] *Zarathustra* I:14.
[5] E.g., *Introductory Lectures on Psycho-Analysis*, p. 121.
[6] *Der Einzige*, however, easily passed the censors: they said it was too absurd to be dangerous (J. H. Mackay: *Max Stirner: sein Leben und sein Werk*, 1898, p. 137).
[7] *Ego*, pp. 194–5.   [8] Ibid., p. 192.

of a piece of writing depends on the State's imprimatur. The will-to-freedom of the type of person who adheres to this morality implicitly recognizes the authority of the State: 'good' citizens take its laws so seriously as to devote much of their energy to changing them. On the other hand there is egoist freedom. Egoists do not ask for permission, they grasp it; the truly free man must 'cheat the State'.[1]

What kind of anarchism can emerge from the debris left by Stirner's critique of practically every type of socio-political organization? This is left to the individuals concerned: they must map their own praxis. Stirner does not lay down a blueprint for social structure, nor even for individual action—neither do Nietzsche or Freud. Nor does he call for 'permanent revolution' which creates its own structures.[2] Stirner is far from the nihilist with his *faute de mieux* attachment to insurrection; he moves from a categorical value base to his appeal for insurrection. This mode of political action is not an end in itself, it is an epiphenomenon of realizing oneself. Politics and the affairs of State are dissociated from the orbit of the individual, and in so far as they cannot be repossessed as his living private property they must be rendered impotent.[3] Thus the individual acts politically, firstly in order to protect his own autonomous development, and secondly, if he is political by inclination, in order to express, and therefore experience, himself.

At the community-scale level of social organization Stirner advocates the *Union*, a voluntary coalition of egoists. Each individual, confident in his own power and his own property, joins with others, recognizing and utilizing their special competences for his own greater satisfaction. The Union, an aid for the whole man, is founded upon the same principle as friendship. The egoist unites with his friend in order to accomplish more, to increase his power, and in a broad sense to heighten his enjoyment.[4] The principle of 'multiplied force' is the sole *raison d'être* of the Union. In 1842 Stirner had suggested the basis for successful association: 'be "each one fulfilled in himself"', then will your community, your social life, also be fulfilled'.[5]

1 *Ego*. We recall Christ's parable of the unjust steward who is dismissed for stealing from his master. Being too old to take up another occupation, and too proud to beg, he cheats his master again. The master, far from being angry when he finds out, praises the old steward for his worldly wisdom (Luke 16:1-11). Recurring through the parables is the theme that life is not just, that the 'good' do not get rewarded for their virtue, and above all, that life must be twisted and cheated if it is to be realized to the full. Stirner is a disciple of the master of this teaching.
2 This slogan was popular among French anarchist students during and after May 1968 in Paris. In that instance the failure to answer the State's question 'What do you really want?' frequently reflected a dearth of positive values.
3 A key Stirnerian theme, to be examined in the critique of *homo economicus*.
4 *Ego*, p. 214.
5 'Das unwahre Prinzip unserer Erziehung', *Kleinere Schriften*, p. 237.

A distinctive feature of individualist-anarchist political philosophy is its indifference to any social totality, whether it be community, society, race, or nation. Stirner's 'organicism' is unerringly ego-centric. It deviates from the Hegelian model at the point at which the self-conscious individual develops an objective social being beyond his personal relationships. This is the point at which Hegel's own drive to discover the 'total' and the 'organic' led him, via Rousseau's conception of the 'general will of the people', to an ultimate synthesis in the harmonious fusion of individual, family, and civil society. For Stirner, the *social* axiom of conservative, liberal, and socialist schools of political thought alike is in itself repressive: it disguises as potentially redemptive an order whose central function is inhibitory of the individual's interests. (We postpone criticism of Stirner's position until the next section.)

Stirner does not, however, advocate a withdrawal from the centres of organized society to form, say, an Owenite utopian community; that would be merely to institute another highly normative social order. The challenge of individualist anarchism is to stand firm, not to seek salvation elsewhere, but to exorcise from consciousness all images of society and of union with large groups, and in the place of the old illusions instate the self and its voluntary personal relations. The battle is thus to be conducted on the plain of ideology.

Martin Buber considers that Stirner is important for his onslaught on substitute reality, but contends that his egoism fails to recognize the mutuality of life, the value of responsibility towards other people.[1] This is the point at which Stirner's philosophical system is most vulnerable. The question broached is a profound one: it resolves ethically into whether an 'I-thou', or a purely 'I' ontology better describes the preconditions for man's most fulfilling experiences. Going to the roots of the ethical alternative, Stirner's psychology cannot cope with the persuasive argument (not put directly by Buber) that there are two, what may be called for convenience, primary human drives: the one drive certainly directed towards self-realization and self-enjoyment, but the other towards union with other persons, or at least one other person—perhaps a drive ultimately to form exclusive heterosexual relationships.

Psychology has not yet devised an adequate approach to the problem of drives. There are at best informed speculations, one of the most impressive of which contains an implicit critique of the Stirnerian position. John Bowlby describes systematically the development

---

[1] 'Die Frage an den Einzelnen' (1936), an article on Stirner and Kierkegaard, included in the English collection *Between Man and Man*, 1961, pp. 60–108, esp. pp. 60–71.

of the young child's attachment to a mother-figure.[1] This attachment is instinctual; its success is decisive for the balanced growth of the child. Individualist psychology is restrictively one-sided to the degree that this drive can be shown to carry through into adulthood, however diversified its targets may become.

Freud took the attitude that man is self-centred, but has an emotional need for community.[2] He preserved Stirner's suggestion that the individual uses other people egoistically, maintaining, in the words of Rieff, 'that satisfaction from an object is but a devious means of self-love'.[3] The egoist axiom is adapted and elaborated into the theory, to piece together relevant fragments from Freud, that there is one primary drive, directed at self-satisfaction, but that a second, subsidiary drive deflects essentially narcissistic impulses outwards, so that objects from the wider community provide satisfactions as if they were the subject's own extended limbs. Love remains narcissistic, but gains a wider compass as the individual learns to find projections of himself and his body in his environment. Thus, to carry the argument further, although a man may be sensually drawn by a dissimilar other, or at a sublimated pitch compelled by the beauty of the other, the enduring bond of intimacy is possible only with an other who reflects one's own character, or in the presence of whom grows an *experience* in which one can express, or realize, some of the multilevelled mystery of one's being.

The anarchism of Proudhon and Kropotkin provides the drive to community with a stronger formulation and an ethical superstructure. Emphasis is reversed: the comrade or the neighbour becomes the primary object and purpose of man's highest drive.[4] Psychology cannot decide categorically in favour of either the egoist principle or the principle of mutual aid; it merely persuades that neither is complete by itself. Nevertheless, we note that the work of the anarchist philosophers who follow a social principle leaves itself vulnerable to the charge that it is no more than utopian ideology. It fails to ground itself thoroughly in sociological or historical analysis, as developed by Marx; it also fails to grapple with the unconscious causes of human conduct, to analyse the roots of individual gratification and fulfilment, and leaves little psychological insight into individual behaviour and social action. Thus the resulting theory can claim neither a firm sociological nor a firm psychological basis.

1 John Bowlby: *Attachment*, 1969.
2 Philip Rieff: *Freud: the Mind of the Moralist*, 1960, p. 222.
3 Ibid., p. 158.
4 This is the orthodox reading of Proudhon, which is however thrown seriously into question by work currently being undertaken by John Hooper in Oxford. Hooper's interpretation places the mature Proudhon much closer to Stirner.

One of Stirner's central tenets, which has been curiously neglected by subsequent psychology, is that of *uniqueness*. Whilst such notions as 'identity crisis' and 'ontological insecurity' have been the subject of elaborate investigation, there has yet been no systematic attempt to determine the degree to which a strong sense of identity depends on a feeling of uniqueness. The question of the relationship of the unique-I to the shared-I is at the core of social psychology. A common antipathy sometimes precludes friendship between two people who are temperamentally similar: perhaps one individual's hypersensitivity to the other's faults reflects both a need to differentiate himself from the threatening other and, by castigating the other, to exorcize symbolically his own faults. To take another case: the only unique action available to Judas is to betray the man who embodies all the virtues to which he himself aspires, and whose living presence thus renders him impotent. It is a commonplace that radical political groups show more intense hostility towards those parties close to them ideologically than to those to whom they are theoretically opposed. Moreover, modern European history suggests, in the repeated examples it offers of people submerging their individuality in the crowd or the mass, that attempts to deny individual uniqueness in favour of group identity release the most brutal and sadistic of the primitive human passions. The sense of unique identity stands, by contrast, as a means of structuring and sublimating primitive drives. Here are strong indications that the dominant ethical emphasis which Stirner places on uniqueness should be able to draw upon wide-ranging psychological support.

Stirnerian anarchism has found two viable styles of life, the one individual, typified by the artist, and the other more directly social. Max Ernst, the German Dadaist, Surrealist painter, is the ideal epitomization of the man Stirner has influenced. Ernst felt an exceptional sympathy for Stirner, finding in him the person who aimed to overthrow single-handedly the whole structure of human belief, one who nevertheless could not cope with the demands of everyday life. *Der Einzige* provided the orientation for Ernst's youth from the time he first read it at the age of fourteen or fifteen: he acknowledged it as a lifelong tie.[1] He even titled a painting of 1925 *L'Unique et sa propriété*. Indeed, the Stirnerian egoist is most fully embodied in artists like Max Ernst, isolated men whose extreme lives are sustained by the force of their imaginations, and an inviolable confidence in their own capacity for revolutionizing human consciousness. Stirner is their philosopher; it is they, moreover, who have done most to define the contours of his praxis.

[1] John Russell: *Max Ernst*, 1967, pp. 17–18.

If Stirner's ideas are to be accorded any enduring social *praxis* it has been in schools. Rudolf Steiner was a devoted follower of Stirner from early in his career. More significantly, there has been no credo which has matched Stirnerian principles more closely than the educational philosophy of both Maria Montessori and A. S. Neill. In these cases, however, there may be no direct influence. Individualist-anarchist ideas are amenable to group experimentation only in schools or communes, communities which can gain a high degree of autonomy from the institutional and ethical constraints of advanced industrial society. It is worth noting that Stirner wrote two pieces on education, and that they contain many of his best ideas outside *Der Einzige*. His theory of the development of the vital individual hinges on a different approach to education, one which stresses the unhampered self-expression of the child. It is one mark of Stirner's contemporary relevance that education along these guidelines is being discussed and innovated on a large scale for the first time.

Stirner does not defend the power of the individual to dominate others. While the individual is to apply his accumulated force to gain what he needs, what he needs is deeply personal and independent of the taste of others—and hence does not depend on proving their inferiority. Implicit in his philosophy of self-realization is what Nietzsche was to introduce as the positive, resentment-free Will-to-Power, the will to overcome oneself.

As Arvon has pointed out, it is only with the *Recensenten Stirners*, Stirner's reply written in the third person to his critics, that the case for the egoist is completed.[1] Stirner writes his 'anticritique' in the calm and reflective tone of a man who, confident of his position, feels free to banter the desperate and futile endeavours of his critics. He now focusses on *interest* as the principal guiding value in human life. His advice is to follow only what one is passionately interested in. At the same time: 'The holy interest is the uninteresting'.[2] Thus *interest* supplements, and encompasses, the twin value orientations of *Der Einzige*, enjoyment and realization. Stirner goes on to deny that he is a proselytizer: he is indifferent to how other men live their lives as long as they do not interfere with him—a principle which at its surface level is distinctively 'liberal'. The egoist is not the enemy of any 'real interest'; he opposes only the 'uninterested and the uninteresting'.[3]

The choice of *interest* as the supreme value provides an essential link in the development of vitalist philosophy. Interest is enjoyment raised up to consciousness, the first order of the sublimation of

[1] Arvon, op. cit., p. 142.
[2] 'Recensenten Stirners', *Kleinere Schriften*, p. 357.
[3] Ibid., p. 375.

instinctual gratification. Interest is the parameter in the *Aufhebung*[1] of pure hedonism into Stirner's theory of self-realization. As interest is stimulated, the whole of individual being is focussed on the object of attention, and the life-provoking bond between the isolated self and the external world is struck. To be absorbed by an 'interest' is to be quickened and alerted by it; it is to become indifferent to all else; it is to become instated as the master of a domain which is worth possessing simply because it is interesting. Man is the measure of all things only so long as his interest in them stimulates his senses and his intellect to grapple with them, to enjoy them, and to understand them. Interest provides the bridge across the chasm between the measurer and the passive to-be-measured.

Indeed, the constellation of a man's interests, the seams along which his energy flows unimpeded—in effect, what psychoanalysis was to call 'libidinized attention'—define the shape of the self. What he communicates to others is what he is excited about, what holds his interest; the self is largely conceptualized in terms of the individual's externalizations of his inner world, that is predominantly in terms of what and how he communicates. Moreover, what he is enthusiastic about he will usually deal with lucidly and intelligently—in this sense 'intelligence' too is a function of interest. Finally, the sense of uniqueness, of completeness, of power, as the superlative resonances of the self, reaches a crest in the wake of an interest, at times of confident and spontaneous action.

Stirner's critique of ideology reaches its climax with the postulation of interest as an ultimate value. Ideology, following this analysis, is the diametrical opposite to interest. It constitutes an order of consciousness which stands against enjoyment and realization. It is not a sublimation in the sense of a 'raising up', an *Aufhebung* of instinctual energy; it is rather a means for the destructive displacement or repression of passion, for the reduction of human possibility. Finally, it is employed to rationalize resentment and viciousness which it itself helps to stimulate. In Freud's model the superego is the repository of ideology.

The next transition in this vein of intellectual history is not a difficult one for the post-Freudian world, that from *interest* to *eros*. However, it was left to Nietzsche, with his 'The degree and type of a man's sexuality reaches to the highest peaks of his spirit',[2] to suggest, and Freud to develop. The patterns of emotional response toward

---

[1] There is no English equivalent for Hegel's usage of the German verb *aufheben* (past participle, *aufgehoben*; noun, *die Aufhebung*); it has the triple connotation of to reject or cancel or negate, to go beyond or transcend, and finally, to take what has been negated up into the higher, transcendent order of meaning.

[2] *Jenseits* 75.

something in which the individual is passionately interested are so closely analogous to the flush of excitement, the ebb and flow of feeling, that a man experiences in close proximity to a woman who attracts him, that they can instructively be called erotic. Groddeck and Ferenczi, Reich and Norman Brown, and in particular Herbert Marcuse have continued this polymorphously instinctual, egoist line on from Stirner. (Nietzsche, as will be discussed, identified himself with ascetic themes which are not to be found in the writings of these psychologists.)

Stirner and Marx

We have observed the anarcho-psychological perspective unfolding in reaction against what it saw as the rise of ideology and its socially pervasive role as an instrument for the repression of passion, and therefore gratification, and for the distortion of consciousness. In the particular case of Stirner the philosophical task was conceived of as taking the works of Hegel, Feuerbach, and Bruno Bauer to their logical conclusions, stripping them of their abstractions, and examining the implications of what remained. In doing this Stirner provoked Marx, with Engels, to write what is virtually an entire book in refutation:[1] this book also claims to be a critique of ideology.

The 'critique of ideology' is as central to the development of Marx's thought as it is to *Der Einzige*. Marx sets out to demolish Stirner's critique in the same manner as Stirner had set out to demolish Feuerbach's: by showing that it never escapes from the vicious circle of devouring its own tail. And indeed the subjection of egoist social theory to the Marxian critique of German ideology provides the most distinct insight into the limitations of Stirnerian philosophy.

Stirner's book and the Marx-Engels reply, taken together, place in vivid relief the issues at stake between the competing statements of man the individual and man the social species-being (*Gattungswesen* in Marx), man in an elemental state of conflict with a constraining society and man uniting with man to create an integrated and harmonious community. A dichotomy implicit in Hegel's philosophy, which was developed after his death by his radical followers, commonly known as the Young Hegelians, comes to a head at this point, marking the final fragmentation of the group and its thought.[2] At the same time an irrevocable schism in social philosophy was established, one illustrating much of the subsequent split in nineteenth-century

1 The section headed 'Saint Max' of Marx and Engels: *German Ideology*, 1965.
2 Engels wrote to Marx on 20 Jan. 1845 after a visit to Berlin: 'The decomposition of the dead body of the "Freien" [the last group of Young Hegelians] seems to be complete' (Marx/Engels: *Werke*, 1956, vol. 27, p. 17).

THE CRITIQUE OF IDEOLOGY

thought.[1] We observe in Marx's reaction to Stirner, and the changing perspective in his work which it helped to stimulate, a tension which will absorb at once creative writers such as Dostoevsky and Thomas Mann, and social and political theorists such as Simmel and Weber. The Stirner-Marx debate has been analysed, but only from the point of view of its importance in the development of Marx's thought.[2] We consider that the debate is important in itself, shedding light on both critiques of ideology and the social philosophies that they represent.

The publication of Feuerbach's *Das Wesen des Christentums* in 1841 was held by the Young Hegelians to mark the key turning point in the development beyond Hegel.[3] (They exaggerated Feuerbach's theoretical significance: his analysis of the alienating displacement of the human essence is no more than a reformulation of the process explicated by Hegel as 'objectification'.) Marx took Feuerbach's notion of religious alienation and generalized it into the spheres of economics, politics, and social structure. But although he still acclaimed Feuerbach's work in 1844 as a 'real theoretical revolution'[4] he had by that time already partly moved beyond it. He writes:[5]

Religious estrangement as such only occurs in the realm of *consciousness*, of man's inner life, but economic estrangement is that of *real life*; its transcendence therefore embraces both aspects.

In Marx's application of Feuerbach's transformative method the dehumanized economic phenomenon 'worker' has become the subject, and 'man' the predicate, of the ontological equation.

1 Earlier writers, Rousseau for example, were conscious of the contradictions existing between such notions as individual freedom and social harmony; yet it is only with Stirner and Marx that the two extreme positions in the debate receive full and painstaking elaboration.
2 By Hook and McLellan. Although R. W. K. Paterson includes a chapter on the Marx debate in his book on Stirner (*The Nihilistic Egoist, Max Stirner*, 1971), it draws heavily on Hook's account, now superseded by that of McLellan, and fails to take account of highly relevant recent Marx scholarship (Avineri, Althusser). It neither examines the text of *Die deutsche Ideologie* in any detail, nor gives more than a highly speculative résumé of the possible significance of Stirner for Marx. Paterson's book, the first sizeable study of Stirner in English, has many limitations: in particular, for our purposes, it fails to recognize the significance of Stirnerian psychology.
3 McLellan (op. cit., pp. 95–113) argues that the two later books of Feuerbach, *Vorläufige Thesen zur Reform der Philosophie* (1842) and *Grundsätze der Philosophie der Zukunft* (1843), exerted a more important influence on Marx. *Das Wesen des Christentums* was most significant as a symbol of the fact that the Hegelian system was not omniscient, that it was vulnerable, and that all who followed Hegel were not doomed to be epigoni. Virtually all of Stirner's references to Feuerbach are to the second edition (1843) of this book.
4 Marx: *The Economic and Philosophical Manuscripts of 1844*, ed. D. J. Struik, 1965, p. 64.
5 Ibid., p. 136.

The *1844 Manuskripte* share many features with Stirner's contemporaneously written work.[1] They contain a notably humanist, ideal image of the happy man, rich in the endowment of his senses, whose work and its fruit are the voluntary creative expression of his essential being.[2] Man is *homo faber*, he who makes his world, untrammelled by repressive social forces; labour is the free development of his physical and mental potentiality; it is his own, affirming and ennobling his being. In contrast, existing labour is seen to be dissociated from both its product and the process of production, it represents a loss of self, and the more alien the object world the poorer is man's inner world.[3] The worker is an object at the mercy of the modern forces of fate, ultimately the division of labour. About the ideology of capitalism, British Political Economy, Marx writes:[4]

Self-renunciation, the renunciation of life and all human needs, is its principal thesis. The less you eat, drink, and buy books; the less you think, love, theorize, sing, paint, fence, etc., the more you *save*—the greater becomes your treasure which neither moths nor dust will devour—your *capital*. The less you *are*, the less you express your own life, the greater is your *alienated* life, the more you *have*, the greater is the store of your estranged being.

Stirner's portrayal of the unfulfilled man, the selfless conformist ruled by sacred externalities, is similarly counterposed against an image of man who repossesses the external world as living property, the man who becomes whole only when his flesh and his senses are valued as highly as his mind, and to the exclusion of his conscience. Stirner, like Marx, regards the will to save and conserve as essentially misanthropic; its correlate, greed, is personified in the bourgeois, who is not a real owner, but the servant of his avarice. The question facing man is not how to acquire life, but how to spend it—enjoy it.

Stirner and Marx, schooled in the same Young Hegelian circle, advance Feuerbach's reformulation of Hegel another stage, but at this point their distinctive negations of the 'slave type' tend in antithetical directions. The Marx of the *1844 Manuskripte* describes a third stage of work alienation, its culmination, the dissociation of man from his own species.[5] Stirner rejects the possibility of social integra-

---

1 The *Manuskripte* were written in Paris between March and August. *Der Einzige* was written largely in 1843 and finished in April 1844; however it was not published before August. The first indication of its publication is in a letter of 19 November from Engels to Marx. There is no evidence that Marx ever met Stirner.
2 *1844 Manuskripte*, p. 141.   3 Ibid., pp. 107–8.   4 Ibid., p. 150.
5 Ibid., pp. 112 ff. Marx's closeness to Feuerbach here belies the originality of his strict derivation from man's concrete labour relations to the nature of his estranged state.

tion, regarding the notion of 'Man' or 'Species' as yet another religious postulate, and develops a theory of moral rather than economic alienation.

Stirner has been largely neglected in the copious literature on the roots of Marxist thought. The fact is that the Marx-Engels critique of German philosophy and socialism, as they subtitled *Die deutsche Ideologie*, allots 60 pages to Feuerbach, a meagre 20 to Bruno Bauer, and 320 to Max Stirner, two-thirds of the entire manuscript.[1] If Nietzsche's claim that only the greatest and most formidable causes are worthy of serious criticism holds any weight in this case, then the influence of Stirner merits careful attention. The composition and tone of the final critique of German philosophy suggests that in 1845 Marx and Engels considered Stirner to be their most dangerous adversary. Their relentless and vicious ridiculing of Stirner cannot be simply passed off as the product of Marx's choleric temperament. 'Sankt Max' is the work of a mind under threat. Karl Löwith in summing up this period writes: 'the only thing radical enough to be compared to Marx is the converse programme of Stirner . . .'[2] Feuerbach himself, in a letter dated in 1844, mentions Stirner as 'the most gifted and freest writer it has been given me to know'.[3] Recently the Polish Marxist, Leszek Kolakowski, asserted: 'Stirner's grounds are incontrovertible.'[4]

David McLellan has indicated the vital importance of Stirner in the development of Marx's thought.[5] He demonstrates the extent to which Marx borrows elements from Stirner; he writes:[6]

> It has been seen quite rightly that the 'Feuerbach' part of the *Deutsche Ideologie* brings this period of Marx's writing to a close, but what has not been seen is that it was the following and longer part entitled 'Sankt Max' that both compelled and enabled this culmination.

Before this time Marx was regarded as a disciple of Feuerbach, certainly by Stirner, who refers to him only once.[7]

Louis Althusser divides Marx's thought between four distinct

---

1 Refers to the numbering in Marx-Engels *Werke*, vol. 3. Marx devotes another 90 pages, approximately, to Bruno Bauer in the earlier work, *Die heilige Familie* (*Werke*, vol. 2).
2 Karl Löwith: *From Hegel to Nietzsche*, 1965, p. 103.
3 Quoted in Arvon, op. cit., p. 130.
4 Kolakowski: 'Vom Sinn der Tradition', *Merkur*, (Dec. 1969), p. 1087.
5 McLellan: *Young Hegelians*, pp. 129–36.
6 Ibid., p. 135.
7 Ibid., pp. 129–30. Moreover, Stirner refers to Feuerbach as a communist (*Ego* (1912), p. 412). McLellan goes on to suggest that Marx's sudden coolness to Proudhon at this time is partly as a result of Stirner's trenchant criticism.

periods. In particular, he stresses that an 'epistemological break' occurred in 1845. In his view the *1844 Manuskripte* mark the end of the early, philosophical and humanistic works. The Marx of 1844 is the 'Marx *furthest from Marx*', on the brink of a threshold.[1] The works of this break are the *Thesen über Feuerbach* and *Die deutsche Ideologie*. Thenceforth Marx writes as a scientist, having transcended the confusion of ideology and scientific theory.[2] Althusser describes the break as a flight from ideology and myth to reality.

For Althusser, Marx, the German philosopher, turns to science when, in pursuing what had been for him the political myth of France and the economic myth of England, he discovers at first hand the brutal, exploitative realities of those countries.[3] The point is overstressed. For a man as rigorously intellectual as Marx, the theoretical problems and contradictions generated from within his work would play no less significant a role in the development in it of a major discontinuity. It is on reading Stirner that he is brought face to face with the contradictions inherent in the position he had reached by 1844, a position, as we have suggested, sharing much in common with *Der Einzige*. They are concerned centrally with the problems of reconciling two dualities—ethics and science, and the individual and society.

In the works of the 'epistemological break', the first works written after reading *Der Einzige*, Marx turns against Feuerbach, rejecting his idealist humanism. Feuerbach is criticized for the religious nature of his thought, which will never spark off any 'real' change in the world. He merely wishes to achieve a correct consciousness, not realizing that his own senses are historically determined, an argument Marx turns against Stirner.[4] Marx has taken over Stirner's critique of a Feuerbach who has failed to go beyond the very idealism he criticized in Hegel, who has made sacred one concept ('Man') as he secularized another ('God' or 'Reason').[5] (However, for Marx it is not that the individual has been sacrificed for the ethereal species-being, but rather that Feuerbach's species-being is ethereal because it embodies no understanding of the ubiquitous significance of the dynamic material relations of history.)[6]

Marx had little difficulty in coping with Stirner's demonstration

---

[1] Louis Althusser: *For Marx*, 1969, p. 159.
[2] Ibid., p. 241.
[3] Ibid., part 2; in particular, p. 81.
[4] *German Ideology*, pp. 57–9.
[5] Althusser (op. cit., p. 72n) finds it remarkable that Marx should have so correctly seen that Feuerbach '*remained a prisoner* of Hegelian philosophy precisely when he was claiming to have "inverted" it'. This comment is illustrative of the ignorance of Stirner's work common among historians of political thought.
[6] *German Ideology*, pp. 29–31, 37, 645–7.

that the basis of Feuerbach's philosophy was idealist; he simply rejected Feuerbach. But *Der Einzige* confronted him with more troubling problems. It presented psychological questions which he could not dismiss with the same ease with which he could expose the cloudy abstractions of Feuerbach, nor with the clear conscience with which he could pass by the attacks of Strauss and Bauer on such 'straw men' as the historical authenticity of Jesus or the modern role of the Church in society. He must have realized that to emphasize individual fulfilment and man's creative potentiality leads danger-ously close to individualist philosophy, and its concern with ethical explanation at a remove from the social process. Stirner posed the nagging question for him: is not the artist the man who comes closest to embodying the unalienated *homo faber*, and is it not he who has liberated himself from the chains of economic relations and an oppressively determined consciousness by notably *individual* means? Moreover, Marx must have realized that implicit in Hegel's dialecti-cal continuum—consciousness, self-consciousness, Reason—is the *hubris* of man becoming God, leading to the logical extreme, Stirner's egoist morality.

Whether there were two Marx's has been disputed. Shlomo Avineri, in a painstaking study of this question, has shown the presence of early perspectives in late works.[1] McLellan, however, has put the counter-argument most persuasively.[2] He draws attention to many passages in the *Grundrisse der Kritik der politischen Ökonomie* (written 1857–8), the rough draft for *Das Kapital*, which elaborate themes of 1844 on alienation, leisure, human need, the 'universal individual', and so on. McLellan argues that *Das Kapital* is only the first of six sections of Marx's planned *Economics*, for which the *Grundrisse* was the ground plan. Thus the change from the *Grundrisse* to *Kapital*, where humanist themes are rare, is not one of methodology, but one of size.[3] The crucial question which McLellan fails to answer is why there is no split in the *Grundrisse* between the 'scien-tific' and the 'humanistic' Marx, between economic discussions and questions of a much wider nature, when *Das Kapital* is definitively split—the 'humanist part' remaining unwritten.

Even if McLellan is correct, and this will never be proven con-clusively, Marx's work undergoes a marked shift of emphasis in 1845. In the introduction to his critique of Proudhon, *La Misère de la philosophie* (1847) (we note that the title parodies philosophy as much as it parodies Proudhon), Marx stresses that he criticizes as an *economist*—as a scientist. Even granting a return in 1857 to earlier preoccupations, *Das Kapital* stands as a published exemplification of

[1] Shlomo Avineri: *The Social and Political Thought of Karl Marx*, 1968.
[2] David McLellan: 'Marx and the Missing Link', *Encounter*, (Nov. 1970).
[3] Ibid., pp. 38–9.

'scientific socialism'.[1] (We may conjecture as to whether the *Grundrisse* is not the reflections of a second, more speculative and philosophical, ethically-concerned Marx, repressed from consciousness (the manuscript was never prepared for publication) by his strongly-endowed scientist superego. There is also an at times unreconciled split in Freud, between the imaginative philosopher-prophet and the scientist.)

We now turn to a detailed discussion of the Marx-Engels critique of Stirner. We have two objectives. First, this critique provides the opportunity to examine in detail the gulf separating a radical socialist sociology from anarcho-psychology. Either standpoint is vulnerable to criticism from the other. Marx's critique of ideology concentrates directly on Stirner; Stirner's critique in turn includes socialist and communist ideals amongst its targets, and hence stands as an anticipatory attack on Marx. Second, and in conjunction, we review the break in Marx's thought which led him largely to renounce questions of individual fulfilment and ethical meaning. That, having read Stirner, he should find himself forced to move part of the way toward the positivist method of the procreators of *homo economicus* is of significance to our fourth chapter.

Engels wrote of Stirner and his newly published book to Marx on 19 November 1844:[2]

> But what is true in his principle, we, too, must accept. And what is true is that before we can be active in any cause we must make it our own, egoistic cause—and that in this sense, quite aside from any material expectations, we are communists in virtue of our egoism . . .

The following April Engels visited Marx in Brussels, where he had recently moved with his family. There Engels learnt of his friend's latest ideas on the materialist theory of history. Then, after a summer visit to England, they began collaboration on their critique of German philosophy and socialism. *Die deutsche Ideologie* was completed in October 1846, but in spite of their own efforts it remained unpublished as a whole until 1932. Marx subsequently wrote:[3]

[1] Nevertheless, Althusser's conceptions of 'reality' and 'science' are crudely scientistic. They preclude the recognition that values must intrude into social analysis at several levels. The concept of science is useful for pointing out differences of degree (as to the amount of empirical confirmation of a hypothesis, and so on), and for describing with some plausibility the crystallization of Marx's own aspirations.

[2] Marx and Engels: *Werke*, vol. 27, p. 11.

[3] Marx and Engels: 'Preface to the Critique of Political Economy', included in *Selected Works*, 1968, p. 184.

We abandoned the manuscript to the gnawing criticism of the mice all the more willingly as we had achieved our main purpose—self-clarification.

The section devoted to Stirner is titled 'Sankt Max' and takes the form of a rambling page-by-page commentary on *Der Einzige*. Sections of rigorous analysis are interleaved with pedantic repetition, heavy jingoistic polemic, and excerpts of Hegelian logic inappropriately applied to aphorisms. The absence of sections haphazardly censored by the hungry mice does not add to the coherence. Stirner is variously referred to as 'Saint Max', he who writes the history of spirits, ghost stories, to the exclusion of all practical affairs, 'Jacques le bonhomme', nickname for the good-natured but simple French peasant, and Sancho Panza, the knight of the woeful countenance,[1] the egoist. The text is liberally enlivened with reworked passages from Cervantes in which the real world makes mockery of Sancho's quixotic illusions. Elsewhere Stirner is regarded as a provincial Berliner whose only experience is of the local beer-drinking philistines, all petty-bourgeois.

The Marx-Engels critique of Stirner resolves itself into three substantive arguments. We shall treat them separately, but in the case of each, piece together the fabric of the argument as a totality before assessing its cogency or value.

The first prong of the critique is devoted to Stirner's history, for which Marx draws on his own extensive knowledge. Stirner, it is argued, offers a history of ideas without reference to actual events and their contemporary social environment. His only pretence to empirical validity comes with his refusal to discuss the nature of old age until he has experienced it himself.[2] He assumes, like all speculative philosophers, that thoughts made independent have always ruled the world, that ideas make material history. History becomes a history of theology, or to use Stirner's language, a history of ghosts.[3] For Marx and Engels the starting point for theory is the history of the practical developmental processes of man; the movement is from earth-bound reality to divine consciousness, rather than the mystical Hegelian effort to descend from the heaven of ideas to the ground.[4]

As an example of Stirner's misuse of historical fact they single out his treatment of Robespierre as a revolutionary priest, obsessed and enslaved by an idea, the generality 'Man', which drives him to inaugurate the 'Terror' as the means to his hallowed end.[5] They contend that worldly empirical interests promoted the guillotine.[6] In general they show Stirner's historiography as unrigorous, often

1 Marx regards Stirner as 'simultaneously Sancho Panza and Don Quixote' (*German Ideology*, p. 97).
2 *German Ideology*, pp. 133-4.   3 Ibid., p. 169.   4 Ibid., p. 37.
5 *Ego*, pp. 81-3.   6 *German Ideology*, p. 190.

vague, and riddled with discontinuities; in places it is no more than a clumsy imitation of Hegel.

These criticisms of the empirical content backing Stirner's history are largely warranted. The historical sections of *Der Einzige* are incomparably the weakest. This philosopher of the self provides a discussion of 'Man' of little accomplishment by comparison to his treatment of 'I'. Stirner's egoist morality, his theory of individual action, reflects in effect an a-historical conception of man, who need be neither modern nor civilized.

The second dimension of the critique is drawn essentially from Hegel's analysis of the unhappy consciousness.[1] It claims that Stirner was as trapped by ideology as his predecessor Feuerbach. Marx and Engels argue that Stirner's egoist is just as much an abstraction as the spooks he exposes (in German the play on the noun *Geist* is readily available: it means spirit both in the sense of 'ghost' and in that of 'mind' or 'soul'). His spirit creates itself, by presupposition, out of nothing. But it must create something other than itself. What? they ask.[2] The individual is a concept without any content to give it objective concrete meaning. The relation of the ego, which posits itself, to the world, as indeed the entirety of his action, is the mere appearance that he creates for himself.[3] His uniqueness is a universal category suspended in mid-air. Once we have defined the egoist as the owner, distinguished by the universal category of uniqueness, nothing remains to be said.[4]

Marx and Engels contend that because the egoist is the creator of himself, the creation, he is imprisoned in a world of reflection, and hence incapable of action.[5] (This is the ascetic moment in Hegel's development of the 'unhappy consciousness', in which the self strenuously shuns the natural world of activity and enjoyment, and withdraws.)[6]

Stirner, they claim, even more than Feuerbach, places exaggerated emphasis on the struggle against illusions:[7]

> . . . In the final analysis this Ego comes into existence because it has the same illusions about the world of the Christian as the Christian has about the world of things. Just as the Christian takes possession of the world of things by 'getting into his head' fantastic nonsense about them, so the 'Ego' takes possession of the Christian world, the world of thoughts, by means of a series of fantastic ideas about it.

Finally, Marx and Engels gibe at Stirner's delusion that, in his

---

[1] Hegel: *Phenomenology*, pp. 241–67.   [2] *German Ideology*, p. 159.
[3] Ibid., pp. 288–9.   [4] Ibid., p. 261.   [5] Ibid., pp. 255, 261.
[6] *Phenomenology*, pp. 263–4.   [7] *German Ideology*, p. 206.

battle against predicates and concepts, he is contending with the real forces determining the world.[1] Idealists like Feuerbach and Stirner have set up straw men, with no actuality in the real world, to destroy.[2] The knight of the woeful countenance persists in tilting at windmills.

The preceding argument hypostatizes the image of the egoist as an absurdity. As Marx and Engels regard Stirner's construction of the communist ideology as a travesty of their philosophy, so Stirner could regard their reconstruction of his own.[3] In the first place, the content of experience is given for Stirner as much as it is for Marx and Engels; he is as hostile as they to ideology which denies rather than mediates experience. Stirner's positive interest in social action is limited to the individual and his relation to the property having genuine significance in his life. From this point of view, thoughts, while they are important parts of the egoist's property, can exist only as media translating the world of particular experience, the world of love, conflict, and consumption. The crux of his argument on the content of experience is that man has no duty to the objects around him; they are real only when he himself invests them with value. Ideas are the vital means of understanding and relating to these objects.

Marx and Engels use Hegel's development of the 'unhappy consciousness' to show the one-sidedness, and ultimate self-contradiction, of Stirner's egoist, *'brooding over himself*, as *unhappy* as he is *wretched'*.[4] The self-positing ego that they examine, fearing the mastery of any other being, dissociates itself from the external world of particulars. In Hegel's analysis the Stoic must master the fearful irrationality, and hence potential dominance, of natural existence. Similarly, the ascetic individual must subdue his flesh, repress his animal needs.[5] Both limit themselves to abstract thought in a detached world of self—this is where Marx and Engels place Stirner. But Stirner argues no less vehemently than they against this extreme type of idealism. He criticizes Hegel and Feuerbach for harping upon 'being', viewing the latter's 'unconquered being' as no less of an abstraction than the former's 'absolute thinking': 'Only *I am* not abstraction alone'.[6] Moreover, sexual prudery, chastity, and sacred wedlock formed a theme of contemporary morality that most caught his critical imagination. In the light of this, it is puzzling that

---

[1] *German Ideology*, p. 256.   [2] Ibid., p. 30.
[3] It is virtually certain that Stirner did not read *Die deutsche Ideologie*. Marx probably kept the manuscript, taking it to England with him. Stirner was quick to reply to all his published critics, and it is most unlikely that he would have consciously disregarded the most trenchant of his opponents.
[4] *German Ideology*, p. 287; quoted from *Phenomenology*, p. 264.
[5] *Phenomenology*, pp. 241–67.
[6] *Ego* (1912), pp. 453–5.

Marx and Engels should have identified his philosophy with the ascetic moment of Hegel's phenomenology. Stirner is an emphatic advocate of the hedonist life in which self-enjoyment is the pure criterion of an action's value. Ascetic by comparison is the Marxian implication that the present is irredeemably miserable unless approached with the pure instrumentalism of the revolutionary.[1]

To avoid a common confusion it must be stated from the outset that the significant dichotomy is not between the isolated individual and society, but between the individual, subsuming the domain of his personal relationships, and, beyond these relationships, abstract society in the large. The dichotomy has parallels with that of Tönnies between intimate, individual-centred *Gemeinschaft*, here in the form of the small group, and *Gesellschaft*.

Stirner is not a philosopher according to Hegel's conception of the man who strives to understand the entirety of humanity and its history. There are many spheres of human activity in which he is little interested, especially those concerned with the action of groups. Moreover, unlike Hegel, he is not interested in the changing structures of a man's consciousness *per se* of his world through time. He most closely resembles the *psychologist*, who, in the image Nietzsche evokes in the Preface to his *Götzen-Dämmerung*, has the task of uncovering the idols of the age, tapping them as with a tuning fork to hear how hollow they ring. Such a psychologist is interested in the puppeteer rather than the gesticulations of the puppet. The motives behind action, the hidden drives which form the mainspring of behaviour, the goals and aspirations which underpin these motives, and the taboos that reinforce them, are the subject matter of his researches. In a given field of perception he is interested in why one individual will choose to see certain things and remain 'blind' to others. And for this a 'history of ghosts', as Marx and Engels parody it, is fundamental.

It is as invalid to accuse Stirner, who works through a psychological analysis of ideology towards his own ethical standpoint, of merely swapping abstract ideals as to accuse Marx, who works through a historical, sociological analysis of ideology, of the same idealist practice. Stirner is more an abstract ideologist than Marx only in that he leaves a less comprehensive and systematic theory. Marx accuses Stirner of losing himself in the arbitrariness of ideology on the grounds that he fails to root his ideas in the historical and social process. But Stirner's work correctly implies that there are ideas which do not merely reflect the social environment, ideas about which it is not adequate to say merely that they are socially condi-

---

[1] However, at least in 1844, Marx holds no explicit truck with asceticism. On the contrary, his critique of Political Economy in the *Manuskripte* (pp. 150 ff.) centres on its ascetic ethic of self-denial.

tioned: there are symbolic orderings of experience which are irreducibly egocentric, products of the individual's self-reflection which mediate his personal drives and his private needs.

Psychology as a human science does not hold to the sociological axiom of Durkheim, that society itself is an irreducible entity with its own ontological reality. It takes the individual, his psychic biography bounded by birth and death, as the primary unit of analysis. There is more, however, to the divide between anarcho-psychology and Marx than conflicting attitudes to the proper focus for social analysis. The writings of Stirner, Nietzsche, and Dostoevksy are governed by their existentialist ethic and its exclusive concern with the few moments in the individual's life, his few experiences, which they consider significant. These are the mystical, the ecstatic moments, those of intense suffering, the crucial turning points at which, often quite inexplicably, the course of a man's life changes direction. This ethic serves as a prism through which the wider compass of human behaviour is viewed and evaluated. There is a parallel orientation in Freud's concentration on the traumatic events which pattern individual biography: they provide the key to human self-understanding, and they can only in a secondary and perhaps partial fashion be related to social process.

Stirner reverses Rousseau's vision of man in the primitive state as being noble, innocent, and free. In the primitive state the individual does not exist. The innocent child is overwhelmed by a colossal and alien world; growing up is the slow process of realizing potentialities, of an embryo finding its latent being as it differentiates itself from the society on which it was born dependent. Through struggling against the authority of society, a youth may reach the mature state in which he has become his own centre of gravity. Nietzsche was to take an identical position with respect to child development, describing maturing as the individual emancipating himself from the 'herd'. He too set himself against the sociological axiom: he criticizes Darwin for overestimating the formative influence of 'external circumstances' at the expense of the form-creating forces within the individual.[1]

Stirner, nevertheless, displays a notion of social dialectic. Just as it is the individual who changes society, through insurrection, so, reciprocally, it is the same society which, according to its own characteristics, defines the egoist's rebellion and patterns his self-realization. However, the dialectical balance shifts. The scales swing continuously in the individual's favour, until the formative influence of society is entirely displaced. Development takes what might more accurately be called a 'skew-dialectical' path. The mature egoist has liberated himself from dialectic: his relationship to society is essentially one-dimensional, with himself the centre of all power and

[1] *Wille* 647.

F   71

influence. Society may still impinge upon him; but it is mediated by *ego*. Stirner does not imply that tensions between the individual's inner forces at this juncture also become resolved. The notion of the egoist is not incompatible with Hegel's idea that dialectic becomes internalized in the mature man.[1]

Stirner's psychology derives from an ethic which stresses the value of behaviour which transcends the patterns that can be predicted by examining previous social conditioning: only when a man goes beyond the identity, the sum of social roles, which can be plotted by sociological analysis does he become an individual—that is unique and creative.[2] The point may be clarified by turning to imaginative literature, and for example observing the technique of Stirner's contemporary, the Russian writer Nikolai Gogol, in his play *The Government Inspector*. All the characters are 'types', caricatures of real human beings, whose most striking facet is exaggerated to the exclusion of all others, very much in the manner in which a sociologist must *type*, through such media as role-analysis, in order to generalize about social behaviour. Gogol, however, with extreme austerity of detail, as if suggesting a full portrait with a single flourish of the sketcher's pen, fractures the 'type' by intimating the individual humanity which lives underneath. To this view men are almost wholly *typable*, but it is only in the fleeting residue, at the moment they transcend their predictable roles, that they become interesting and human: the contrast between the morass of the predictable, and the subterranean flicker of something more, endows Gogol's characters with a deep tragi-comic pathos. Stirner's assertion is that the first, 'social', dimension, without the leavening of the second, is merely a surrogate form of religious and moral ideology.

For Stirner the individual is unabashedly the categorical imperative, and hence, in a second sense, Marx and Engels are right to

---

1 Such crude, speculative theories of human development are of limited interest today, and must be evaluated within the context of the detailed research carried out by modern psychology, and in particular the traditions of Freud and Piaget. Stirner's contribution at this point is significant as an outline theory, one which contrasts with alternative social philosophies, which provides a vivid sketch of one ethical perspective and thus something of a framework for later, more empirically substantive theories. We note, incidentally, that Piaget draws on a Durkheimean image of man.

2 This is not to argue that sociologists have not been aware of the difficulties inherent in the Durkheimean axiom. George Herbert Mead, for example, develops the distinction between 'I', the uniquely individual self, and 'me', the social self dependent on how others perceive and respond to the subject (*Mind, Self, and Society*, 1967, pp. 173–8). Alfred Schutz, in his *The Phenomenology of the Social World*, discusses 'type-transcendent behaviour'. Max Weber defines sociology as the study of social action, whose central locus is the individual actor (*The Theory of Social and Economic Organizations*, ed. T. Parsons, 1964, p. 88).

label him as an ideal. But, as has been pointed out, to go beyond good and evil is not available to man. The critique of Stirner as a German ideologist hinges in part on the false belief that it is. Marx and Engels had learnt, probably from Stirner himself, that moral philosophy was not essentially different from theology. Notions such as 'ego' and 'unique' could be described as *religious* in that their content depended on the subjective evaluation of the relative quality of different types of human experience. The *quality* of an experience— its noumenal intensity, its sensual abundance, or however it is described—can be assessed only in the same manner in which the individual subjectively makes value judgments about phenomena external to him. The actor/observer can compare it with other experiences only by making judgments as imprecise ('unscientific'), and as open to subsequent revaluation, as moral rankings of good and evil.

Die deutsche Ideologie stands as a vehement rejection of this subjectivist method and its attendant concern with ethics. Individualist philosophy is accused of losing itself in ethical sophistry. The critique of German ideology prepares the way for a turning back to the scientist habits of mind of Smith, Bentham, and Ricardo: while Marx attacks their *laissez-faire* ideology and implies that it distorts their economic analysis,[1] he takes up the method of Political Economy in order to produce a more comprehensive and objective analysis of the capitalist system. Ethics is thereby reduced to the role of providing passing criticisms of various consequences of the historical process, and in particular of the nineteenth-century advance of capitalist society: Marx does not need to introduce value judgments into a purely descriptive analysis. However, to justify his radical optimism he must assume that qualitatively better social arrangements emerge with time: thus, like the positivists, he is driven to make a progress assumption, and, indeed, like Bentham, one grounded in economics. In order to comment on what would constitute qualitatively better arrangements he is forced to return to ethics, with its subjectivist foundations.[2]

Necessarily, Marx and Engels cannot respond to the mystical, irrationalist core of Stirner's existentialist ontology. They can dismiss it as religious; but they too enter the 'religious' domain of the categorical imperative. They can resort to Hegelian logic by endeavouring to show that the concept 'ego' is vacuous; we have seen that

---

[1] Avineri, op. cit., p. 158.

[2] The attempt to fuse the Hegelian model of historical dialectics, the concerns of positivist science, and the progress assumption led to the absurdity of Engels in his *Anti-Dühring* (1878) rejecting, in spite of his sound knowledge of the science of his day, both the second law of thermodynamics and Darwin's theory of natural selection.

the ensuing argument does not convince. Finally, as we now examine at greater length, they can attack this ontology from their own materialist standpoint.

Whereas the second dimension of the Marx-Engels critique of Stirner was based on logical objections to the egoist, the third centres on the argument that his philosophy is quintessentially ideological in the sense that it distances itself from an understanding of the determining role played by the material forces of history. Egoist praxis is thus grounded on illusion. At this point Stirner's critique of ideology from the standpoint of individualist psychology, and Marx's from the standpoint of historical materialism, come into direct conflict and turn most critically against each other. Moreover, Stirner here receives his most formidable criticism—from Marx, the social historian and economist. 'In revolutionary activity the changing of oneself coincides with the changing of circumstances.'[1]

Marx and Engels argue against Stirner that the development of the individual is inextricably bound up with the evolution of society. Private property, for example, is necessary for certain stages in the development of productive forces in an economy; it cannot be significantly changed, not to mention abolished, until congruent productive techniques are established. The economic relations of rent, profit, and enforced labour fetter the individuality of the majority, whose freedom depends upon their destruction.[2] The egoist morality, they write, bears a theological character; Stirner will never understand the possible means of strengthening man until he has studied the material relations which govern his behaviour.[3] Man is not simply a creation of his own consciousness; on the contrary, the structuring of mind is an epiphenomenon of the structuring of matter. Because of such needs as the relation between the sexes, exchange, and the division of labour, men had to form unions with each other.[4] These needs defined their tasks and vocations from the outset;[5] in particular, the division of labour subordinates man, segments his abilities, and thus determines him in his fractured being. Marx and Engels outline the pervasive influence of the social factors:[6]

> The development of an individual is determined by the development of all the others with whom he is directly or indirectly associated, and . . . the different generations of individuals entering into relation with one another are connected with one another . . . the physical existence of the later

---

[1] *German Ideology*, p. 230.   [2] Ibid., p. 248.   [3] Ibid., p. 386.
[4] Ibid., p. 481.   [5] Ibid., p. 312.   [6] Ibid., p. 482.

generations is determined by that of their predecessors, their own mutual relations being determined thereby.

Stirner, the argument continues, imagines that one can become an egoist by the philosophical trick of changing one's consciousness. His book continually reiterates the theme that alienation can be successfully overcome by means of profane introspection on one's sacred ideals; hence rebellion takes place in the head, no hand ever being raised. Ideas make history, ideas overthrow despotism, and ideas change property relations.[1]

Marx and Engels contend that the true egoist appears as an ideal unattainable by the majority of individuals.[2] The majority, the workers, need to congregate in order to assert their interests, their common goal, which can be achieved only by mass action against the repressive might of the capitalist class. Marx and Engels dispute that individual interests will undergo alienation when they become transformed into class interests.[3] Rather, they believe, the individual is strengthened in identifying with a like-minded class. An interest is not the product of thought, but of life, and the 'general will' may well coincide with the 'particular will'. When one class has always ruled, the practical task of the rising class is bound to appear to its individual members as a universal task.[4]

Stirner's programme of action, the argument continues, is quite impractical. Certainly he understands that the wealth of the banker is alien, and the evil of existing class relations lies in their mutual idolization of money, but he naïvely imagines that the truth of money can be willed away;[5] he seeks to reform property relations, but restricts his remarks to the agricultural sector, conveniently disregarding large-scale industry;[6] he believes that the propertyless presented their rights to the owners as a gift, and all that remains is to reclaim the gift;[7] he argues that the workers need only to rebel, failing to see the futility of such amateurishness in the face of the organized power of the propertied class.[8] The scantiness of his historical knowledge preserves his illusions for him. For instance, Marx and Engels claim, it was impossible for the German peasant to organize himself communistically, in spite of Stirner's injunctions, because he lacked the means of instituting collective husbandry, an essential precondition of the communist association.[9]

Even in the case of the artist, the critique continues, uniqueness is socially determined. Stirner refers to Raphael as the type of man who most needs to develop in a society without hindrance.[10] Marx and Engels counter that Raphael was dependent on the nature of the

---

[1] *German Ideology*, p. 273.   [2] Ibid., e.g. p. 282.   [3] Ibid., p. 265.
[4] Ibid., p. 313.   [5] Ibid., pp. 419, 218.   [6] Ibid., p. 420.
[7] Ibid., p. 397.   [8] Ibid., p. 425.   [9] Ibid., p. 385.   [10] *Ego*, p. 178.

division of labour in the Rome of his day, the demand for painting, both in terms of quantity and taste, and, at the most mundane level, a number of assistants to help with the actual painting.[1] There was nothing total about his individuality. They add that Stirner's example of a born poet, prevented by unfavourable circumstances from developing to his full potentiality, entirely substantiates their point.[2]

The crux of the argument is that Stirner's notion of consciousness is badly distorted. In reality, the many-faceted structure of mind is not simply an individually generated phenomenon: it is historically, socially, and culturally influenced.[3] Stirner is not interested in the social conditioning of consciousness, and consequently he has no conceptual means of analysing social change. The development from child through youth to man takes place against a static, invisible, social backdrop.

Finally, they mock at Stirner's quixotic subjectivism. The State is a fact and cannot be imagined away when it places one of its subjects, Stirner for instance, in a debtors' prison. They do not recognize his distinction between the inner freedom that even a slave may enjoy and physical emancipation from social constraint; their concern is with iron fetters, not moral ones.[4] They find ridiculous his experience under the whip of the cruel master, quoting it in italics:[5]

> But it is *my* bones that moan under torture, *my* fibres that quiver under the blows, and *I* moan because *my* body moans. That *I* sigh and shiver proves that I have not yet lost *myself*, that I am still my own.

'What cunning', they ask, 'will he use if the State declares his thoughts to be contraband?'[6] It is all very well to leave to Caesar what is Caesar's, but Caesar may decide to stop feeding Stirner, and if he crucifies him in spite of his indifference, then where is Stirner's uniqueness? In *Das Kapital* Marx quotes from *The Merchant of Venice:* 'You take my life,/When you do take the means whereby I live'.[7] In short, they conclude, Stirner has to treat the difference

---

1 *German Ideology*, pp. 430–1.
2 *Ego*, p. 227; *German Ideology*, p. 465.
3 *German Ideology*, pp. 132–3.
4 The distinction is most clearly expressed in Marx and Engels' own words:
   'Yet *Absolute Criticism* has learnt from Hegel's *Phenomenology* at least the art of changing *real objective* chains that exist *outside me* into *mere ideal*, mere *subjective* chains existing *in me*, and thus to change all exterior palpable struggles into pure struggles of thought' (*The Holy Family*, Russian trans., 1956, p. 15; also, *German Ideology*, pp. 23–4).
5 *German Ideology*, p. 332; *Ego*, p. 113.
6 Ibid., p. 390.
7 Karl Marx: *Capital*, trans. E. and C. Paul, 1933, p. 526.

between the personal and the material as holy.[1] He does not accept material necessity; the bonds of the empirical world are too mundane to impair effectively his inner freedom. The point is pressed home with a cruel reference to Stirner's hapless venture into the dairy trade: 'Thus Stirner the "ragamuffin", "the man of ideal wealth", arrives at the desperate decision to carry on trade with the curdled, sour milk of his thoughts.'[2]

The individual-society dichotomy is not an intellectual sophistry. The existence of a continuing dialectic between the individual and his society, each making, determining, and changing the other, is not in dispute. Nor is there dispute over whether social action should be analysed psychologically or sociologically: it would be perverse to deny that both are necessary. But the dichotomy is pivotal at the level of praxis, as illustrated by the contrast between the activities of Marxist political groups, with their focussing interest in the economic infrastructure, and Freudian psychology which devotes its attention to the individual and his private capacities for salvation.[3] Moreover, many, if not all, key social problems can be meaningfully approached in terms of a disjunction between the private psychological needs of individuals and the institutional needs of the means of production and their socio-economic superstructure.

Between the individualist and the socialist or communist there is little common ground. The former believes that freedom and fulfilment in life are to be achieved only in a personal way through growing self-awareness of the repressive forces trammelling the individual psyche. Liberation is, in the language of psychoanalysis, a release from the powers of the superego, erosion of the bad conscience, exposure and comprehension of the guilt-weighed taboos inhibiting free expression. For Marx and Engels self-help is meaningless outside the context of social revolution.

Stirner need not deny that man is heavily conditioned by his environment. His description of the mature egoist, who has successfully moved beyond the unreflected realism of the world of objects and the mesmeric mystery of a world of ideas, should be accepted as itself having an idealistic component: that is, it will never be fully realized. Stirner's egoist is an end, indicating the way to its own perfection, and an 'ideal-type' in Max Weber's sense. No man can achieve total emancipation from his social conditioning.

[1] *German Ideology*, p. 409. [2] Ibid., p. 390.
[3] There have been a number of theoretical attempts to synthesize psychoanalysis and sociologically oriented conceptual models (Reich, Parsons, Marcuse, Habermas), but none has yet found any enduring practical realization. We limit our discussion in this section to the division between Stirner and Marx and avoid, apart from voicing some sceptical inferences drawn from the argument, the wider question of the possibility of the two traditions being synthesized in praxis.

Stirner's views on freedom are pertinent to his concept of 'liberation': 'And, if you become free from everything, you would no longer have anything; for freedom is empty of substance'.[1] The achievement of *real* freedom invariably leads to the emergence of new tasks and new constraints, just as the discovery of the cause of an event leads back to another, prior one. This view of human struggle is Hegelian: the past is not simply left behind, it is *aufgehoben*. In the terms of the ancient philosophical problem, there is no incompatibility between determinism and free-will. The individual has the free choice for responsible action within the limits set by necessity. (What is important is not that he can choose consciously between different courses of action—anarcho-psychology disputes the possibility of such 'rational' choice—but that his passions are free to *flow* unimpeded.) The same constraint, say a speech impediment, will have different significance for different men. Not all stutterers follow Demosthenes, who in resolutely fighting his 'necessity' became an outstanding orator. The finest liberation and the most free expression may well develop only when the individual has to pit himself, with great self-discipline, against conditions of forbidding constraint. The egoist, as a phenomenon immanental in the physical world, attacks his constraints in this individual way; he is defined by his striving towards his *ideal*—this ideal is the 'egoist' in the second, unattainable transcendental sense of one who has overcome all constraint.

One of the glaring limitations of Marx's sketchily drawn outline of the man who has transcended his alienated state is its failure to distinguish between the situation wherein man is free from external constraint, and the higher state in which this freedom has been creatively utilized.[2] Man, ideally the productive animal, does not automatically produce when he has been liberated from the capitalist nexus.[3]

---

1 *Ego*, p. 110.
2 Such a dichotomy is glossed by Avineri (op. cit., p. 89) when he writes: 'Marx's way to socialism is not a collectivism which subsumes the individual under an abstract whole; it is rather an attempt to break down the barriers between the individual and society and to try to find the key to the reunion of these two aspects of human existence'. Avineri fails to note the absence of a Marxist psychology.
3 Marx never precisely specifies the nature of this liberation. In his discussion the time scale of real change remains ambiguous. It is unlikely that he regarded significant changes of consciousness as being possible within the same generation; throughout his work revolution usually appears as the natural culmination of a lengthy process of social adjustment, contradicted in its purpose if violence becomes necessary (Avineri, op. cit., pp. 187–8, 268 ff.). The existence of an extensive sociological literature on the problem of leisure, and the capacity to use it in an affluent society, is one indicator of the critical division between potential freedom and actual fulfilment (in particular, the work of Mumford, Fromm and Riesman).

In *Die deutsche Ideologie* Marx and Engels equate personal inner freedom with freedom in society. The former is precluded by the absence of the latter, and obversely, the establishment of communal harmony and mutual social integration is the precondition for personal liberation. For Stirner such equations linking the individual and society are mere chimeras, the striving to create equilibrium in one domain as wrongheaded as the expectation that this order could transpose itself into the other.[1] The hope for personal redemption following from social revolution is for him the dual of an original projection of individual powers on to alien externalities, that is the abdication of self in the face of a rigid social structure. A new society will not usher in a new self. The estranged ego projects its own disorder on to society and expects the restructuring and integration of the self writ large, the society, to reflect back on to the source of consciousness. Stirner regards this flight from self as a form of suicide, the dissolution of identity and uniqueness. He notes: 'if I cannot or may not write something, perhaps the primary fault lies with *me*'.[2] The mature man is one who accepts full responsibility for his condition. Whereas Marx's vision of *homo faber* becomes inoperative within social chains, Stirner's man *makes* his own freedom.

There is a strain in Marx of the cleric, of the vulgar moralist. He paints the capitalist and the bourgeois as incarnations of evil; it is they who are responsible for the woes of mankind. The dismissal of the individual's responsibility for his own misery is the quintessence of clericalism: it will be Dostoevsky who accuses science, in this case economic science, of relieving man of personal responsibility for his acts. From the immoralist standpoint Marx has taken the part of the revengeful type, unable to cope with uncertainty, whom Nietzsche stamped with the cry: ' "How can *I* help it that I am wretched! But somebody must be responsible, *otherwise it would be too unbearable!*" '[3] There are scapegoats for man's fallen social state: Marx *blames* the capitalist and the bourgeois, and thereby justifies his own identification with the forces for *good*.

In Stirner's scheme of things Marx is a post-theological moralist: he chooses, optimistically, to resolve the problem of original sin through an ethical commitment to the redemptive power of human History. Marx is as conscious as Stirner, in his own different way, of the limitations of utopian socialist ideology. But his own attachment to a progress assumption about History is as vulnerable to the

---

1 Stirner would say that the primary condition for a better standard of education is not better administrative structures or better class-rooms but more talented, individual teachers.

2 *Ego*, p. 190.

3 *Wille* 765. Cf. 'An admirable evasion of whoremaster man, to lay his disposition on the charge of a star' (*King Lear* I:ii).

Stirnerian critique as any socialist ideal. Marx subordinates the individual to the new God, History: history itself is moralized. The profound Hegelian sense of history as amoral is lost, not by Marx the descriptive economic historian, but by the *alter ego* which shadows his entire intellectual endeavour, which retains the moral enthusiasm of the utopian socialists. Our contention is that the virtual suppression of ethical discussion after 1845 produces the semblance of purely descriptive analysis, dressed in the mantle of positivist objectivity, analysis which is, in fact, strung to a framework of crude, because unexplicated, moral assumptions. One of the most consequential analytical breakthroughs pioneered by the anarcho-psychological perspective, and in particular the work of Nietzsche, was to make its own ethical commitments explicit, and thereby subject them to critique. The analytical power of the framework for moral discussion which resulted, one in which ethics and descriptive investigation proceed integrally to each other, and the insights it provided into the epistemological status and the psychological function of value judgments, strongly vindicate the adoption of a self-reflective methodology in the human sciences.

Stirner is mistrustful of the grouping tendency in man; indeed, his own discussion of the Union of egoists, the coalition forming the sole unrepressive group unit, reads as half-hearted, an appendage to his theory. Certainly, he admits, in many conflict situations the interest of the individual may well coincide with that of the many, and group action appear as the only means of redressing an iniquitous balance of power. Then it is natural to band together, much in the nature of warriors in mutual coalition against a common foe. Stirner would simply warn that the group is an unnatural affiliation for the individual, it goes against his healthiest instincts, and he should be constantly on guard against the growth of group morality and conscience.[1] While the dictator Nero must be opposed, it is the spontaneous indignation and will of the egoist, not the moral ought of the liberal, which will dethrone him.[2]

Marx assumes that economic relations determine the psychological characteristics of the individual, that his motivations are cast essentially in economic terms, and hence that the transcendence of economic constraint, of commodity scarcity and exploitative capital-labour relations, will automatically provide for the emergence

---

[1] Cf. Freud's analysis of emotionally charged group behaviour as the demise of personal responsibility resulting from the projection of the individual superego on to the leader, whose demands and morality are simultaneously introjected by the individual as a surrogate superego (*Group Psychology*). Nietzsche had made the point, as a corollary to his critique of morality, that the origin of morals lies with the thought that 'the community is more valuable than the individual' (*Menschliches* II:i:89).

[2] *Ego*, pp. 68–70.

of a 'non-alienated' generation. A state of estrangement from meaningful life, of fragmentation, runs the implication, is reducible to a failure of man, *homo faber*, in relation to his work. The only way forward is through pervasive economic change. This picture succeeds only partially in reproducing the condition of man in society: it is lacking at the levels both of description and prescription. Firstly, as description it fails to recognize that ideology (and hence power and authority) is rooted in psychological needs, and that it is structurally incorporated into the individual's consciousness through the formative stages of socialization. The psychology of the unconscious, one of the first contributions to which was Stirner's assertion that every Prussian carries his gendarme in his breast, exposes, as inadequate, analysis of such political categories as 'authority' in terms of overt, physical power relations. We will later examine, moreover, some psychological constraints inherent in human nature which Nietzsche and Dostoevsky posit as precluding the possible realization of most utopian hopes. The anarcho-psychological perspective, anticipating Freud's work, penetrates the problem of ideology more profoundly than Marx's critique in that it demonstrates that fantasy, illusion, and the need for moral systems are all embedded in the individual psyche, irrespective of the nature of the society which determines their particular colouring. This perspective shows that a concept of liberation, to constitute more than an unrealizable wish, must subsume an understanding of the psychological origins and function of ideology. It accuses Marx of proceeding under the delusion, to borrow an image from Freud, that he can predict the drift of an iceberg from taking observations of its visible mass and of the surface currents flowing in its vicinity. He fails to take account of the range and depth of individual experience, with which no historical generalization can cope. Stirner's riposte is that social activity is a mirror of the individual's inner world, and to generalize about the former one must understand the latter.

Marx, like Bentham and Comte, believed that a rational social order could be achieved. Following Hegel, he argued that each process in history has its own rationality, and each of these processes, in turn, reflects a higher rationality. But, while Marx accepts this more universal plane of rationality, he neglects to step in the other direction, towards the more microscopic: the psyche is not a significant entity for historical materialism. After 1844 there are no more than rare passing intimations in Marx's work as to the conduct of apolitical leisure and domestic life. There are objective, leaving aside temperamental, reasons for Marx's failure to discuss behaviour outside the political arena of the class struggle. He views the individual as insignificant, an atom powerlessly swept along within the self-determining process of history. He holds, moreover, that the capitalist production-consumption nexus allowed negligible scope for the proletarian's self-realization: therefore the worker's political task, overthrowing the dominant class, constituted his only meaningful mode of action.

The life of the individual, as Hegel explained, however atomic it appears when viewed in isolation, also develops its own logic. Psychology devotes itself to this plane, to its rationalities and absurdities, and to the individual's ability to reconcile his aspirations with the constraints of his environment. In bypassing what is virtually the entire domain of psychology, as we have construed it, which is not to deny his astuteness as a political psychologist, Marx neglected the individual's capacity to grow and mature, to master his environment in spite of its constraints, to learn from his suffering, to relish and enjoy life in the midst of necessity, and indeed to call this his freedom. Marx's analysis is thus limited in its prescriptive range: it does not exhaust the available paths to redemption.

In retrospect, it appears that Marx renounced a series of psychological insights, with which he was confronted in 1845 on reading *Der Einzige*, ones which pointed forebodingly in one direction. He, moreover, expurgated his own bad conscience for rejecting psychology by venting his spleen on Stirner. Stirner was for Marx the convenient scapegoat, the external object onto which to project an unresolved inner conflict, for exorcising the psychological man he knew that he should consider more thoroughly.[1] Hence the vicious intensity of the Stirner section of *Die deutsche Ideologie*. The dilemma that Marx faced over individualist psychology acted as a crucial factor in the epistemological break postulated by Althusser: the consequence was that he moved abruptly closer to the positivist habits of mind whose economist exponents he had attacked in 1844.

Marx and Engels disclose their antipathy to Stirner's emphasis on self-enjoyment in a ponderous joke: they decline to dwell on 'the more or less dirty forms in which the "self" in "self-enjoyment" can be more than a phrase'.[2] This is suggestive of an embarrassed reaction to the anarcho-hedonistic programme, with its attendant ludic principle, a reaction consistent with their evasive attitude to the entire domain of individualist psychology. *Der Einzige* confronted Marx with the implications of some of the hints in his own *1844 Manuskripte* at the possibility of a non-alienating mode of work which was to be more in the nature of play (implications which have

---

1 An isolated line appeared in Marx's notebook in the middle of 1845: 'The divine egoist as opposed to egoistical man' (*Selected Works*, p. 670). Perhaps he was toying with the idea of developing the Stirnerian theme; if so it was quickly suppressed, and the possibility remains but this indistinct cipher in his *Werke*.

2 *German Ideology*, p. 460.

found recent elaboration in such works as Herbert Marcuse's *Eros and Civilization* (1955)). Marx's response was to deny in blanket fashion the possible practical relevance of this entire anarchist perspective.

Marx and Engels' comments on Raphael are inadequate. It is not certain whether they suggest, by the emphasis that they place on Raphael's dependence on environment, that the social and economic conditions created by the communist revolution will be more conducive to the maturing of like genius. The substance of Stirner's argument, and Raphael stands as a paradigm for the egoist, is that any man of rare talent is recognized as such by virtue of his originality, his uniqueness, although he may be precariously dependent on his supporting environment. The great individual is, by definition, never the predictable product of a planned environment. 'The unique person will work himself forth out of society all right, but society brings forth no unique person.'[1]

Nietzsche puts the anarcho-psychological point more aggressively: 'to let oneself be determined by one's environment is decadent.'[2] He also suggests, with historical credibility, that wilful, creative individuals like Raphael may be most prevalent in the midst of the unegalitarian turbulence and violence of a Renaissance Italy.[3] The case of Raphael is thus anti-socialist on two fronts.

Nietzsche takes a position virtually identical to Stirner's on issues which separate him from Marx. In the case under discussion, that of the unique artist:[4]

Against the doctrine of the influence of the milieu and external causes: the force within is infinitely superior; much that looks like external influence is merely its adaptation from within. The very same milieus can be interpreted and exploited in opposite ways: there are no facts.—A genius is not explained in terms of such conditions of his origin.

In Nietzsche's terminology, the sociologistic axiom legitimates 'herd morality': only types, not individuals, are reducible to laws.[5]

Marx and Engels have, nevertheless, rightly made the point that Stirner does not discuss the significance of different social preconditions for the egoist. Patterns of individual behaviour do change through time. Nietzsche, in his *Zur Genealogie der Moral*, however,

---

[1] *Ego*, p. 178.   [2] *Wille* 49.

[3] Georg Simmel repeated the suggestion made by numerous nineteenth-century literary figures that a degree of social alienation suits the artistic temperament, and moreover is a prerequisite for self-consciousness (*The Sociology of Georg Simmel*, ed. K. H. Wolff, 1964, p. 418). Nietzsche had proposed that the aims of culture and civilization might be in opposition (*Wille* 121).

[4] *Wille* 70.   [5] Ibid. 684.

introduces a historical notion of the individual by showing its dependence on the development of the 'ascetic ideal'.

Stirner can reply in subjectivist kind to the self-explanatory criticism that his individualist philosophy, as the ideology of the petty-bourgeoisie,[1] has the effect of enforcing the political *status quo*. From his antithetical conception of significant social change he accuses the socialist of working towards an abstraction. He warns that the 'law-abiding' mind is so firmly implanted that revolutionaries want to subject man to a new sacred law. What is more, 'soon we no longer hear anything but the clashing of the swords of the disagreeing dreamers of freedom'.[2]

The history of socialist movements in industrial societies has somewhat vindicated Stirner's tartly dismissive scepticism. The problem at the core of socialist theory is how to innovate general welfare principles in a meaningfully democratic way into a society which is too complex structurally either to be readily adaptable to such principles, or to be unequivocally receptive to a government wishing to implement them. Hence the inevitability of contention over how the general principles apply to particular problems and over what degree of coercion is warranted in order to institute and maintain a socialist government. In essence Stirner sets up the debate which will be pivotal to Koestler's *Darkness at Noon*, that between Stalinist methods, justified by the long-term revolutionary goals, and the anarchic, humanist values of the individual. Stirner suggests that Stalinist methods, in one form or another, are inherent in the attempt to reform society on the large scale, that authoritarian structures will never wither of their own accord.

But Stirner's praxis is also problematical; as Marx and Engels stress, it lacks realism. Egoist philosophy is one-sided. Whereas Stirner has insights into some of the psychological origins, functions, and effects of social institutions, he does not show any systematic grasp of their historical development, nor of the manner in which they influence individual behaviour. He evades an honest recognition of the inevitability of the State and its constraints. His work could be neither theoretically nor practically available to the nineteenth-century working man. The one-sidedness of his vision is epitomized by his exhortation to egoistic insurrection, a tactic quite impotent against the organized power of the capitalist system. Stirner has little conception of the future patterns of social and economic development. The individual is virtually powerless in confrontation with any of the key institutions of twentieth-century advanced industrial society, whether they be the oligarchical business

1 *German Ideology*, pp. 234, 256, 328, 404, and 418; also Löwith, op. cit., pp. 103–5.
2 *Ego*, p. 114.

THE CRITIQUE OF IDEOLOGY

corporations large enough to influence the national economy, the State apparatus itself, or the mammoth party machines which compete for control over the political system. Marx, who does painstakingly develop a systematic, philosophically and empirically well-grounded, theory, can at this point accuse Stirner of abstraction. It was not until Freud that psychology became adequately developed as a theoretical discipline; Freud also succeeded in spelling out some of its social and political implications.

Stirner could today make a partial rejoinder to the criticism that his work takes little cognizance of real social constraints. His views are more widely applicable in an advanced industrial society in which relatively few people live on or near a subsistence standard of living, and where, in terms of a Durkheimian dichotomy,[1] moral questions are more salient than purely economic ones. Economic constraints on individual action are potentially lesser at higher levels of affluence. Egoist philosophy with its stress on anarchist individualism becomes more relevant the more 'doing your own thing', setting up co-operatives in which individuals work just enough to provide the necessities of life, and simply working 'part time' by choice, become economically viable.

The case for Stirner having failed to provide a total social theory is telling. And yet at another level, one notably akin to his own style of anarchism, his work can be redeemed from the charge of one-sidedness. The point has already been made that his theory is realizable by individualists such as artists, and in certain institutions such as schools: but as such it is relevant only at the margins of society. His work is potentially of more socially pervasive significance. Stirner's political praxis is quixotic. It accepts the established hierarchies of constraint as given; they have their own life, they generate their own momentum, and in this, although not labile to radical change, they constitute part of the theatre housing the individual's action. Solzhenitsyn's work provides powerful empirical verification of Stirner's extreme assertion, ridiculed by Marx and Engels, that the slave may, in spite of his manacled limbs, become one of the freest of men: it suggests that only in the prison camp or the cancer ward will man come to recognize the true dimensions of his freedom, and realize them.

The egoist uses the elements of the social structure as props in his self-expressive act. Herein lies the meaning of Stirner's anti-utilitarian, immoralist challenge to the established order of punishment: 'a mighty, reckless, shameless, conscienceless, proud crime'.[2] The provocatively anarchic, wilful assertion of the parodic dancing of the

---

1 Émile Durkheim: *Suicide*, trans. J. A. Spaulding and G. Simpson, 1952, p. 252.
2 *Ego*, p. 152. Nietzsche, mocking well-educated 'good people', calls for 'a real lie, a genuine, resolute, "honest" lie' (*Genealogie* III:19).

Dadaists in the streets of Zürich in protest at the madness of the First World War is representative of this Stirnerian praxis. Where there is no scope for conventionally rational communication the individual chooses his own means, however quixotic, of expressing himself and asserting his political beliefs. It is only from the perspective which holds that the social order can and must be *systematically* changed that individualist anarchism can be charged with one-sidedness.

The work of both Stirner and Marx provides insight into social action and social process. Analysis can help to decide between the two standpoints by clarifying their relative usefulness, in terms of the range and depth of their explanatory power, their coherency, and their consistency. But the task of relative evaluation ultimately reaches a level at which the so-called objective world appears as a different phenomenon according to the perspective chosen. The world that Marx criticizes is not the one that Stirner describes. The nature of society, the various facets of the individual, the creative potentialities of either, are inextricably bound to the vision of the particular philosopher.

In order to conclude this discussion we must distance ourselves from the particular arguments and admit that, in spite of a painstaking comparison of the different perspectives of Stirner and Marx, the scales of judgment can be conclusively tipped only by as subjective a standpoint as that taken by the protagonists themselves. For, what is at stake is the plausibility of one of two conflicting myths, sacred and totally identified with, one of two mutually exclusive categorical imperatives. Were one to convince Marx that economic forces have not behaved according to his laws, his vision would still stand as a psychological map of the tension in every man between evil self-aggrandizement and good, satisfied creativity[1] — Marx would merely need to change his empirical parameters. On the other hand, a State can refuse to employ a Stirner because of his subversive ideas, it can throw him in debtor's prison, it can so weaken his morale that a fly's bite kills him, and yet if he is as obstinate in the face of necessity as Job he will rightly not recant his faith. We are in the sphere of ultimate values where 'science' can play only a subsidiary role. There is another, what might be termed 'mythological', dimension to 'truth', and to ask for the scales of judgment to be tipped in favour of Stirner or Marx is to fail to realize that ethically neutral enquiry cannot produce a definitive resolution here; the question which is in effect being asked is the *religious* one, in the words of Max Weber, 'Which of the warring gods should we serve?'[2]

---

1 Robert Tucker: *Philosophy and Myth in Karl Marx*, 1961, ch. 15.
2 Max Weber: 'Wissenschaft als Beruf' (1918), included in *From Max Weber Essays in Sociology*, ed. H. H. Gerth and C. Wright Mills, 1948, p. 153.

Nietzsche

So far we have constructed the lower storey of the anarcho-psychological critique of ideology. It remains to add the upper one. Although its dimensions are projectively governed by those of its supporting structure it embodies a more complex and sophisticated view of the role that morally charged ideas play in social action. The diverse and rather unsystematic writings of Friedrich Nietzsche present an orientation to ideology remarkably similar to that of Stirner. At the same time Nietzsche's analysis supersedes that of his predecessor.

Nietzsche informs the psychological dimension of the anarcho-psychological perspective with a wide-ranging, yet profound and deftly detailed scope. In his general psychology, that is in the hundreds of aphorisms which disinter with uncanny precision the traces of motivation backing individual perception and action, the quality of his insight far surpasses that of Stirner; it will be matched only in the work of Freud, if then. Moreover, although the volume of his output far outstrips Stirner's five hundred significant pages, his mastery in individual works, by themselves, is unparalleled. Nietzsche is the exemplar of anarcho-psychology also in cultural-historical concerns. In so far as these distinctions remain tenable, anarchist themes are the preserve of Stirner; his work is definitive in questions of specifically social, political, or economic substance. He also has the indisputable claim to have initiated the individualist affirmation: he was the first to mount a categorical rejection of all that is abstract, absolute, aggregated, that is—supra-individual. This rough division of labour does not hold, as we have already gone to some length to show, in respect of the pivotal psychological themes and dichotomies which course through Nietzsche's work: unlike his multitude of fragmentary insights into human motivation, these recurring themes are prefigured in *Der Einzige*. We turn now to a systematic examination of the advance that Nietzsche pioneered for the anarcho-psychological critique of ideology. Most of the major facets of his philosophy are involved, and emerge as projections from a common centrepoint, one which is equally central to Stirner's schema—the master-slave dichotomy.

Hegel's master-slave dialectic is one of those nuclei in the history of thought which, once discovered, is seen to hold the key to a diverse range of prominent, hitherto opaque and unconnected, problems. So important to the radical consciousness of the time did it become that the direction of philosophical departure of the greatest German thinkers for several following generations could be read in how they oriented themselves to it. This is true for Stirner and Nietzsche, as it is for Marx. Stirner transforms Hegel's dialectic into a duality, that of *egoist* and *cleric*. Hegel had described, in the primal state of human interaction, the slave being driven to reduce the anxiety that he suffers at the hands of the master; but this slave learns to distance himself from his oppressor through his labour. Self-consciousness originates at the time when he finds he can enjoy his labour as a self-expression, as a representation of a meaningful sense of self which enables him to transcend the logic of domination. For Stirner the genesis of self-realization is crucially different. He regards pleasure, satisfaction, and joy as providing the momentum for a man's higher activities; *anxiety* is not one of his parameters. The implication is that the egoist, who ideally does manage to pursue his interest and express his power, does not suffer seriously from anxiety; anxiety is identified by Stirner with repression and morality, it is a symptom of a lack of egoism, it is the emotional currency of the cleric. Stirner does not, however, answer the question of what prevents the cleric from harnessing his aggression egoistically.

The egoist, like Hegel's master, seeks to control his environment, but actively out of self-propelling exuberance, rather than reactively in a desperate attempt to cope with a hostile world. He is aggressive in order to win and protect his own, and perhaps, additionally, as Nietzsche puts it, he attacks in order not to conquer or harm, but to know his own strength.[1] Unlike Hegel's master he is not a slave of his own mastery; his future is not restricted to a one-dimensional need to dominate. On the other hand, the poverty of the cleric is both the cause and the effect of his serfdom; his condition contains none of the seeds of liberation which it does in Hegel's model. Stirner has in fact inverted the fulcrum of Hegel's philosophical system.

We are at a crossroads in nineteenth-century intellectual history. Here radical psychology and radical sociology branch off from the same trunk. Also parting along the same two branches are what were to become the guiding intellectual concerns of the two schools, concerns on the one hand with questions of value and individual meaning, with what Marx would have deemed 'religious' questions, and on the other with large-scale historical, as well as socio-economic explanations. The only man to make significant progress in bringing these two traditions in social thought together again was to be Max Weber.

The original step that Stirner takes is to conceive of the slave's alienation in moral terms; the revolt of the slave-type leads not to creative labour, but to a bastion of moral dogma. The psychological critique of ideology stresses that the category 'alienation' serves to conceptualize primarily a distortion in moral, not economic, conditions, one in which the socially-determined bad conscience represses the more spontaneous human essence. That Marx should have followed and adapted Hegel, and not Stirner, in his terminology, is of crucial significance. His conviction that the hope for a better

[1] *Menschliches* I:317.

society lies with the underprivileged, depressed, proletarian class, and not with the controllers, who for him are slaves to their own power in bourgeois society, is a direct elaboration of the master-slave dialectic in socio-economic categories.[1]

At its first level Nietzsche's exposition of the master-slave dichotomy is precisely that of Stirner: the slave is Christian, his alienation is structured in terms of morality, it is detailed by means of psychological analysis, and it is typed in terms of the 'ascetic priest'.[2] Above all, this slave is utilitarian, he always calculates, and he has the cold heart that Stirner associates with ideologues. Although Nietzsche's descriptions of the slave-type are restricted to general psychological terms, they portray quite distinctly a character combining the traits of Stirner's cleric and *homo economicus*. It was left to Max Weber to make the connection between the two types more explicit in his history of the Protestant ethic and its relationship to capitalism.

Nietzsche's starting point is the query as to whether morality itself does not present the greatest danger to human society. Perhaps what has hitherto been praised as 'good' is 'a seduction, a poison, a narcotic, through which the present was possibly living *at the expense of the future*'.[3] According to Nietzsche's history of morality there was originally an aristocratic age in which the terms 'good' and 'bad' were employed to describe noble, high-spirited, self-affirming action, and alternatively that which was plebeian, uninspired, and utilitarian.[4] Only late in human history did the relationship of the noble to the common become moralized. Simultaneously the egoist-altruist dichotomy took possession of human consciousness.[5] The early product of, and in turn catalyst for, this transition was the priest; with him emerged the *reactive* type, he who, in the absence of spontaneous passions to direct his actions, applies his intellect to create a network of moral, religious, and metaphysical rules to guide his conduct.[6] The reactive emotions—pity, compassion, and humility—are endowed with supreme virtue; altruism is established as the moral yardstick for social interaction. Finally, a second type of reactive emotion—vengeance, envy, and resentment—takes root

---

1 Hegel's *Phänomenologie* does, on other levels, point towards the psychological tradition. The analysis of the role of *Angst* in the development of self-consciousness provides a powerful influence on Kierkegaard, and anticipates Nietzsche.
2 Although threads of Nietzsche's argument are to be found in all of his works, we concentrate our attention on his *Zur Genealogie der Moral* (1887), where he treats the master-slave morality in greatest detail, and most systematically.
3 *Genealogie*, *Vorrede* 6.
4 Ibid. I:2–5.
5 Ibid. I:2.
6 E.g. Ibid. III:10–11, and *Menschliches* II:ii:350.

at a deeper level, and erodes the remaining capacities for impulsive, expressive action: 'the slave revolt in morals begins by "resentment" turning creative and giving birth to values'.[1]

The argument continues with a psychological analysis of bad conscience, priestly revenge, cruelty, punishment, and resentment towards the egoist, roughly along the lines which have already been discussed in reference to Stirner. Nietzsche, however, also takes up Hegel's theme that anxiety is at the root of consciousness; at this point the analysis becomes highly intricate. Nietzsche maintains that it was in a desperate attempt to avoid pain, to evade the cruelty and hostility of his neighbour, that man was driven to sharpen his wits, to extend his memory—to think.[2] But this same struggle to reduce tension also gave birth to morality; thereby it provided community with its most powerful nexus, its most resilient self-preserving bond.[3] Nietzsche, like Stirner, is led finally to differentiate the universe of human action into two broad classes: the one aristocratic, powerful, hedonistically vital, later egoistic, creative, irreligious, and a-social, the other structured and rationalized according to a strict moral code, Christian, utilitarian, reactive emotionally, and community-centred. Developing Stirner's un-Hegelian interpretation of alienation as a moral phenomenon, he equates the tenacity and vitality of a people with its capacity for progressing 'beyond good and evil' to the 'sovereign individual'.[4]

But Stirner's dualism becomes a dialectic in Nietzsche's analysis. Positive dimensions are discovered in what was unambiguously destructive at the first level of meaning. The Hegelian postulate is amplified into the view that European culture has been nurtured in the soil of the slave's attempt to master his hostile environment: the priest with his *evil* introduced the seeds out of which man grew 'interesting', 'complex', and 'deep'.[5] Ultimately Nietzsche does not criticize the slave morality itself, but a society in which the priest has gained too much power, where the creative forces of the master are in danger of becoming completely repressed. It is this advance of the naïve conception that morality and social constraint, and the instinctual renunciation that they enforce, are fully ameliorable that prepares the way for Freud's insights into the psychological nature and necessities of civilization. Nietzsche's analysis here provides the supreme example of psychological ambivalency at work. Indeed, in

---

1 *Genealogie* I:10. This section provides the crux of Nietzsche's analysis of *ressentiment*, in which he uses the French concept for want of a German equivalent. English translators (e.g. Kaufmann) have preferred to retain the French. We see no reason for not using the legitimate English equivalent, 'resentment'.

2 Ibid. II:3–5, 15–16.　　　　　　3 *Menschliches* II:ii:44.
4 E.g. *Genealogie* II:2.　　　　　　5 Ibid. I:6.

so far as Hegel invented the dialectical method, Nietzsche becomes, at this point, an original and sophisticated Hegelian.[1]

Another prominent Hegelian theme reappears in a striking new guise in Nietzsche's work. Hegel endeavoured to circumvent Kant's categorical imperative by setting up a supra-ethical model: he established History as an objective process unfolding according to its own inner laws. He maintained that individual historical events, however barbaric or atrocious, however destructive of human life or the finer achievements of civilization, cannot be judged. They form but a necessary moment in the process as a whole. In isolation they have no meaning, ethical or otherwise. In any case, a phase of persecution and massacre might be the precondition for the later flowering of a rare and beautiful culture, if this is the direction in which one's private values lead one.

Nietzsche transplants this orientation into the soil of individual morals. He titles the first essay of his *Zur Genealogie der Moral*: ' "Good and Evil", "Good and Bad" '. He retains moral categories, rejecting only the highly charged, moralistic 'good' and 'evil'. He explicates his preferred distinction between good and bad individuals as non-condemnatory of the latter. A 'bad person' is merely devoid of what Nietzsche personally considers to be noble or virtuous qualities; he is not morally evil. Nietzsche's aim is to make the process of forming moral judgments visible, to defuse morality of reactive emotion, to render it prescriptive in no more than a low subjective key. It would be futile, tactless, and cruel, he suggests, to try to change a bad person, one with whom one does not empathize; his formula advises: 'Where you cannot love, pass by'. No one should be blamed for what he is; there is no point in lamenting fate. Nietzsche goes further. He described the 'eternal recurrence' as his greatest discovery: one of its dimensions was *amor fati*, the acceptance of all events as necessary and of equal importance. This principle is antithetical to all moralism, it is Hegelian in being deliberately non-prescriptive.[2]

With his categories of 'good' and 'bad' Nietzsche does in a meaningful sense step outside the circle of morality, however blurred its circumference remains. Given the constraint that human conduct depends on discriminating between different objects, different actions, and different modes of thinking, Nietzsche's preference is for aesthetic rather than ethical criteria of judgment. His life-long

---

[1] Hegel, commenting on the Adamic myth, stated with anticipatory significance: 'This is a deep truth, that evil lies in consciousness', (*Philosophy of History*, p. 321).

[2] There are many traces in Hegel's work of themes to which Nietzsche will give central prominence. For example, in the *Encyclopaedia* appears the sentence: '*Alles* endliche *ist dies, sich selbst aufzuheben*'.

wrestling with the problem of morality drives him ultimately to choose the beautiful rather than the good. Thus it is that his central socio-historical concern is with *Kultur*; thus it is that he scorns ethical commitment to individual happiness and social melioration; and thus it is that he singles out the politically optimistic philosophies of liberalism and socialism as mutilating human reality through their ideals. Nietzsche's qualms about humanist ethics stem from his fatalist conviction that man does not have the power, by means of conscious choice or application, to improve the quality of his life. 'Quality' is an aesthetic concept, and the 'beautiful', whether in the form of a human creation or of an exemplary individual, is supra-historical—it can neither be predicted nor prepared for. Man is more than an animal only in that he finds expression for the beautiful. Additionally, it is significant merely that he may recognize and praise that beauty which moves him. The ugliness of the ideological lies in its legitimating the pursuit of the trivial: it has no rapport with the essence of beauty, nor with its elusive origins. This view finds support in *Genesis*: the garden is the realm of pure beauty from which man is expelled when he becomes interested in ethics, in the fruit of the tree of knowledge of good and evil. The return into paradise, the homecoming, depends on him penetrating the veils of morality to glimpse again the lineaments of lost beauty.

Nietzsche's dialectic has many facets. For example, it extrapolates a direct relationship in the case of the philosopher between instinc-tual repression and the quality of his thought. The philosopher attaches himself to a desensualized ascetic ideal in order 'to gain release from a torture'. He chooses thought as his unique means of salvation. But out of this dismally repressed world of thought emerges the sense of an independent, ontologically valuable exis-tence, a sense of the centrality of the persona. Here man becomes interesting—the *individual* is a cultural-historical phenomenon, the polar opposite of the instinctual 'noble savage'.

Nietzsche paraphrases the philosopher's credo: 'Let the world perish, but let there be philosophy, the philosopher, *me!*'[1] Stirner, thus even more than himself, is placed in intimate kinship with the priest. Another facet of the dialectic is outlined in the case of the artist. With his 'terrible egoism', his confidence in the ultimate value of his work, he is *not* a victim of a strong bad conscience, but he does contribute to its general development. Society is driven to moral condemnation in its struggle to neutralize the violence and freedom of the artist. Nietzsche provides numerous other applica-tions of his thesis; he does also epigram its very Heraclitean funda-mental mechanism:[2]

[1] *Genealogie* III:7.   [2] Ibid. III:9.

> Every smallest step on earth has been paid for by spiritual and
> physical torture: . . . not only every progressive step, no! every
> step, movement, and change has required its countless martyrs,
> . . . Nothing has been bought more dearly than the modicum of
> human reason and feeling of freedom that are now our pride.

The same socio-cultural conditions produced both the most negative,
life-denying force in modern Europe, the ascetic priest, and the
possibility of the most positive, the *Übermensch*. Both types are
confronted with a world undergoing rapid secularization, and
experiencing an expanding capacity for self-consciousness, at once
balanced by a waning in generic exuberance. Both turn their aggression, with their consciousness, in upon themselves. But the one
disinters emptiness, ugliness, and undifferentiated waves of anxiety,
he builds defences and channels his aggression outwards again—this
time with cunning and with malice. His life-style leads eventually to
a 'castration of the intellect'.[1] The other has driving resources to cope
with his new inwardness, he finds himself able to harness his violence
in the form of self-overcoming, and gradually begins to enjoy his
power of Will, his capacity for self-definition.

The concept of the *Übermensch* focuses Nietzsche's individualist
ethic. The emphasis is on the character of a man; dominant is the
Goethean view that nature, which is not directed towards any end,
terminates in a unique personality. Nietzsche has transformed the
medieval belief that the vitality and quality of a society is dependent
on the strength of its ruler, or, as Machiavelli put it, on the *virtu* of
its Prince: he argues that all that passes in the life of a society is
ephemeral and banausic except for the presence of great personali-
ties, of men like Goethe himself who seem to forge their own
destinies, who seem to move unhampered by those burdens of
existence which keep most men from rising above the vicissitudes of
their daily toil.

The *Übermensch* possessed qualities which set him apart from the
egoist. Essentially the egoist is more of a hedonist. While Stirner's
philosophy carries a strong ontological interest in self-realization,
and the egoist's *modus vivendi* depends on how much power he can
exert, this Will-to-Power is directed outwards in order to gain the
property he desires. Will, as a means to self-discipline, is mentioned
in *Der Einzige*; it is also present in Stirner's conviction that satisfaction depends on the wilful exploitation of all of a man's own resources. But we find fewer traces of the ascetic, stoical inflexions of
Nietzsche's tenacious and defiant Will-to-Power, his 'self-overcoming'. There is less of the extreme will-affirmation of Ibsen's *Brand*
(1866), an anticipation of the Nietzschean Will which caricatures it.

[1] *Genealogie* III:7.

Absent also is the stress on the mastering of strong (Dionysian) passions, and their refinement through sustained (Apollonian) control. Although Nietzsche's description of Goethe, the man who came closest to embodying the *Übermensch*, 'he disciplined himself to wholeness, he *created* himself',[1] could plausibly be read into *Der Einzige*, this image of man creating himself is woven by Nietzsche inextricably into a warp of instinctual constraint. It points to the hypothesis that culture is purchased at a great price in terms of emotional repression. Stirner was more naïvely optimistic about the compatibility of individual maturity and gratified desire. He does not recognize that the creative spirit might derive from a psychic constitution which shares features in common with seventeenth-century Puritanism.[2]

Both Stirner and Nietzsche place primary importance on the individual *creating* himself; both stress notions of process and flux, of realization and becoming; both disdain unimaginative, unplayful, and instrumental action. Their anarchism rejects external authority on the grounds that it inhibits exploration and invention by providing the individual with set patterns of action. In all, both philosophers point towards the central value of creativity: the artist is the most appropriate paradigm for either the egoist or the *Übermensch*. Indeed, Nietzsche's Dionysian-Apollonian dialectic stands as a definition of the creative process. Its structure can be discerned in Freud's theory of the primary (id) and secondary (ego) processes at work in dream formation, as it can in Ehrenzweig's more recent psychoanalytical theory of art.[3] It initiates a tradition in aesthetic theory which we might call anarcho-psychological, that is, a tradition which argues for a balance between the two psychic functions at work, and emphasizes that too much rationality is ideological in both reflecting and perpetrating a repression of the primary process, thus stifling the imagination. These views have today become a truism in a number of schools of educational philosophy, as they have in existentialist-influenced branches of psycho-therapy.

Schopenhauer had singled out boredom, chronic weariness of the

---

[1] *Götzen-Dämmerung* ix:49.

[2] In *The Scarlet Letter* (1850), Nathaniel Hawthorne portrays the ambivalency of Puritan virtues with a deftness and subtlety which parallels Nietzsche. He sketches how overwhelming grief can instil a type of sympathy which is vital for social cohesion, and alternately, how unbridled, natural passion nurtures the wilful, social isolate. He links the suffering of intense guilt with the growth of inspiration and wisdom. He also links the acceptance of a burden of guilt with the development of character and self-integrity. Hawthorne, like Nietzsche, identifies the existence of ego, of human complexity, and of psychic depth, with a biography of instinctual stress and repression.

[3] Anton Ehrenzweig: *The Hidden Order of Art*, 1970.

spirit, as man's greatest vice. This was a prophetic sentiment to find a melancholy echo from many of the prominent imaginative writers of mid-nineteenth-century Europe (Baudelaire, Turgenev, Mallarmé, and Fontane stand out). No one charted more intensely or insistently than Nietzsche the terrain left between the 'death of God' and nihilism, the death of life. Yet the resigned pessimism of Schopenhauer ran counter to his own temper. His search for a plausible cosmology was underpinned rather by a romantic Stirnerian type of faith in such a realizable ultimate value as *interest*, the psychological antonym to boredom. He criticizes Schopenhauerian aesthetics for not freeing itself from Kant's moralistic: 'that is beautiful which gives us pleasure *without interest*'. Nietzsche prefers Stendhal's sketch of the beautiful as 'une promesse de bonheur'.[1]

Nietzsche's categories are often internally branched into opposing currents, the one positive and affirmative, the other inherently destructive. This is true for 'nihilism'. The sustained self-questioning of the *Übermensch* may leave him at times in a position in which no fixed points remain, in which there are no criteria left for ordering the world, or ranking alternative modes of action. However, an undertow of driving, Dionysian instincts is strong enough to carry him through this intellect-mediated void. A wholly different kind of nihilism threatens the priest: if he puts his God in question he is left with nothing, unless he can find a surrogate 'saving lie' such as bourgeois morality. (This morality arises as the socially legitimated defence against incipient nihilism, the reverse side of the same coin.) His life had previously been one of norm-governed reaction to his environment; but now the ego through which he responded to the external world has lost its moral struts, and collapsed; his spontaneous impulses are dead, and so he has no means of orienting himself. Nietzsche's social pessimism stems from his Stirnerian belief that to remove repressive social and economic constraints is merely to 'free from'. The priest who has lost the resilience of youth cannot be helped; his polymorphously playful and imaginative energies have been emasculated by a long conditioning to the ways of the old order; he would be liberated into a sea of undifferentiated boredom and anxiety. Only the man whose desires and passions are intact has a future.[2]

[1] *Genealogie* III:6.
[2] There are obvious and powerful applications of this general theory. Ehrenzweig argues from his experience of teaching art that the problem of the schizophrenic is that he is too frightened to 'dedifferentiate' fully—that is, to open himself to the full force of his unconscious fantasies. Thus the schizophrenic is seen to be afraid of the nihilistic void that Nietzsche predicts will remain when a rigid world-view is discarded. Of great contemporary significance is the theory's implication that any attempt to break with the past, or with existing social structures, is a failure if it leads to a

Nietzsche's *Genealogie* is directly relevant to this study as an extension of the immoralist critique of ideology. It also outlines the historical significance of the slave morality. Nietzsche argues that by the nineteenth century the 'ascetic ideal' had become the last weapon available for combating the exhaustion and boredom which he delineated as the key symptoms of the contemporary decline of European civilization. A devitalized people endowed the priest with great authority in a last attempt to discipline themselves, to command their own destiny. Nietzsche saw in the Protestant ethic, in both its religious and secular (economic) forms, a final protest before the emergence into dominance of the ordered, bourgeois world of the 'last man'—he who will pay any price in tedium for comfort and the absence of tension.[1] Even the *élan* of the 'captain of industry' was to fade before the bourgeois dream, as also characterized by Stirner in terms of addiction to moderation in all things. The rise of the bourgeois ethos was qualitatively different from any earlier phase in the history of the ascetic ideal, for it brought with it *nihilism*. Nietzsche prophesied that the future course of this nihilism would determine whether Europe was to survive.[2]

The task of assessing the usefulness of this psychological genre of cultural history, to be later exploited by Spengler, lies outside our rubric. If its psychological connections help to define the present then it is, at least, justified at one level. On the other hand, it may be significant that no detailed psycho-history of nineteenth-century capitalist Europe has yet been written. Our next chapter, on epistemology, will touch, although obliquely, on the problem of historical knowledge.

There can be no doubt that Nietzsche's primary analytical concerns were psychological. The guiding assumption, one which he took over from Schopenhauer, that intellect is subordinate to Will, provided clear indication that his passion would be for psychology. What is more contentious, taking him as a founder of an anarcho-psychological perspective, is the claim that his social and political inclinations were anarchist.

Nietzsche defined his task, and therewith he believed the task of

bored, listless, and colourless style of life; assertive and enduring innovation, like the mastering of a new environment, requires the confidence and discipline which are founded on exuberant emotions.

[1] *Zarathustra, Vorrede* 5. From Nietzsche's diverse writings we can piece together a coherent conception of 'bourgeois man', one which is psychological, based on the analysis of prominent psychic traits rather than a history of economic relations. The bourgeois is simply the contemporary embodiment of the slave.

[2] Jung was to consolidate this prophecy, e.g. 'About a third of my cases are not suffering from any clinically definable neurosis, but from the senselessness and aimlessness of their lives' *Collected Works*, vol. 16, 1966, p. 41).

every philosopher and psychologist, to be the relentless search for new values and their hierarchy of significance. The preparatory endeavour, to which his own life-work was devoted, lay in sounding the accepted values of the time in order to hear how hollow they rang. His work, as a result, bears that uniquely anarchist quality observed in Stirner's assault on all structures of supra-individual authority. He is the master of psychological iconoclasm. A driving hostility to any unquestioned order of authority determines his social attitudes. He evaluates social action according to its relationship to what he regards, like Stirner, as the key dichotomy between the individual, as ultimate value, and society—in his terms, the 'herd', any group or institution.[1] He too dismisses the State as a purely negative phenomenon.

George Brandes, the first man to lecture on Nietzsche, christened his philosophy 'aristocratic radicalism'. The reference is not to the traditionally ruling dynasties of Europe, nor to some ancient pantheon of heroes: Nietzsche preaches an aristocracy of the individual. In political terms his position is individualist anarchist. He differs from Stirner only in placing a more élitist emphasis. However, he admires Napoleon not specifically as dictator or conqueror, but as a man who, in the continuous conflict of Wills which constitutes human life in society, incarnates 'aristocratic' virtues. Napoleon, like Goethe, is a creator, an initiator; it is inevitable that such men will impose their authority over others. Nietzsche's supreme anarchist prescription is that the most powerful men should turn their Wills against themselves: dedicated to 'self-overcoming' they should place the ultimate order of authority, their own egos, in question.

Copernicus and Darwin undermined man's image of himself as the 'measure of all things'. Newton provided him with a new hope which the Benthamite tradition was to transplant into social theory—that of 'man as the measurer of all things'. Thus the possibility was revealed to man, who had been disinherited from *being* at the centre of the universe, that he might be able to *know* how to work himself back there. Science, at the same time as it destroyed his ontological security, gave him the tools for reapproaching Eden—through eating of the fruit of scientific knowledge he gained the faith that through eating again and again he might be saved. Stirner and Nietzsche put this last endeavour into critical question. They interpret the 'Will-to-Truth' as having become a priestly defence against impending nihilism, Christianity's 'last metamorphosis'. They ascribe to history a monumental a-rationality, an overwhelming absence of design, an ineffable fortuity (Darwin's influence on Nietzsche). The dialectic is recast: man is the prey of chance, he is a

1 *Wille* 679.

time-bound speck enclosed within an infinite universe of time and space.[1] The only coherent destiny available to him requires that he takes 'himself as the measurer of himself' —there is one measurer and only one to be measured.[2] The faith which is not a defensive illusion, and thus the only viable connective for the self-conscious psychologist, is a faith in the significance and tenacity of the individual ego. And, if Nietzsche's psycho-history is valid, then the ideals of *Einzige* and *Übermensch* provide European man with his last integral vision of himself and what he might do.

The high and sustained pitch at which Nietzsche defends the individual against social forces, against the 'slave' and the 'herd', is illustrative of the centrality of his opposition to socialism. Indeed, Lukács has read Nietzsche's whole life work as 'a continuous polemic against Marxism and socialism'.[3] Although he never read Marx or Engels, and his specific references to socialism were rare, his critique of compassion (*Mitleid*), which is fundamental to his psychology, stands as the blatant negation of any socialist-humanist ethic. To deny the compassion for the underprivileged which lies at the root of socialist humanism is to rob it of both its psychological and its ethical thrust. Nietzsche analyses compassion, a reactive emotion, as the issue of anxiety and unhappiness, a symptom not of humanity but of sickness and self-disgust. It reeks of the hospital; it is one of the main signposts on the road to decadence and nihilism. Compassion does not heal, it infects. Nietzsche counters with a spartan intellectual ruthlessness: even the type of friendship which is based primarily on mutual aid is corrupt. He combines, in effect, Christ's harsh sayings: 'let the dead bury their dead' and 'narrow is the way, which leadeth unto life'. To compromise these truths, to release one's compassion or one's sympathy (*Mitgefühl*), is to invite nihilism.[4]

As Lukács notes, Nietzsche posits a historical progression from Christianity to the French Revolution, to democracy, to socialism.[5] The critique of Christianity frames critiques both of liberal-rationalism and of socialism. And there is a sense in which Nietzsche's castigation of liberal-rationalist habits of mind is a prelude to a more fundamental attack on socialism. He regards the Bentham-Mill tradition as based on a sterile misconception of the human condition, a misunderstanding of the power and function of reason: it is

---

[1] *Menschliches* II:ii:14. A view vindicated by modern molecular biology.
[2] Cf. Kafka's central parable: *Vor dem Gesetz.*
[3] Georg Lukács: *Die Zerstörung der Vernunft*, 1962, p. 273.
[4] Max Scheler provided an early defence of certain types of compassion, from a Schopenhaurian perspective, as not being grounded in resentment in the way Nietzsche had maintained (*Zur Phänomenologie und Theorie der Sympathiegefühle und von Liebe und Hass* (1913)).
[5] Lukács, op. cit., p. 324.

geared to the reactive values of liberty, equality, and social utility.
But socialism brought the threat of a more profound distortion of the
human essence by directly taking up the Christian inversion of
noble ethical imperatives, even to the extreme of investing the
underprivileged with unique qualities of virtue, and elevating the
act of sympathizing with their abject state to the level of an ultimate
value. Nietzsche warns that here is the supreme consummation of the
European bad conscience, and Christianity's highest achievement:
for the strong to kneel down before the weak.[1]

Many of Stirner and Nietzsche's key critical themes, when shone
through a systematizing lens, focus as a critique of ideology. These
themes are centrally concerned with the conceptions men have of
themselves, their goals, their obligations, their satisfactions. Com-
pounded, they form an attack on European society which isolates the
rise of various types of self-destructive false consciousness as man's
contemporary problem: the contention is that his self-images have
become governed by ideologies and have thereby separated him from
his real desires, masked his true face. This is an existentialist, not a
Marxist, formulation. The critique presupposes that it itself constitutes a first stage in the emancipation from ideology. For Marx such
an enterprise condemns itself as ideological.

Stirner and Nietzsche's critique serves also as the ground in
which their own positive revaluations grow. Their image of man
emerges from psychological analysis of the nature, function, and
consequences of beliefs held to and introjected, under the delusion
that they support the individual. The ideals of egoist and *Übermensch*
are similar, but not identical. Their common anarcho-psychological
traits have now been detailed; their position counter to liberal-
rationalist and socialist ideals is shared. But, in so far as Nietzsche
advances the view that every positive is infused with a negative, that

---

[1] I have discussed the case for implicating Stirner's work in the roots of
European fascism in my introduction to *Ego* (pp. 11–17). Although such
notions as '*Übermensch*' and 'slave morality' are peculiarly amenable to
translation into fascist slogans, the Nietzsche case is parallel to that of
Stirner. In a society in which there is no equivalent to the bonds of
commitment joining feudal lord and serf, that is, in a predominantly
individualist society, a romanticist philosophy which emphasizes self-
realization and the individual's striving to create his own glory, if projected
into the political arena, is in danger of being commandeered to legitimate
militant fascism. Thomas Mann has provided a level-headed assessment of
Nietzsche's relationship to fascism ('Nietzsche's Philosophy in the Light of
Recent History', included in *Last Essays*, 1959). He argues that 'Nietzsche's
rhapsodies on the selective and culture-saving function of war strike us as
the fantasies of an inexperienced child, offspring of a long era of peace and
blue-chip security which was beginning to bore'. He concludes that Nietzsche,
at bottom a non-political, an innocent intellectual, did not create fascism,
but sensed and recorded its imminent arrival.

every great human achievement is precarious, and is made at the price of severe instinctual constraint, the critique of ideology has gained a new complexity, and the *Übermensch* as an ideal-type has superseded the more embryonic *egoist*.

3 The critique of knowledge

The critique of absolute truth

Stirner, Nietzsche, and Dostoevsky all concern themselves individually with problems of knowledge; in particular they probe into its origins, its reliability, and its utility. The question of whether knowledge is a force for the individual's emancipation from authority, above all his own social and psychological conditioning, or whether, as legend has it, it itself compels man's expulsion from the Garden of Eden, is central to the critique of ideology. Nietzsche's work stands out as providing an extensive critique of knowledge which analyses both its logical foundations and its psychological functions. His critique has the added virtue of being ruthlessly self-reflective.

The anarcho-psychological critique of ideology progresses logically towards a repudiation of 'absolute truth'. 'Truth' is another humanist ideal like 'Man' or 'Freedom'. The iconoclast moves from the hall of the liberal god to the connected hall of its rationalist brother. But the argument at once becomes more difficult, for to attack truth is to put in question the very means by which the reflective process is conducted.

Nietzsche, like Hegel before him, is at pains to point out that epistemology is caught in its own tautological circle, eating its own tail. There is no starting point: knowledge cannot stand outside its own boundaries, and therefore cannot define itself. A true meta-theory of knowledge is impossible. Both Hegel and Nietzsche grapple with critical philosophy, which, in the terms of Habermas, 'demands that the knowing subject ascertain the conditions of the knowledge of which it is in principle capable before trusting its directly acquired cognitions'.[1] In his *Phänomenologie* and in his *Logik* Hegel developed

---

1 Jürgen Habermas: *Knowledge and Human Interests*, 1972, p. 7.

a method of thinking which reflects back on itself. It does not depend on an origin: any starting point is adequate and will lead through the necessary logic of the argument, which is a self-contained totality.

Nietzsche's strategy is quite different; but it is not, finally, worked through into a fully elaborated and fully consistent epistemology. We take our cue, in setting out to map this strategy, from the critique of morality. We have stressed that, although great sophistication can be gained in the analysis of ethical systems, the categories of good and evil, in one form or another, are binding: the possibility of a genuine metatheory of morality is not available. Even psychology has its ethical presuppositions, as the discussion of Stirner in relation to Marx was at pains to point out. A metatheory of morality would be legitimate only if the existence of a hierarchy of absolute, and hence unconditioned, truths were established. They would then provide a framework of supra-ethical categories. The primary ambition of Nietzsche's critique of knowledge is to expose just such an exercise, and there include much of the history of Western thought, as a sleight of hand, an efficacious deception. This critique sets out to demonstrate that 'truths' are fictions masking moral commitments.

Nietzsche's case is often impressionistic, haphazard, and polemical, rather than argued. Nevertheless, there is a system to be pieced together from behind the unsystematic appearance, one of radical pertinence to the conduct of the human sciences. The critique of truth can be broken down into two phases: an analytical critique from the sceptical standpoint that all knowledge is subjective, followed by a psychological investigation of the origins and the functions of knowledge.

Nietzsche poses the question: What is thinking's reality?[1] The first phase of his argument responds to the more specific: How is knowledge possible? His answer is a simple negative: knowledge in the sense of incontrovertible conclusions about a 'real world' is not possible. Much of his subjectivist scepticism at this point moves in the shadows cast by Berkeley, and more especially Hume.[2]

The 'objectivist fallacy', which constitutes in fact a metaphysical assumption, is subjected to repeated castigation: there is no self-contained, ordered, objective reality, nor consequently any isomorphic relationship between its 'facts' and propositions about them. The keystone of Nietzsche's attack on this positivist fallacy, which has found no more pervasive representation than in the Benthamite notion of rationality, is that there is no 'thing-in-itself', no object independent of man's cognition, unconditioned. We can know

---

[1] *Wille* 484.
[2] Parallels between Hume and Nietzsche are drawn by Danto in his outstanding study, *Nietzsche as Philosopher*.

things only as they are conditioned by the cognitive process;[1] the radical tenet of Nietzsche's scepticism, distinguishing him from Kant, is that there is no reality mediated by this process. Knowledge creates objects, it does not discover them. Thus man patterns and orders the meaningless chaos which is external to him; he introduces meaning, he interprets, but he does not explain.[2] Put in other words, man schematizes, designates, simplifies, abstracts, distorts; but he does not know.[3] He is constrained, as in Plato's cave, to a world of appearances. The dichotomy between an apparent and a true world is a false one; it reduces to the true antithesis between the world, which is apparent, and nothing.[4]

The laws of logic are also down-graded to the status of fictions. Given that no objective criteria exist by means of which logic and truth can be evaluated, logic itself can claim merely to provide convenient, but arbitrary, rules for communication. Nietzsche's first concern is to question the habit of causal thinking. He points out, anticipating modern linguistics, that language forces upon us the belief in subjects and predicates, the assumption that wherever there is an event or an action there is a doer, a first cause.[5] His immoralism quips: 'I am afraid we are not rid of God because we still have faith in grammar'.[6] In the section of *Jenseits von Gut und Böse* which inspired Groddeck and Freud's notion of *Das Es*, Nietzsche proposes, in a paradigmatic case, that a thought comes when *it* wishes, not when *I* wish.[7] The subject or the ego can rarely be said to initiate. The only causal chain which is not a purely abstract fiction is 'the sequence of thoughts and feelings . . . becoming visible in consciousness'.[8]

The implication is that thinking in terms of causes is not merely a method of creating an illusory objectivity, but that it unnecessarily obscures the world which we inhabit. (We postpone discussion of the assumption implicit in Nietzsche's desire to build a more appropriate logic: that a 'real world', which we *can* learn to understand, exists.) He suggests that there are only effects. To say, for example, the 'lightning flashes' is to introduce an imaginary agent into a description of a happening.[9] Rather, 'a "thing" is the sum of its effects, synthetically united by a concept, an image'.[10] The way is now prepared for the unifying principle which founds all life: the Will-to-Power. This Will is not so much a causal factor as an existential 'it', a dynamic core presence.

The argument runs counter to the axiom of ego-psychology that the individual, at best, is a conscious agent who directs his own action. Nor will it sanction Sartre's ethic of individual responsibility,

---

1 *Wille* 555 and 560.   2 Ibid. 604.   3 Ibid. 515 and 554.   4 Ibid. 567.
5 *Jenseits* 20.   6 *Götzen-Dämmerung* III:5.   7 *Jenseits* 17.   8 *Wille* 523.
9 Ibid. 531.   10 Ibid. 551.

which presupposes the existence of a capacity for conscious choice. Nietzsche is not, however, repudiating his erstwhile attachment to an egoistic principle:[1]

> Even in the domain of the inorganic an atom of force is concerned only with its neighbourhood: distant forces balance one another. Here is the kernel of the perspective view and why a living creature is 'egoistic' through and through.

The Will as life-force is utterly egoistic, or in Stirner's preferred, and less ambiguous, terminology, unique and individual. Stirner's 'I have founded my affair on nothing' should now read, more in the style of Groddeck, 'It has founded my affair on nothing'.

There are moments, however, when Nietzsche suggests, without developing his suggestion, that causality may be a useful fiction. He is less ambiguously condemnatory of the law of non-contradiction. He views this cornerstone of Aristotelian logic as an unnecessary epistemological crutch, a manacle on creative thought. This law, which he associates with positivist science, depends on the false assumption that knowledge might be comprehensive. But, once the world is recognized to be a multi-faceted and only partially comprehensible phenomenon, there is no compulsion to deny propositions which may contradict one another on one of the levels of their application.[2] Nietzsche is defending, by contrast, what we have introduced as the indispensable 'half-truth'; he replaces formal with paradoxical logic.

The critique of metaphysics proceeds by incorporating an empiricist moment. Nietzsche repudiates Kant's notion of 'pure reason' on the empiricist grounds that all of reason's categories are of sensual origin, derived from the world of concrete experience.[3] Nietzsche denounces Kant's style of thinking, its cumbersome abstracted intellectualism; he viewed Kant's obsessively regulated personal life as a concomitant of idealist metaphysics. But his specific critique of *a priori* categories is unconvincing. Indeed, he not only fails to discredit Kant's notions of the 'transcendental idea' and of 'pure reason', but he repeats in less precise form a number of Kantian assertions—for example, that knowledge is completely dependent on empirical experience, and that understanding is an intuitive process of imaginatively representing the appearance of objects which can never be known in themselves.

Nietzsche's primary contention *contra* metaphysics is that philosophers have placed an unwarranted trust in concepts, they have absurdly overestimated consciousness.[4] He poses the question again and again of whether the whole of conscious life is not a reflected

---

[1] *Wille* 637.   [2] Ibid. 516.   [3] Ibid. 488 and 530.   [4] Ibid. 409 and 529.

image, of whether thought and belief bear any relation to active life other than that of providing it with an *ex post* signature. This querying of *homo sapiens*' cardinal assumption about himself intensifies Hegel's reflection that the owl of Minerva takes flight at dusk, that the time for philosophy is when the action is over—Nietzsche's sounding of knowledge is potentially far more radical, and self-annihilating, than Marx's contention that hitherto philosophy had failed to change the world.

Stirner's ambition to tarnish what he called the seductive 'glitter of the idea' anticipated Nietzsche's attack on metaphysics.[1] *Der Einzige* develops Feuerbach's argument that idealist philosophy, indeed all metaphysics, is religious. It contends that idealism, which is interested in things only to the degree that it can find *reason* in them, fragments man's natural wholeness. Life is more than thought: what a man feels, and what his senses awaken in him, are more indispensable to his life's fullness than subsequent reflection on their significance. Both Stirner and Nietzsche have elaborated Faust's opening speech in which he bemoans his wasted years in academia: this speech is Goethe's own impeachment of Kant and Hegel. Philosophy proceeds always under the risk of making a fetish of thinking.

A fruitful approach to the history of ideas is to investigate the changes that occur in what different ages and different groups isolate as problems of crucial significance. The problem that beset all the Young Hegelians, and defined their mutual interest, revolved around the question of what remains if one no longer believes that philosophy and religion are compatible.[2] Christianity, on this view, formed but one dated moment in a secular historical process. The radicalness of Stirner's response to this problem, one which takes him beyond his Hegelian environment to Nietzsche, is to mount a psychological attack on religion which then extrapolates into an attack on philosophy. He thus abolishes the original problem, and prepares the ground for its successor, which Nietzsche will formulate in terms of the questions: Why do men need knowledge? and secondly, Given that knowledge has no reliable basis, can men do without it?

The second phase of Nietzsche's critique of truth is, characteristically, psychological. Now, leaving behind his first, Kantian question, How is truth possible? he asks: Why do men need knowledge? In answer, he counterposes against other epistemologies the proposition that knowledge is gathered because it is indispensably useful. Principally under attack is the rationalist theory which holds that knowledge is to be gained and valued for its own sake, as an objective phenomenon in itself. Nietzsche denies any 'body of truth'.

[1] *Ego*, p. 246.
[2] Brazill: *The Young Hegelians*, p. 222.

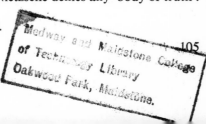

Utility is truth.[1] The question to be asked of knowledge is not how true, but how useful it is. According to Nietzsche's purely instrumental notion of truth—truth is no end, only means—it is judged by the ultimate criterion of whether it enhances the individual's power and vitality. It has, at root, a biological function, that of preserving life.[2] One of the key manifestations of the Darwinian instinct for self-preservation, as Nietzsche interprets it, is the need for stability of belief, for a comprehensive, ordered picture of the world.[3] Concepts, like moral beliefs, are signs creating a meaningfully differentiated environment in which to live. The final assault on metaphysics thus reduces its categories to desires, interests, and instincts.[4] Stirner had directed a similar subjectivist attack against Hegel, arguing that each individual understands the world according to his own particular needs.[5]

But, if utility is thinking's ultimate criterion, then a 'lie' may be more effective than a 'truth'. Opposing himself to the Enlightenment, Nietzsche writes in his notebook in 1886 that man needs lies in order to live. Two years earlier, in *The Wild Duck*, Ibsen had defended the 'saving lie', the self-deception which renders life bearable. Nietzsche himself speculates that the constitution of things may be hostile to the presuppositions of life.[6] (Throughout this discussion language verges on the threshold of nonsense. To be consistent to his argument in its strongest form Nietzsche should deny all significance to the concepts 'truth' and 'falsehood'; but he chooses to employ them, again under the unstated, and perhaps unrecognized, assumption that there is, framing the fictitious trees, a real wood.)

Nietzsche calls his theory of knowledge *perspectivism*: the complex of perspectives within the individual, here his inner drives, which resolve through social interaction into a final equilibrium—the *gestalt* perspective defining that individual—decides the character of appearance. Knowledge is preconditioned by interests: thus the task is to decide whether it is at the service of egoistic interests or inverted, tortured, self-retarding 'interests'. Nietzsche even employs Stirner's language: the conceptual apparatus is directed not at knowledge, but at 'taking possession of things'.[7] Stirner had argued that the *truth* of a thought is the degree to which the individual makes it his property, and uses it as a means to the realization of his desires and ambitions.

Stirner is at this point instructive. He points to the logical problem inherent in Descartes' rationalist *cogito, ergo sum*: in this schema, he

---

1 *Wille* 484. The degree to which Nietzsche is at variance with English Utilitarianism will be pointed out in the next chapter. His concept of the 'useful' is utterly different from that of Bentham.
2 Ibid. 494. Nietzsche elsewhere makes the self-preservation principle subordinate to the Will-to-Power (*Wille* 650).
3 Ibid. 507. 4 Ibid. 579. 5 *Ego* (1912), p. 454.
6 *Wille* 583. 7 *Wille* 503.

asks, what presupposes thought? Thought must dogmatically presuppose itself. His own ontology sets out to repudiate the Hegelian, as much as Cartesian, conception of the 'Will-to-Truth' as providing the unique thrust behind the pursuit of the essence of being. It counters with the existentialist: 'I am creator and creature in one'.[1] Stirner posits the owner as the sole presupposition for thinking. Ownership of thought depends on the thinker not subordinating himself to a 'ruling thought'. This is peculiarly difficult, argues Stirner, anticipating Nietzsche, for language itself is a network of 'fixed ideas'. Truths emerge only when language is reworked and possessed individually, when thoughts are absorbed, lived with, alternatively kept in and rejected from mind.[2] The Will-to-Truth is thus a clerical virtue; it represents, in Nietzsche's words, 'the impotence of the will-to-create'.[3] Descartes is placed at the head of this rationalist tradition which leads to Bentham, Comte, and Mill. Horkheimer and Adorno will point to Bacon rather than Descartes as the key Renaissance figure standing at the head of modern rationalism.[4] Like Nietzsche, moreover, they trace the Enlightenment back to classical Greece: Nietzsche attacked Socrates as the first 'theoretical man'.

Stirner first broaches the question of epistemology in his 1842 article, '*Das unwahre Prinzip unserer Erziehung*', in which he transforms Hegel's dialectic with a series of vivid aphorisms into a theory which posits knowledge as a dynamic *process* rather than a related series of static facts. The transformation is carried out through the injection of the phenomenon, *Will*.[5] It is striking that Stirner came to this orientation independently of Schopenhauer, whom he would not have read. If man is to remain the creator and master of his world then, Stirner maintains, every knowledge must die. All that has been accepted, that has taken on the secure guise of the 'fact', must return to a state of flux, or be rejected. This *Will* of Stirner's, this restless probing of all given knowledge, this endless questioning, and this continuous bending towards new understanding, uniformly point towards an ultimate valuing of the man who makes himself all-powerful—the egoist embodiment, to take the short jump to Nietzsche's category, of the Will-to-Power. Stirner writes that knowledge ought to be the ego itself—that is, subjective, living, and self-illuminating. But such non-alienating knowledge is only possible for the ego which, while it has 'founded its affair *on* nothing', has founded itself *through* its Will. Both Stirner and Nietzsche find in

---

[1] *Ego*, p. 250.   [2] Ibid., pp. 241–6.   [3] *Wille* 585.
[4] Max Horkheimer and T. W. Adorno: *Dialektik der Aufklärung*, 1969, esp. pp. 11–12.
[5] The relevant section is included in *Ego*, pp. 239–41. See, in particular, my footnote to p. 239.

the Will their answer to nihilism: only an instinctual Will to self-mastery and self-realization can give direction and significance to human life for him who has rejected all supra-individual values. This affirmation of the life-force, or the *élan vital* of Bergson, does not see the Will turning back on itself and destroying the ego; here is the point of departure from Schopenhauer's pessimism.[1]

The genealogy of Nietzsche's notion of the Will-to-Power is intimately bound up with his theory of knowledge. Perspectivism does not escape from the epistemological vicious circle. Nietzsche never formally resolves the problem of how alternative perspectives can be discredited by a standpoint, another perspective, which can claim no firmer logical foundation than they themselves. As Danto points out, there is little for us, if we hold this position consistently, but to insist on our own perspective, and perhaps impose it if we can.[2]

Nietzsche's response to this dilemma is, in part, consistent. He holds that, just as we need the categories of 'good' and 'bad' in the parallel domain of moral thinking, we need epistemological categories. Moreover, our knowledge *is* substantive as long as it is not overestimated, as long as more is not claimed for it than it actually achieves. The 'expedient falsification', the 'shrewd misunderstanding', the indispensable fiction pave one of the pathways to power.[3] No one could live without such 'articles of belief' as 'bodies, lines, surfaces, causes and effects, motion and rest, form and content'.[4] The strongest formulation of the thesis that knowledge must be creative asserts that [we think *mythologically*.[5] Concepts at their best are mythical symbols, constructs for selecting the high points of experience, the type-transcending moments when the individual sheds the clerical mean, when he initiates and defines, when he renounces his idols. Mythologies mediate the Will-to-Power; thus they are the vehicle for the highest truth.

But there are signs of Nietzsche suspending his disbelief, and asserting the Will-to-Power as the absolute principle of life. It is more than a perspective; it is the basis from which other perspectives are judged as more than misunderstandings, as the poorer of fictions.

The Will-to-Power is the principle which presupposes itself. The

---

[1] R. W. K. Paterson makes a central point of identifying Stirner with nihilism. His argument depends on a failure to distinguish between social values, which Stirner does reject, and personal values, to which he is more overtly committed than any other philosopher. The dark pessimism, the hesitancy of Will, and the disaffection with life symptomatic of the nihilist are not to be found in Stirner—rather the contrary. Schopenhauer, with his constant doubts about the existence of any value, was a nihilist; Turgenev's Bazarov, Dostoevsky's 'underground man', his Stavrogin and his Kirilov were closer to nihilism.

[2] Danto, op. cit., p. 77.   [3] *Wille* 584.   [4] *Wissenschaft* 121.
[5] *Jenseits* 21.

individual is his Will, the force which at the same time determines his becoming. Nietzsche's doubts as to whether beliefs cause anything, or whether there are such things as conscious intentions which precede actions, lead him to spotlight his conception of *Das Es* as the nucleus of all life, a Freudian *id* superordinated to total dictator. The whole of instinctual life is the development and specialization through expression of this Will; pleasure and pain are its derivatives.[1] Even self-preservation is a secondary instinct, an indirect, if frequent consequence of 'giving vent to force'.[2] Moreover, Kant's *a priori* categories are displaced by an *a priori* Will-to-categorize. Nietzsche's vitalist empiricism amplifies a revaluation of the human body: Will is patterned at its source among bodily needs and bodily functions.

Nietzsche includes in his critique of knowledge an attack on what may be the most basic of all the assumptions which underpin the cognitive process: the monistic conviction that backing the world of existence and becoming is some grand unity, a hierarchy of consistent truths all deriving from a unique and incontrovertible first principle.[3] He describes monism as a form of decadence.[4] For the sceptic there is neither aim, being, nor unity: the world is valueless. Perspectivism nurtures a pluralist vision of competing cosmologies. Yet the Will-to-Power restores aim, being, and unity to life: Nietzsche turns three-quarters-face back to monism. He is not merely employing a linguistic convention. To stand back from his critique and view it as a whole provokes us to enquire: Is it psychologically possible for man to live by a non-monistic cosmology? In other words, does not reason which mediates personal experience break down at the point at which it has to accommodate two genuinely incompatible life-principles? The consequence of such a breakdown is a type of schizophrenia.

Cast in this light, the dialectic appears as the means at the disposal of consciousness for maintaining the unity of a world perpetually in danger of disintegrating into contradictions. Indeed, there has been no more self-consciously monistic thinker than Hegel: all his ultimates are fantastic unities. Similarly, tragic drama, in which the hero is destroyed by irreconcilable opposites, finds its unity in the encompassing imaginative form, the play itself. The unfolding acts of Nietzsche's critique of absolute truth are borne by a structure which finally resists its own tendency to annihilate itself. The critique thereby provides an unmatched psychological insight, at the level of both general principle and subtle detail, into what it means to seek and to employ knowledge; but it fails in its initial ambition, to abolish the absolute, or rather to neutralize the individual's need for a unique absolute.

---

[1] *Wille* 688–715.   [2] *Jenseits* 13.   [3] *Wille* 12.   [4] Ibid. 600.

The critique of empiricist, positivist truth

A repudiation of metaphysics leads into either the garden of utter scepticism, or the modern market-place of positivism, where the rule is that knowledge is the preserve of the empirical sciences. Anarcho-psychology, as it has been outlined so far, retains an ambivalent relationship to both metaphysical and sceptical standpoints. We now examine its perspective on positivism, the methodology of liberal-rationalism, noting that although empiricist themes were employed in the critique of metaphysics, they were strictly concerned with emphasizing the primacy of concrete individual experience, and bore no relevance to the question of systematic science.

Stirner makes only oblique references to science; his interesting comments relate specifically to English Political Economy and his own economics, and will be discussed in the next chapter. Nietzsche maintains an ambivalent attitude to science. Perspectivism applies equally to empirically as to metaphysically derived knowledge. He maintains that all sense impressions are permeated with value judgments: for example, whether they are useful or harmful.[1] He gives repeated illustration to the contention that we see only what we want to see. The general target for attack is the 'cult of objectivity' which holds that affects can be removed from knowledge.[2] Nietzsche thereby denounces positivism for its objectivist fallacy, in effect arguing that metaphysics is inextricably wedded, in the form of moral dispositions, to empirical science. This genre of scepticism has found substantiation in recent years in the theory of Thomas Kuhn that the development of natural science has been governed more by paradigms, in a sense fashions, than by a systematic historical progression towards perfect knowledge.

But Nietzsche at the same time praises science for emancipating itself from morals, for being less guilty than most metaphysical systems of spinning webs of pure abstraction.[3] It has better satisfied his demand that knowledge should not pretend to be more than instrumental. He approves of the science which he defines as 'the transformation of nature into concepts for the purpose of mastering nature', for it belongs under the rubric 'means'.[4] That is, he approves as long as the human Will retains control.

Empiricism is a more potentially useful fiction than metaphysics. Nietzsche himself, as a psychologist, accepts the evaluating principle of empirical falsification: his aphorisms claim to map accurately the empirical universe of concrete human experience. Moreover, empiricism is less prone to reducing itself to moralism. Nietzsche's orientation is similar to that later developed by Weber, who empha-sizes that 'functional rationality', reason applied instrumentally to

---

[1] *Wille* 505.   [2] Ibid. 612.   [3] Ibid. 63.   [4] Ibid. 610.

realize predetermined ends, has a superior claim to objectivity. Both theorists are then concerned about who will choose the ultimate ends, and how. Science gives rise to technically exploitable knowledge, but not to normative knowledge. Nietzsche puts it that the scientist is at best an instrument, a useful slave: he does not command or decide, he is not a whole man.[1]

There is a tendency for Nietzsche to take the positivist attitude that knowledge is the preserve of the empirical sciences. Yet he never accepts the positivist claim to objectivity, and, moreover, he leaves open the question of which manifestation of the Will-to-Power science enhances. Two points are worth noting in conclusion. First, he transforms a defence of empiricism, having argued that 'eyes and fingers speak in its favour', into a meditation on the Platonic way of thinking.[2] He associates Plato, who made a point of resisting obvious sense-evidence, with a rare and noble type of enjoyment, one quite alien to contemporary Darwinists, physicists, and physiologists, and what Nietzsche deprecates as their 'rough' world of machines and bridges.

Second, the very tone of Nietzsche's prose, like that of Stirner, its surging exhortatory cadenzas, the staccato of its pungent aphorisms, the intricate harmonies of its concentrated poetic ambivalencies, its rhetorical flourishes, and above all its anarchic, dissembling and reassembling thematics, is prescriptively anti-scientific. The methodical construction and verification of connecting hypotheses belongs to another universe. Nietzsche's method resonates his own personal rhythms; it is deliberately individual, and develops as a critique its incompatibility with both idealist philosophy and positivism.

For our purposes, Dostoevsky takes up the discussion where Nietzsche leaves it off, asking the pivotal question whether empirical science has served to enhance or retard the creative power and vitality of man. Like Stirner and Nietzsche, Dostoevsky's concern is with the psychological question: What are the consequences for the individual and the quality of his life? But Dostoevsky's status in the perspective unfolding as anarcho-psychology is not unequivocal. The vast corpus of secondary literature that his work has stimulated has commonly distinguished between the Christian writer and his atheist, immoralist, anarchist *alter ego*, as projected in the characters of Raskolnikov, before his conversion, Stavrogin, Ivan Karamazov, and above all the narrator of the *Notes from Underground* (1864). This division is perpetuated by Dostoevsky's followers, represented most notably by Berdyaev and Ivanov, who develop the Christo-mystical dimension, and by Shestov, who sides with the anarchist underground man and develops his ideas into what is the most incisive modern philosophical statement of irrationalism.

[1] *Jenseits* 207.   [2] Ibid. 14.

Dostoevsky develops one side of his Christianity as a specific critique of egoism, and a complementary defence of compassion and self-abnegation as cardinal values. This runs counter to anarcho-psychology. The case is different with regard to the no less central way in which he employs Christian themes to articulate mystical, noumenal values. Here is extension rather than negation of Nietzsche's affirming emphasis on the fusion of Dionysus and Apollo, of intoxication and dream. Indeed, Nietzsche's aestheticism, his celebration of the artist, is only at one degree of sublimation removed from a mystical ethic. It is Rilke who will bridge this gap, by making of the lovers and their fleeting, ecstatic and divine, moment the paradigm for both the artistic experience, that of dancer and singer, and the mystical experience, which he represents in the metaphor of communing with angels.

Dostoevsky does not concern himself with an epistemological critique of truth. He accepts that the equations of mathematics and the laws of natural science are in some sense true. He focuses attention exclusively on the psychological effects of these equations and laws: like Stirner and Nietzsche, he analyses how human interests, as he explicates them, undergo distortion and suppression. The *Notes from Underground*, the key text for his critique of knowledge, may be read as the frantic meditations of a man trying to live with the conviction that truth and value have become incompatible. He has no doubt that in such a situation truth must be abandoned; but he fears that values, isolated from supporting fictions, may not be enough to live by. Our concern at this point, however, is merely to examine his critique of empirical science, his claim that it had become the cardinal subverter of human interests.

Dostoevsky would have rejected as idealistic Nietzsche's view that science ought to be a purely instrumental activity carried out within a human metaphysics, and thus at the service of man. He holds that science is value-creating, that the instrument defines the end: inherent in the enthusiasm for science are the vices of the industrial society which it has made possible. The utilitarian values of the new technological order are the logical and necessary correlates, confirmed by practical success, of the empiricist impulse to number and to calculate, the positivist drive to find a law for every interaction. The Western concept of Reason itself is the root cause of the evils of industrial civilization: its method programmed the political and social perversions of utilitarianism. Dostoevsky adds the Stirnerian point that to expect an applied science and a non-rationalist, non-utilitarian ethic to combine is to underestimate the pervasive force of the *idée fixe*. Implicit in the *Notes from Underground* is a view of technological determinism: as Weber was later to formulate it, economic institutions in industrial society develop *sui generis*, gathering their own momentum and determining by their own evolution the patterns of social change. Dostoevsky's extremist conclusion is that either science must be scrapped *in toto*, or man will succumb inevitably to the machine. Some of these themes have been taken up this century by T. W. Adorno. The argument is conducted simultaneously as a critique of ideology and a critique of the mechanical and institutional embodiments of that ideology. Empirical science, taken in conjunction with its moral and theoretical presuppositions, is inseparable from utilitarianism: together they form the ideological framework for the construction of technological-industrial society.

Dostoevsky continues Stirner and Nietzsche's anarchist defence of individual life as essentially unknowable, as flowing from a noumenal source which defies conceptualization, as resistant to all equations. The rise of science has been corrosive of the free-will manifest in this image, it has sought to make calculable and predictable that which is unpredictable. This science has progressively cut man to fit a Procrustean bed in which there is no space for wilful acts. The underground man calls for an anarchist demolition of the new authority.

Scientific laws, or what Dostoevsky calls with some irony the laws of nature, enclose whoever accepts them like stone walls. Their total power of explanation negates the individual, subordinates him to their ubiquitous authority. They neutralize his will by whittling away his sense of uniqueness:[1]

> In me, anger disintegrates chemically like anything else, because of those damned laws of nature. As I think, the anger vanishes, the reasons for it evaporate, the responsible person is never found, the insult becomes an insult no longer but a stroke of fate, just like a toothache, for which no one can be held responsible.

This passage broaches two of the modern psychological impoverishments for which positivist science and technology are held responsible. Firstly, Dostoevsky maintains that all human passions, not just anger, will be dissipated once scientific laws are found for them. The impulsive, contrary creature capable of ecstasy is being metamorphosed into an 'organ stop', able to manipulate itself with perfect precision: soon there will be no more adventure, finally no more action.[2] Not only will man lose his free-will, but amongst the 'graphs, timetables, and test-tubes' he will stop desiring—desire depends on the unplanned, intense passion, on the fleeting, paradoxical unknown. Dostoevsky's vision of hell oscillates between Nietzsche's image of the 'last man', bored but comfortable, existing in a perpetual

[1] *Notes from Underground*, p. 103.
[2] Ibid., p. 109.

slumber, and at the other extreme, an image of a demented, gratuitously sadistic and also bored, nihilist.

This critique of science is necessarily unscientific. Yet the natural and the human sciences have produced evidence which supports Dostoevsky's evocative analysis. Psychologists call 'habituation' the well-known phenomenon of the senses becoming progressively insensitive to a repeated stimulus. We do not hear the ticking of the clock in our room, but we do hear that it has suddenly stopped. Familiarity does not usually breed contempt, but indifference. It has recently been found that single nerve cells in the mid-brain of a rabbit fail to respond to a tone sounded on a frequency of a thousand cycles after several repetitions.[1] It is a sociological commonplace that an increasing division of labour, by reducing the range of each man's activity, aggravates the problem of work boredom. It is not a great extrapolation from these findings to Dostoevsky's general point that the sciences draw upon, and legitimate, a drive and a disposition of mind which are directly inimical to the conditions which favour human interest, curiosity, absorption, and thus fulfilment.

The second point broached in the passage quoted from the *Notes* concerns individual responsibility. Once anger has been objectively classified, it is taken beyond man's control; he is exonerated without a struggle, like a machine which breaks down. Now he is no longer responsible for his actions. Dostoevsky later, in *The Brothers Karamazov*, focuses his critique of empiricism, and in particular the charge that it erodes individual responsibility, on the rationalist French physiologist, Claude Bernard.

Bernard, in what still remains a trenchant, lucid, and significant book, *Introduction à l'étude de la médecine experimentale* (1865), outlined his view of the experimental method with reference to physiology. He was convinced that physiology would become the central science of man. He claimed to be the first experimental biologist to insist on the study of the inner, organic environment (*milieu intérieur*).[2] Through understanding the physico-chemical processes within the human body he predicted that the totality of human behaviour could be explained—an assumption of absolute determinism, without which, he stressed, there can be no science.[3] He opposed the vitalist notion that there is some spontaneous, irreducibly human essence with which science cannot deal: 'the spontaneity of living bodies is simply an appearance and the result of a certain mechanism in completely determined environments'.[4]

---

1 Arthur Koestler: 'Literature and the law of diminishing returns', p. 43. *Encounter* (May 1970).
2 Claude Bernard: *An Introduction to the Study of Experimental Medicine*, trans. H. C. Greene, 1927, p. 76.
3 Ibid., p. 68.   4 Ibid., p. 61.

Bernard admitted that there was one level of existence from which he was barred: but he claimed that no man could ever know the first cause or the essence of a thing.[1] The scientist will never answer *why* questions.[2] Nevertheless, immediate causes are accessible, and absolutely determined: the *how* of things can be explained in terms of the 'material causes of phenomena'.[3] Bernard's programme finds an extensive modern realization in B. F. Skinner's 'technology of behaviour'.

For Mitya Karamazov, Bernard's science forges the chains with which the modern world will replace the authoritarian barbarisms of the old.[4] Physiology could have been used in his defence at the murder trial, but its effect would have been to remove human responsibility, excusing the murderer as a 'victim of his environment'. Mitya would rather take the responsibility for a crime he did not commit than allow this 'chemistry' to gain credence in human society.[5] He stutters with incredulous frustration about the 'nerve tails' in the brain as he paraphrases Bernard: 'and that's why I contemplate and then think—because of the little tails, and not at all because I have a soul'.[6]

One year before the publication of Bernard's treatise on methodology the underground man had struggled with the problem of first causes and explanation in almost identical terms. Dostoevsky, a vitalist *par excellence*, did not choose his devil's advocate for empiricism carelessly; he not only anticipated the argument that Bernard was to make famous, but foresaw its prophetic significance for an age preparing to embrace scientific determinism as its new religion. He accepted its prognosis, but inverted the evaluation of its implications. The underground man, like Bernard, can never find a first cause for anything; he too is left with only the deterministic laws of nature.[7] But, unlike Bernard, or Turgenev's Bazarov (1862), who was portrayed as the prototype for the *nihilist*—believing in nothing, and yet finding some meaning in the pursuit of empirical science—he has no faith in science as a therapeutic. Indeed, he predicted that the panacea promised by the positivists would turn into a prison.

There are two counter-arguments to scientific determinism; they

---

1 Claude Bernard: *An Introduction to the Study of Experimental Medicine*, pp. 29, and 67.
2 Ibid., p. 80.
3 Ibid., p. 67.
4 In his *Summer Impressions*, especially the third chapter, Dostoevsky had defended the vital barbarity of Russia against the effete refinement and aestheticism of the West.
5 *The Brothers Karamazov*, pp. 690–1.
6 Ibid., p. 691.
7 *Notes from Underground*, p. 103.

represent respectively the two sides of Dostoevsky's critique of natural science. His defence of individual responsibility connects with the argument that man has free-will, that he has the capacity to initiate and to carry through significant choices. This is in one sense a rationalist humanist position, emphasizing the determining power of human consciousness and denying that all human acts can be reduced to prior causes: it posits that there exist first causes, some of which are within human control. The underground man would like to accept this argument, but finds it implausible. The most that he can claim, and then with reservations, is that man is wilful and capricious — but this is the 'freedom' to rebel, and as such heavily conditioned. The same dilemma is faced by Mitya Karamazov; his different response illustrates the passionate nature of Dostoevsky's attachment to the myth of personal responsibility. Dostoevsky fears that if science undermines this myth then no check on man's brutish and rapacious nature will remain.

The second counter-argument holds that although man does not have the power of freely conscious choice, although his destiny is beyond his own control, neither does science have any control. Man is not personally responsible, but neither can he be programmed. The anarcho-psychological perspective generally takes this line, maintaining that the *milieu intérieur* is ultimately unknowable, that reason is impotent in the face of the complexity of the human organism. The curse of science is thus not that it removes free choice, a fiction in any case, but that it imposes a self-image on man which makes him less than he is, which makes him forget the anarchic, playful, noumenal core of his humanity.[1]

Dostoevsky's first argument, as we explicated it, accusing science of reducing man to a machine, takes this latter orientation to determinism: it presupposes a vitalist or mystical ethic, rather than the ethic of personal responsibility. It posits that before Bernard science had offered only partial explanations of man and his place in the universe; there had remained a place for the mysterious and the noumenal. But now this science was penetrating man's most private inner world and fitting equations. Ultimately it is this noumenal realm, that of the Stirnerian *presence*, which Dostoevsky seeks to preserve. Science would be justified if it helped man to contact his own mystical depths. But its effect was precisely the opposite, to substitute itself for the hidden god; it thus operates as a charlatan revealer of being.

[1] It is possible to take this position and still hold to an ethic of personal responsibility, as appears to be the case with Freud. The ethic is then not autonomous, but rather a useful fiction, reducible in the terms of Freud's own theory to such factors as the biologically and socially determined development of the individual's superego.

The dichotomy between truth and value distils into one between positivist truth and faith. What Stirner had called the 'seductive glitter of the idea' had materialized in the form of machines, which could produce bread of whatever type desired, and at the cost of little effort: thus *truth* had been powerfully vindicated. This truth was now readily demonstrable, its proof visible and useful. The technological miracle was in the process of displacing the personal, inner miracles of insight, grace, and revelation. The gains of the way of faith were too difficult and too precarious set next to the concrete realizations of science. Dostoevsky's Grand Inquisitor puts the point to Christ that men will choose as their saviour he who can turn stones into bread. The victory of the industrial revolution and the values it embodied was thus inevitable.

The Christo-mystical indictment of science rests on the assumption that man is, at his best, driven towards the organic and the whole, towards an orientation to his environment in which all is integral and one. Western science has instated the drive to analyse as the vehicle of progress. The flower can no longer be admired as a prototype of the marvellous coherency of the universe: science does not 'see a World in a grain of sand', but reduces the world to many grains of sand. Dostoevsky's charge is that what he regards as the accelerating wave of social secularization and scientific progress is not merely combating superstition, but abolishing all noumenal values: he warns repeatedly in his works that the man who is utterly disenchanted by life will become bored and vicious, that civilization which advances too far will turn to barbarism.

The argument that the empiricist, utilitarian drive to quantify destroys that which is most valuable in the human condition has ready extensions. Just as an absorbing commitment to rational-empiricist truth precludes the possibility of mystical ecstasy, it precludes tragedy—as portrayed in Western literature. In a universe in which joy and grief are calculable there can be no conception of tragic experience; disaster must alternatively be understood as miscalculation, the result of conspiracy rather than chance or psychic inevitability or fate. The high point of the repression of the tragic experience, from the anarcho-psychological perspective, was the Enlightenment: what has been pithily caricatured as the age whose greatest men wore the 'smile of reason' paid a high price for its elegant wit and sanity—those men could neither laugh nor weep, their play was manacled.

Dostoevsky's critique is directed primarily at the natural rather than the human sciences. He did, however, frequently express doubts about the science of man's inner world complementary to physiology, that of psychology, his own superlatively cultivated defence. These doubts appear as corollaries to his general fears about empiricism and its threat to the ethic of personal responsibility; they suggest that his attitude to the other human sciences would have been similar. His view of psychology is equivocal: he grants that at least it remains 'two-edged', that it never proves anything absolutely. Psychology's descent into the *milieu intérieur* is fanciful, haphazard, and full of ambivalency compared with the path of Bernard's iron determinism.

Taken as a whole the anarcho-psychological critique of positivism denies that there are absolute or objective empiricist truths; positivist truths are at their best instrumental aids at the service of externally determined problems or goals. More significantly, the critique attacks the view of Bentham and Comte that science holds the key to human progress. Positivism, and its practical manifestation, technology, prepare the way not for social melioration, but for the psychological degeneracy of the individual.

Irrationalism

Anarcho-psychology advances beyond a straight scepticist critique of absolute, metaphysical and empirical, truth: each of its theorists places positive value on the capacity to live without knowledge, to live somehow in active opposition to it. We define 'irrationalism' as the purposive denial of rational processes and their ends, impelled by an iconoclastic drive which is valued in itself. This school of thought, which founds itself precisely in order to undermine thought, is conditioned by the belief that rationality, or at least the Will-to-Knowledge, is embedded in the human condition, and thus cannot simply be ignored. If one is not with *Reason* then one must live in active and sustained opposition to it.

Irrationalism, from the anarcho-psychological perspective, is the necessary consequence of the belief that truth and life are often incompatible. 'Truth' is viewed as binding the individual to a hierarchy of authority whose centre of gravity lies outside himself: it thus acts as a means of self-alienation. Irrationalism is a harsh philosophy which grants no dispensation for human frailty. The 'saving lie' is now viewed with unambivalent hostility: indeed, 'truth' is held to be a form of such a lie. Nietzsche focuses his discussion of fictions with the assertion that man must have the courage for what he really *knows*,[1] which, paradoxically, is the knowledge that there is no knowledge, that all apart from Will is chaos.

That the tree of knowledge and the tree of life grow apart is an unstated presupposition of Stirner's metaphors for man at his best: the bird in the height of its song and the flower, without self-reflection, giving fragrance. The case is identical for Nietzsche's image of

[1] *Götzen-Dämmerung* i:2.

the dancing star, or his affirmation of the artist as against the man of knowledge. A philosophy which portrays life as an expression of force, as Will-to-Power, bears an inherently irrationalist bias. At the basis of the principle of the Will-to-Power is the dichotomy between being and becoming. Nietzsche's primary stress is on becoming, on change, on striving to go beyond, on the future. The Will's relation to being is construed in the subordinate form of 'Become who you are!' Nietzsche structures his epistemology within an ontological attachment to becoming: hence his reluctance to embrace fully any mode of knowing. One of his notes posits:[1]

> The character of the world in a state of becoming as incapable of formulation, as 'false', as 'self-contradictory'. Knowledge and becoming exclude one another.

Heidegger paraphrases Nietzsche's argument: 'The true world is that of becoming, the apparent world that of the fixed and constant'.[2] The domain of *being* is that of the already happened, of the static, of the assured. Knowledge results from the process of reflecting backwards; irrationalism holds that this paralyses. Dostoevsky argues that knowledge, whether it take the form of a mathematical equation or one of the laws of nature, because it is incontrovertible, stands as an immovable constraint on man's freedom, against which all he can do is bang his head, like the cretin butting the brick wall in Breughel's painting of the *Netherlandish Proverbs*. Dostoevsky saw reason mesmerizing mankind: man was in danger of 'Euclideanizing' himself. Shestov puts the point, characteristically, with evocative succinctness: 'Grant Reason one single assumption, but one proposition, and finita la commedia'.[3]

Shestov is the most caustic of knowledge's critics. He is included in this study because his writings often best represent the anarcho-psychological side of Dostoevsky. For him the *Notes from Underground* is the true 'Critique of Pure Reason'. He writes of the 'living, restless, insubmissive, tortured and—by that very fact—great Parmenides', who became a mere stone endowed with consciousness once his 'truths' began to content him.[4] Shestov takes this as a paradigm for what philosophy does—merely acts as a tranquillizer. He analyses Kant's devotion to the synthetic *a priori* judgment as an escape from the important questions of God, free-will, and immortality. Kant knew that his metaphysical system could not even hint at answers to these questions, so there was good reason for not asking

---

[1] *Wille* 517.
[2] Martin Heidegger: *Nietzsche*, 1961, vol. 1, p. 617.
[3] Lev Shestov: *All Things Are Possible*, 1920, bk 2, sec. 17.
[4] Lev Shestov: *Athens and Jerusalem*, pp. 90, 116. This is Shestov's last and major work, completed in Paris in the year of his death, 1938.

them with more than passing reference. The Nietzschean point is that few philosophers have dared to think in the categories in which they lived.[1] They have generally attached themselves to the irrelevant abstractions which Feuerbach associated with religion: few have asked the questions of the underground man.

The Parmenides parable has another facet. One reason why Dostoevsky selects the identity twice-two-equals-four for attack is that such a rational truth has a quality of purity and clarity which outshines the goals of alternative endeavours.[2] Once men believe that there are absolute truths, ones which can be known unambiguously, then the apple on the tree of knowledge will become the irresistible focus for all desire and all striving: it is seen to hold the possibility of ultimate revelation. For Dostoevsky such faith in rational truth is the most nefarious of all delusions. He preaches irrationalism as the only means whereby the individual can preserve himself from subservience to the rationalist ideology: if it so pleases him twice-two is five, he likes it that way. This is intellectual anarchism at an extreme which verges on the splintering of its own scourge—the cognitive process.

The truth which paralyses Parmenides is likened to the Medusa because it distracts, and thus provides escape, because it absorbs, providing delusory revelation, and thirdly, because it is trivial. Stirner, Nietzsche, and Shestov all castigate Descartes for his refusal to look into anything which is not *clare et distincte*.[3] What is clear and distinct is trivial: this axiom is at the core of their repugnance for rationalist or positivist habits of mind. They hold that the price of Reason is too high: too much is lost or denied in the distortions and simplifications which are prerequisite to the construction of rational propositions about human action. What is learnt is dwarfed by the deviously complex reality. Irrationalism, to make such assertions, must hold to a notion of noumenal or intuitive truth, one which does not utilize orthodox logical thought processes. For Stirner and Nietzsche psychological truth has something of this quality; for Dostoevsky and Shestov the truths of the soul, mystical truths, provide the frame of reference for dismissing rationality.

But Reason can be inhuman in a more overt way, as a defence against feelings of compassion or sympathy. Raskolnikov, in Dostoevsky's *Crime and Punishment*, after feeling intense pity for a helpless fifteen-year-old prostitute, and doing everything in his power to protect her from seduction, suddenly starts to think that there must be a *percentage* of prostitutes in every society. Better that

---

[1] Lev Shestov: *Athens and Jerusalem*, p. 230.
[2] Stirner had made this point in 1842—the passage is included in *Ego*, pp. 230–4.
[3] Nietzsche: *Wille* 533; Shestov: *Athens and Jerusalem*, p. 75.

this girl, who is probably beyond reform in any case, than his own sister, should make up the percentage. Raskolnikov starts to reason and sociologize at the moment his involvement with the particular human being breaks. His pity is now mediated by Reason.[1] This example complements Dostoevsky's attack on the inhumanity which results from the embodiment of Reason in technological, industrial society, and its utilitarian ideology.

Both Stirner and Nietzsche show some reluctance to abandon knowledge completely. Their work exhibits strong strains of irrationalism, and yet they maintain a basic allegiance to logical thought processes—with Stirner's caveat: 'I am not willing to be a slave of my maxims'.[2] This is not the case with Shestov: his irrationalism is unequivocal.

Shestov seeks to expose the triviality of the field of experience to which rational truth is restricted. He argues that the significant moments in a man's life defy rational comprehension. Causal explanation acts as no more than feeble rationalization when the whole of a life's experiences and emotions are involved. Shestov discusses Tolstoy's character Ivan Ilych, all his life a rational man, who suddenly loses his old interests and becomes fascinated by death. In this situation no connection can be established between the emergent force driving the man towards the unknown, severing him from his past, and the facts that were previously known about him.[3] At the most, Shestov holds, philosophy can help man to bear with equanimity what fate decrees.

From this standpoint, the purpose of dialogue is only in an insignificant, masking sense to discover rational truths, to communicate knowledge. Discourse is the most elaborate and refined ritual man has created for expressing his love and his hate. Shestov clothes his sublimation theory of speech in an imperative:[4]

> When you are listening to a friend . . . remember that though your friend desires it, he cannot express himself save by readymade forms of speech. Look well to the expression of his face, listen to the intonation of his voice—this will help you to penetrate through his words to his soul . . . Do not fasten upon contradictions, do not dispute, do not demand argument: only listen with attention.

Prose is thus poetry gone flat, a sterile wooing lacking in the reson-

1 *Crime and Punishment*, pp. 64–9.
2 *Ego*, p. 213.
3 Shestov: *In Job's Balances*, 1932, pp. 121–38. By contrast Freudian psychology must of necessity assume that such connections can be made. There are, nevertheless, moments in Freud's work at which he confesses the precariously hypothetical nature of psychological insight.
4 Shestov: *Anton Tcheckov And Other Essays*, 1961, pp. 140–1.

ances of joy or passion. The truth of words lies in their art. The final transition in the devaluation of rational discourse would isolate music as the only language adequate to man's deepest purposes.

Shestov maintains that if man is going to reflect, as is his natural inclination, then his reflections ought in some sense to mirror the contradictions and absurdities which his fate bestows upon him. This epistemological imperative is satisfied only within the logic of dreams—a logic also recognized, respected, and interpreted by Nietzsche and Freud, but from a rational-analytical framework. Dostoevsky's novels, Shestov asserts, operate according to this logic, as it was formulated by Tertullian:[1]

> Because it is shameful, I am not ashamed; because it is absurd, it is absolutely credible; because it is impossible, it is certain.

Shestov, through dismantling a large part of Western philosophy, claims to move from Athens, where men seek for knowledge by the 'light of reason', to Jerusalem, where men live by the 'darkness of faith'.[2] Although an atheist, he shares much with mystical traditions: faith precedes truth, faith comes by 'grace' alone, and in this man is at the mercy of fate. Shestov's notion of faith borrows from both Kierkegaard's 'absurd' and Nietzsche's 'Will-to-Power'. It is simply audacity, the *hubris* needed to live unconditionally, in spite of fate. It is less the fate of the anchorite mystic than of the pretty peasant girl who sees the venerable sage Thales walking along, meditating the secrets of the universe, failing to see a well down which he falls: she laughs.[3] Shestov stakes his defiance on the peal of her laughter: it mocks the relentless necessity of fate, it does not recognize the determinateness of the human condition. The only necessity now is to dare, even to the absurd limit of choosing twice-two to be five. This is the ultimate extreme of Stirner's philosophy: only the egoist has the resources, if anyone does, to bear, finally to enjoy, an all-permissive, non-rational universe.

There is no answer to irrationalism: it allows no right of reply. Part of its task is to abolish the categories, both epistemological and psychological, which might be used against it.

Critique of Nietzsche's theory of knowledge

The common sense of an educated Western man who had an informed interest in the study of history, who drew on his reading of Freud in his own personal life, and who used the domestic appliances

---

1 *In Job's Balances*, pp. xxiii, 53.
2 *Athens and Jerusalem*, p. 232.
3 *In Job's Balances*, p. 77.

which scientific knowledge has made possible, would rebel against much of the anarcho-psychological critique of knowledge. His doubts deserve serious attention, if the critique is to stand as more than a rhetorical outburst against modernity. Discussion is here restricted to the most comprehensive and self-reflective formulation of the critique: Nietzsche's epistemological theory. Dostoevsky's orientation is not greatly different, except where it is irrationalist. As has been said, irrationalism is irrefutable: at the most, a sober citizen might point out that one of the challenges of life is to take on *all* of its necessities and vicissitudes, including the 'realities' of earning bread and ensuring the maintenance of some kind of social and political equilibrium.

Nietzsche cannot deny that the natural sciences have generated cumulative, technically exploitable knowledge: the distinction between knowledge and illusion is to this degree preserved, although it may be illusion that this knowledge is in any sense 'good'. Nor can he deny that the human sciences, whilst they are conditioned by the interests, the norms, and the language of the particular culture which fosters them, provide knowledge which is widely communicable within that culture, and held by significant numbers to unlock the text to their own social and individual pasts. These are not, to the letter, criticisms of Nietzsche: he recognizes both the instrumental power of positivist science and the value of 'mythological' thinking. What they do suggest is that his repudiation of the distinction between knowledge and illusion is unwarrantedly sceptical. The landscape lit by human understanding is not so bleak. From this starting point we now take up Jürgen Habermas's critique of Nietzsche's theory of knowledge. This critique constitutes the final chapter of the one outstanding recent attempt to survey the problem of knowledge as it emerged through the history of German philosophy.

Habermas's pivotal contention is that Nietzsche reduces the possibility of knowledge to two mutually exclusive extremes: positivism, which is objective but which fails to take account of human interests, which produces and legitimates technical knowledge, and mythology, which is relevant to life, but not objective.[1] Nietzsche never resolves the contradiction of refusing to accept a non-positivist concept of science and, at the same time, insisting that theory must be constructed in the service of life. Habermas believes that reliable knowledge which mediates human interests is possible; he asserts that objectivism is simply science's false understanding of itself. He accuses Nietzsche of remaining trapped within this positivist identification of science with objectivism. As a result, for science to

---

[1] Habermas: *Knowledge and Human Interests*, pp. 290–300.

become useful it must sacrifice all objectivity. Nietzsche's theory of knowledge proceeds by denying knowledge itself, rendering it incommunicably subjective through psychologizing human experience:[1]

> The methodological reduction of science to an interest in self-preservation serves not for the transcendental-logical definition of possible knowledge but for the negation of the possibility of knowledge as such.

Habermas suggests that the distinction between knowledge and illusion dissolves only if it is held that interest and instinct are immediately identical.[2] Then pure subjectivism would reign. The point seems to be that interests are social as much as they are egoistic, and that as soon as there is consensus amongst a group of people about what constitutes their mutual interest they can proceed to gain and utilize knowledge relevant to that interest. This knowledge is objective in that it is meaningfully communicable, unlike the monologue of Narcissus as he gazes at his own reflection. It is more difficult, although not impossible, to argue that there are individual interests which are not reducible to instincts: but for this the Freudian theory of the sublimation of libido must be countered.

Habermas's final point is that 'Nietzsche is so rooted in basic positivist beliefs that he cannot systematically take cognizance of the cognitive function of self-reflection from which he lives as a philosophical writer.'[3] But at least Nietzsche denied the critical power of reflection from the standpoint of self-reflection itself, and not from the false position of the positivist and his objectivist illusion about the exclusive power of the empirical sciences. He thus prepared the way for a viable self-reflective epistemology, one in which 'The knowledge-constitutive interest in mastering nature would establish the condition of the possible objectivity of natural knowledge'.[4]

Habermas, as it were, synthesizes the extremes that Nietzsche could not bring himself to reconcile. He integrates the virtues of metaphysics and positivism, defining objectivity in a sense that renders reality knowable. He spells out the grounds for a metaphysical understanding which includes factual relations, and controlled observation which includes personal, symbolic interaction.

Habermas is guilty of some hypostatization: Nietzsche is not so systematically wedded to positivism as the critique insists. Indeed, his attitude to empirical science remains consistently ambivalent: he recognizes that its claims have a certain truth, but he also recognizes

---

1 Habermas: *Knowledge and Human Interests*, pp. 296–7.
2 Ibid., p. 298. 3 Ibid., p. 299. 4 Ibid., p. 296.

the claims of nominalism—that there is no reality to which our mental categories correspond. He does not fully endorse any of these claims. They are half-truths, and must be articulated as such. What Habermas acknowledges as Nietzsche's self-reflective psychology is a lifelong testament to the viability of non-positivist knowledge.[1] Nietzsche's theory of knowledge is neither systematic nor conclusive enough to be separated off from his own method. That would be to deny the essence of a uniquely and pioneeringly self-reflective thinker.

Moreover, it would be wrong to stress Nietzsche's positivism as the main reason for his, at most, sporadic, apart from an early essay on history, interest in the human sciences. The prominence in his day of Darwinian theory, of physics, and of physiology, and the relative absence of the human sciences as they are known today, conditioned his interest in science.

What cannot be disputed in Habermas's critique is the suggestion that Nietzsche does not seem to want 'reliable knowledge', that he prefers a confused and irreconcilably divided theory of knowledge to a homogeneous one. Just as he went too far in his critique of Christianity, to the point of fanaticism, he goes too far in his critique of truth. He fails to recognize, except obliquely in brief exhortatory references to the necessity for the individual to gain mastery over his instincts, the substantive sense of rationality. There are untold cases in every community and in every individual life in which knowledge is employed with objective consequences in the service of human interests. A community, for example, in deciding that it needs a new bridge, in planning and building that bridge, is engaged in problem-solving in more than the restricted positivist sense.

The individual, too, is capable of acting in a substantively rational manner when he is faced with concrete problems, and when the relevant knowledge is largely technical: problems such as whether to build a house, or whether to join a political party. The case is altogether different when the focus is on self-knowledge. Then the pervasively difficult question, central to any humanist theory of

---

1 Moreover, Nietzsche writes approvingly in many places of the philosopher and the sage, and their non-positivist pursuit of knowledge. For example, in distinguishing two types of philosopher, he presents both in a favourable light. The first type wants 'to ascertain a complex fact of evaluations (logical or moral); . . . to master the world of the present or the past by concentrating and abridging the multiplicity of events through signs: [his] aim is to make previous events surveyable, comprehensible, graspable, and usable . . .' (*Wille* 972). The work of this philosopher is the vital prerequisite for the task of the second type, who employs the past for the benefit of the future, who legislates the evaluations. Habermas would have to concede that this image of the philosopher, and the implied concept of reliable knowledge, is kin to his own.

education, to psychoanalysis, and indeed to any attempt to integrate knowledge self-reflectively into life, is involved: the question of whether self-understanding provides a means of changing ourselves, or whether, as Shestov puts it, it merely helps us to bear with equanimity what fate decrees. It is not obvious that Nietzsche was deluded in favouring the latter view, and leaning towards irrationalism. Habermas's critique hangs in part on this unresolved point. The fact that most interesting problems lie between the two extremes, that of purely instrumental, technically exploitable knowledge, and that of self-knowledge, does not obviate the need to answer Nietzsche's epistemological challenge: that our self-understandings are merely *ex post* fictitious crutches. For all but purely instrumental problems depend on value assumptions about the efficacy of knowledge.

The clue to an understanding of the tangle of threads which is Nietzsche's epistemology lies in his own troubled relationship to concepts of absolute truth. The paradox he lives with, and tries to think himself through, is that he is driven by an irrepressible Will-to-Truth, and yet everything he knows, by means of cognitive process, by means of giving rein to this Will, tells him that there is no absolute truth. But his accumulating knowledge, that everything is vain and illusory, does not inhibit his searching. His instincts rebel against the one conclusion which is the more confirmed the more he looks in detail at what men have thought, of why they thought it, and of what it is possible to think: the conclusion that there is no absolute. It is as if knowledge and the drive to know operate on different planes, which never intersect. Many of the contradictions in Nietzsche's own thought, and the fact that he often evaluates ideas and thinkers from contradictory standpoints, derive from this fundamental division within himself.

Implicit in Nietzsche's scepticist, nominalist attack on rational truth is a conviction that a substratum of firm and unassailable knowledge exists. Otherwise, all his invocations against false interpretations of the world would be absurd: the genuine perspectivist can communicate only with those who hold the same perspective. The hundreds of aphorisms directed against those who take their truths for absolute read as the exasperated outbursts of a man who feels somehow cheated, who feels that the real path to truth is being obscured or lost by misguided men working under the sway of illusions.

Nietzsche's Will-to-Truth connects him with mystical religious traditions. He rejects Christian, metaphysical, ethical, and positivist orientations to truth as degradations of the real pursuit, as perversions of the profoundest of all myths. Running through his endless search for transvalued values and for the *Übermensch*, through his sustained lifelong psychological examination of the human condition, is the legendary *leitmotif* of the knight riding after the Holy Grail.[1] One difference is that Nietzsche's concerns are more directly anthropocentric than those of most religious quests; his 'looking through a glass darkly' is astringently trained on himself. His work does not, as a result, suffer from the abstract cosmological language into which mystical writing often lapses: the noumenal is left undescribed.

Given this context, it is not surprising that Nietzsche shows little interest in the rationality which men employ in their daily lives. One source of his irrationalist leanings is his camouflaged Romantic yearning for noumenal rather than phenomenal knowledge, and his consequent uneasiness before the apparent solidity, but inadequacy, of the latter.[2] The finest mystical poetry, through its suggestive images and tones, points to a realm of utter privacy, of purely narcissistic, and therefore incommunicable, wonder lying at the core of noumenal experience. From a perspective governed by this recognition, knowledge which claims to be either precise or exhaustive is sham.

The sense of the presence of some sublime hidden truth shadows all of Nietzsche's work. Both the image of the *Übermensch* and the value of the Will-to-Power are attempts to give shape to this truth. Moreover, the resulting split in his concept of knowledge articulates itself in terms of ambivalencies in his work. For example, his attitude to the 'human, all-too-human' oscillates between acceptance of human frailty and a demand for something less mortal. To the principle of *amor fati* is counterposed the *Übermensch*. The significance of Truth in this garb is that a society, a people, or an age is justified only if it produces exceptional men, men who transcend the 'human, all-too-human' and its dependency on phenomenal knowledge. In his first book, Nietzsche, in pondering the question of why tragic drama, through projecting the bleakest images of human destiny, had the effect of inspiring, elevating, and intoxicating, posited an aestheticist answer. It is sublimely beautiful, he suggested, to witness men confronting the tidal forces which sweep them along, and bearing the impenetrable contradictions which ensue, even though these men finally succumb in the same way as do their own

---

1 Significantly, it is the mystical poet Hölderlin whom Heidegger places beside Nietzsche as the second focal point for his own epistemological meditations. We also note that one measure of the existentialist tradition's indebtedness to Nietzsche is the fact of Heidegger using his work as a map by which to set and test his own bearings: Heidegger has published in the region of two thousand pages devoted explicitly to Nietzsche.

2 Many of Max Weber's leading concerns are governed by a parallel ethical dichotomy, that represented in the contrary figures of the charismatic prophet and, to take one of the manifestations of the other, the bureaucrat —he who is involved in 'the strong and slow boring of hard boards'.

disintegrating structures of meaning. A generalization from this theory of tragedy, spelt out more explicitly in Nietzsche's later works, holds that the only substantive *Truth* is that immanent in the lives of tragic heroes, or, to use his preferred categories, in the lives of powerful as distinct from decadent men. Nietzsche conceives of beauty, one of Will's fruits, as the supreme revelation of Truth. Heidegger rephrases the Nietzschean perspective: beauty is 'what tears us out of the oblivion of being, and grants us a view of that being'.[1]

Whilst the drive, or the Will, to find a plausible mapping for absolute truth follows this course, another discussion is conducted on the plane of knowledge. Nietzsche's knowledge is reliable at one level—as psychological insight into human motivation. This knowledge serves two important functions. First, it provides his contention that Will is the primary principle of life with empirical support; it thus also strengthens his derivative ethical attachment to the *Übermensch* as the embodiment of Truth. To this degree we are forced to qualify the disjunction which we posited between the two planes on which his life and work operate, for here his knowledge works in the service of resolving his ethical quandary. But the second function which his psychological knowledge fulfils reinforces the disjunction. Nietzsche's compounding statements to the effect that knowledge cannot help men in their choice of action, that it merely consolidates the past—the world of being rather than becoming—imply that the only consolation which reflection can offer takes the form of the 'saving lie': knowledge does not satisfy the Will criterion, that what is worthwhile enhances and intensifies. Where there is a need for knowledge, it is useless: it is useful merely in the fundamentally trivial domain of technical problems.

This nihilism with respect to knowledge must reflect a personal recognition on Nietzsche's part that however great an insight he gained into the nature of moralism and reactive emotion he would never exorcise the spirits of moralism, of resentment, and of compassion from his own breast. He would have been profoundly sceptical of Kleist's axiom, fundamental to all the human sciences: 'We must again eat from the tree of knowledge in order to fall back into the state of innocence'. A sense of the irreversibility of original sin is prevalent in his work. At the best the individual can learn to bear his 'bad', and thereby perhaps tame it a little. The way has now led from the level of detailed psychological knowledge to that of intuitive, irrational Shestovian knowledge.

Nietzsche does, at first glance, appear to work by the assumption that the demon of doubt will be exorcised in the process of reducing

---

[1] *Nietzsche*, vol. 1, p. 228.

philosophy to that doubt itself. What should also be recognized is that the faith in the efficacy of knowledge which lies implicit in most of his writing derives not from his cognitive insights, but from his instincts. His argument taken in itself develops no effective counter to the nihilistic canon which it explicates: doubt is rather negated by the passion with which Nietzsche writes about it. Indeed, the urgency and vitality of his prose precludes any association of his epistemological scepticism with a melancholic nihilist disposition. His notion of the Will-to-Power articulates his sense of a life-force in himself which flows almost irrespectively of how sceptical his knowledge becomes.

Moreover, his work contains little desperate scepticism or strident lament about the vacuity of existence. His finest writing, on the contrary, bears with it a *pudeur*, a respectful discretion before the unknowable core of what is human: it is as if his knowledge, in removing distortions to his vision, unlocked one last door of consciousness, leading into a subjective state simply of wonder. Although these mystical undercurrents remain unstated in his work, they pattern his orientation to truth, and in particular his essential incompatibility with nihilist philosophy. Nietzsche's resentment against ideologues and those who follow false paths of knowledge stems in part from his frustration at there being others with whom he would never communicate because their obtuseness or insensitivity prevented them from discovering this kernel in themselves of respect for the life-process.

This resentment may also flow from a more immediately personal source. Perhaps Nietzsche placed extraordinarily high value on the uniqueness and originality of his own thought, and correspondingly viewed less insightful philosophies with extreme hostility, because he realized that judged by the criterion of absolute truth his own aphorisms could claim little better status that those of other men, that they were superior merely in the ultimately superficial sense of style, of being more elegantly or subtly phrased. To this view his resentment is a symptom of a disquietude which followed his recognition that truths are none other than the actors in the theatre of fictions, that there was nothing substantive to distinguish his own insights from the crude self-understandings of the simple peasant. The last stroke of Nietzsche's critique, the one which most severely throws his life and his work out of equilibrium, looses the god of self-knowledge from its legitimating moorings: it had become apparent to him that the function of self-knowledge as a therapeutic and self-formative force derived not from its convergence with absolute truth, but from its narcissistic power to tranquillize.

Viewed in this context, setting up a dichotomy between the Will-to-Power and the Will-to-Truth appears as an attempt by Nietzsche to disengage himself from what he saw as his own futile striving after Truth, an attempt to shift the plane of knowledge into conjunction with the plane of faith, of unconditioned Will, of Shestov's pretty peasant girl. His knowledge tells him that his own dominant drive is directed at an illusory goal; so he castigates it as decadent, and affirms by contrast a self-centred and self-contained force which does not need external objects against which to test and evaluate itself.

Recognition that Nietzsche was driven, in spite of himself, by a Will-to-Truth permits a second reflection. Both Nietzsche and Dostoevsky create their art within the thought-dialectic itself between imprisoning walls and freedom, between ideology and the revaluation of all values. Life is rich and exciting for them precisely where it is difficult, where it provokes thought and yet remains disdainfully impenetrable. Little would remain if the walls were removed: Nietzsche and Dostoevsky depend on the negative. It is perhaps an unstated recognition of this which makes both of them hostile to social reform, and deeply suspicious of any notion of progress. Their own experience impresses upon them how dependent highly civilized man is on his cage: struggling with its bars is the most absorbing antidote to boredom that nature has granted him.

Nietzsche's critique of knowledge, taking it in the wider sense of both what is explicitly argued and what lies implicit in his own method, permits two relatively unambivalent and positive conclusions. First, just as tragic drama is one of the high arts of living, so is philosophy.[1] At its best, philosophy is the means used by one type of exceptional man to represent himself, to tell his tale with the uncompromising honesty which renders it hauntingly beautiful. The reflective process is in this case vindicated:[2]

> Gradually it has become clear to me what every great philosophy so far has been: namely, the personal confession of its author and a kind of involuntary and unconscious memoir; also that the moral (or immoral) intentions in every philosophy constituted the real germ of life from which the whole plant had grown.

Nietzsche implies that the search for knowledge conducted on any other basis, for example that of positivist science, is not fundamentally serious.

It is important to recognize that the knowledge generated by philosophy, as Nietzsche constitutes it, is not purely subjective: as in the case of tragic drama, others are free to learn from it. Nevertheless, this is the self-exploratory, self-creative knowledge of the artist, not the less personal, more systematized knowledge of science,

[1] *Wille* 449.   [2] *Jenseits* 6.

with its greater concern for the factual past and for objects external to the individual.

The second and related conclusion provides the lynchpin to Nietzsche's entire methodology. Nietzsche believes that men will, like himself, pursue knowledge irrespective of whether it can be shown to be useful in the unmoralistic context of 'good' and 'bad', at the service of the 'good' Will-to-Power. We are condemned by our natures to pursue knowledge. But Nietzsche, as we have discovered, also gives a number of reasons for approving of this pursuit. His work recognizes the force of the Will to-Truth, the need for knowledge, and the benefits of knowledge. It also recognizes the dangers inherent in knowledge: its ideological propensities, its susceptibility to being overestimated. In sum, his philosophy stands as a working synthesis of these alternating currents. His anarchic reconciliation generates knowledge which is never allowed better than probationary, exploratory status, knowledge which is permanently tentative, which puts itself in question as it advances. He demands more than self-reflective knowledge in Habermas's sense: his working hypothesis is that only knowledge that annihilates itself on one plane as it establishes itself on another will achieve more than mere deception. He builds doubt into the model.

The Nietzsche-Habermas confrontation reproduces that of Stirner and Marx in that the two standpoints do not communicate, they man searchlights whose fields of illumination rarely intersect. In Nietzsche's words, the germs of life from which the two philosophies grow are different. His own work leads him to doubt both the insightfulness and the utility of total, systematic social theory. On the other hand, for anyone who does not share his enthusiasms, the absorbing concern with the concealed absolute must appear incomprehensible: obsessive and futile. The analyst interested in practical social or historical problems will wonder why, once the positivist illusion has been exposed, and the nature of the limited objectivity of the human sciences has been spelt out, further attention is paid to what he regards as the now obsolete question of absolute truth.

For Stirner, Nietzsche, and Dostoevsky knowledge must contain an irrationalist, self-abolishing component; to be true to life it must convey a sense as much of the dissolution as of the construction of meaning. Their epistemology bridges the gap between philosophy, in particular its traditional concern with bodies of consistent and reliable propositions, and that poetry which concentrates on experience which eludes precise rational formulation, which challenges systematic knowledge by remaining obstinately within its interstices. The anarcho-psychologists repudiate the assumption that in order to theorize a philosopher must suspend his disbelief. Thought which does not incorporate disbelief leads to 'bad' fictions; it is

131

symptomatic of philosophy which operates at a distance from affective life, unpoetically.

It may be that the mainstreams of philosophy and sociology, like that of theology, have avoided Nietzsche because of his insistence on the inseparability of epistemology and a subjective ethics. Mystical poetry, the natural point of culmination for any theology, shares one feature in common with most philosophical systems: it splits the world of human experience in two and operates solely within one of the segments. In its case, the domain of the mundane, the sensual, the material is neglected; in the case of philosophical systems the domain of the private, the affective, the subjective is neglected. To take Nietzsche seriously is to participate in a mode of thinking, of thinking about thinking, and of living with thought, whose only ground is the subjective experience of the thinker. There is no alternative level of reality to which the participant can resort if he decides that he wants to terminate the journey.

Nietzsche's endeavour bears two qualities which combine to render it uniquely invulnerable to being encompassed, or 'understood', from another philosophical standpoint: it is persistently self-reflective, and it centres on the mutual and inseparable interaction of one man's highly personal life and thought. Even Danto's deft and insightful interpretation of Nietzsche as a philosopher is deficient, for it fails to take account of the man behind the work, and the psychological currents underlying his search for truth. To examine Nietzsche's philosophy purely in terms of its internal consistency or its empirical credibility is to neglect the central dynamic which governs its motion. Nietzsche is different from a Shakespeare or a Dostoevsky as an imaginative writer in that his own character and its driving preoccupations can be read, almost like a watermark, from his work. And among modern philosophers perhaps only Wittgenstein has lived the unfolding of his own thought with a comparable intimacy: Nietzsche, once he resigned his professorship in Basel, lived out of one suitcase, reading little, travelling alone from single room to single room, from Genoa to Sils Maria to Turin, rarely meeting friends, and then briefly, his notebooks his only steady companions.

Nietzsche's theory of knowledge stands as a paradigmatic statement of the issues at stake in the problematic relationship, which has been of singular prominence in twentieth-century Western literature, that between consciousness and concrete experience.[1] There are two poles, both of unusual strength in Nietzsche's character, which create the tension which gives his work its unique pungency: at the

---

1 To mention only one significant example, one of the rare cases in which the philosophical critique of knowledge is advanced: Kafka illustrates through his stories and parables what happens when conventional habits of perception and understanding become irrelevant to the task of ordering experience.

one extreme is the search for pure truth, for origins, for the pivot of existence, for traces of the transcendental, and at the other, a ruthless self-honesty, a refusal to go beyond the realm of the concrete individual, to disengage from the facts of daily living and its emotional vicissitudes. The latter pole saves him from self-righteousness or the type of crude moralism into which Tolstoy frequently lapsed; the former saves him from cynicism or nihilism.

4 The critique of *homo economicus*

Stirner's redefinition of property

Anyone trying to piece together a radical social philosophy in mid-nineteenth-century Europe had, before all else, to decide his attitudes to the rapidly emerging phenomenon, 'economic man'. In particular he had to pit himself intellectually against the increasingly dominant liberal-rationalist ideology emanating from England. The rationalist drive to classify and to quantify and the utilitarian drive to maximize material happiness were combining with the effect of increasing the scale and the efficiency of industrial production at exponential rates. The 'rationalization' of work processes, the increasing division of labour, demanded that men be useful in increasingly specific ways, and irrespective of personal interests other than the need to earn a subsistence wage. The utilitarian concern with saving time ultimately served to streamline the whole gamut of social interaction. Human interests, dissociated from individual gratification, were progressively subordinated to the economic calculus.

Thus Marx accepted the axiom of English Political Economy that the foundation of social structure is economic, but proceeded to redefine economics in terms of his alternative conception of human interests. Thus Stirner contemporaneously sought through redefining the concepts 'property' and 'possession' to constitute economic behaviour as a function of his ethical principles. Thus Dostoevsky launched a savage and blanket attack on liberal-rationalist ideology and praxis.

Stirner alone establishes a positive anarcho-psychological economic theory; there is no subsequent advance upon his formulation of how men are to trade with each other. The crux of the task he sets himself is to give an unabstract living meaning to the concept 'property', to rediscover man's proper-ties. Above all he sets out to

134

construct an alternative to Adam Smith's rationalist-utilitarian model. Unfortunately English cannot adequately translate the German title of his book. *Ein/eigen* which translates as *one/unique/ proper* forms the root of both *Einzige* and *Eigentum*. Thus the impression is conveyed of the unique one and the uniqueness of his property.

Private property, Stirner holds, exists by grace of the law. Regulated and ratified by the State, it is the State's property on loan to the individual.[1] The distinction between egoistic freedom and negative freedom pervades the analysis. Property is bound by conditions, and, as in the case of marriage, possession must be circumscribed by law; 'But property is *my* property only when I hold it *unconditionally*: only I, an *unconditional* ego, have property, enter a relation of love, carry on free trade'.[2]

Symptomatic of Stirner's method is his radical reinterpretation of the abstract economic term 'free trade'. No longer does it serve as the technical description of a relation between tariff laws and the import of commodities, but draws its meaning from the life and aspirations of the individual. This is not to deny the need in a community to plan the 'balance of payments', but to suggest that such economic manipulation is secondary activity, and should be carried out with a minimum of fuss, as it plays no role in the real interests of the individual. Stirner seeks to devalue economic activity which is not germane to the enjoyment of life; this entails a critique of *homo economicus*, the cleric in mercantile clothing.

Stirner's concern never deviates from the essential *value* of things, the significance they have for their proprietor; the matter of deeds of ownership is trivial to real possession. Ownership is a function of the satisfaction derived from consumption, in effect, the owner's power over the consumer-good.[3] The pauper is he who doesn't value himself,[4] the rich man of the Gospels he who has to find prestige in the quantity of his possessions. (He envies Lazarus when it is too late.)

From this point of view the value placed on an article and the possessor's self-valuation are inseparable. For example, let us consider an idealized picture of the French family which sits down for three hours to eat the main meal of the day. It takes the consumption of food as the starting point for an elaborate intercourse which will include the savouring of a series of varied, yet carefully complemented dishes, the relation of anecdotes, and a lively repartee on the affairs of the day. The meal has been transformed into a

---

[1] *Ego*, pp. 160–70.   [2] Ibid., p. 162.

[3] Stirner may have taken his cue from one of Goethe's epigrams: 'What you have inherited from your fathers, Earn it, in order to possess it' (*Faust* I:682–3).

[4] *Ego*, p. 163.

medium for the rich expression of the life of the family and the individuality of its members. Where Stirner writes of 'free trade' he refers to consumers creating their own code of commerce (also, we may take it, in the erotic sense), finding the mode of consumption which suits their particular needs, and thus building a house on the foundations of *their* 'creative nothing'. And unless man realizes his 'creative nothing', Stirner adds, there is nothing. The utilitarian and otherwise meaningless act of eating a meal can be turned into a stage on which the most satisfying of human trade can ply; and it is our thoughts, our affections, our spontaneous expressions, much more than the fruit of our trade with the greengrocer, that we enjoy trading freely. Dostoevsky will make the point that we do not build palaces merely to shelter ourselves from the rain; we also have to live in them, and for the cultivation of that *art* a utilitarian heritage is a liability.[1]

This failure to realize the worth of property is usually due to what Stirner types as State ownership. The labourer exhausts himself for nothing but the smooth running of the State;[2] there is the debilitating contamination effect which Marx noted in his *1844 Manuskripte*—after work the labourer is too tired to enjoy his leisure. He no longer has the real power to choose in his life. Stirner points in the same context to the alienating phenomenon of conformity in consumption. Whenever a man does not act out of pure self-enjoyment, whenever there is a sense of his conforming to someone else's judgment of the good and the worthwhile, without his having experienced for himself the validity of that judgment, the choice is not fully his own; he is then in the service of a phantom, an *ought*, which can always be traced to the influence of the State.[3] Only the mature egoist transcends the State's monopoly on choice; only he has the resources for realizing his 'free-will.' In fact, *Der Einzige* can be read in its anticipation of existentialism as an exercise in differentiating *determined* phenomena (ideals, idols, fetishes, morals) from those that are *free* (egoistic possessions).

Stirner does not advocate the abolition of money; he realizes that some means of exchange is necessary to keep resources flowing. In any case: 'it is not the money that does you damage, but your incompetence to take it'.[4] The lust for 'filthy lucre', and the passion for accumulation, preclude the calm enjoyment of possessions; the frantic restlessness which they inspire indicates how unegoistic

---

[1] *Notes from Underground*, p. 119.
[2] *Ego*, pp. 102–3.
[3] Stirner at times uses 'State' as no more than a convenient shorthand for supra-individual authority in the post-Christian world. It nevertheless retains the specific associations attributed to it in the critique of ideology.
[4] *Ego*, p. 185.

is this drive in search of a new master—money.[1] Avarice for money is closely related to avarice for time; Stirner poses the complementary value question: 'For whom is time to be gained?'[2] His criticism is not only directed against the existing structure of labour. He suggests that pleasure, taken at one's own place in one's own time, has been forgotten, and by communist and utilitarian alike—they both value property itself, who owns it and in what quantities, above all else. Labour is rarely the enjoyable product of one's 'ownness'; but even where men recognize that their work is not satisfying in itself, they forget that its value to them is no more than as the means to the enjoyment possible when it is finished, when the chores are completed. Stirner here ventures into the field of the anti-hedonistic, Puritan ethos of capitalism as it reveals itself in the hoarding of money, the possessive retention of feelings, and the compulsion to save time.

According to Stirner real price is not determined by the market forces of supply and demand; each person counts for how much he feels he is worth.[3] The value of an individual lies in his uniqueness, which by definition transcends all comparative standards. So he accepts no predetermined value, he sets his own price. Moreover, value does not grow at all in the manner of its economic analogue, the price for a specific commodity: price inflation is not generated by any intrinsic improvement in the quality of the goods.

The problem of how to make comparisons of value has beset all economic theories, *laissez-faire* and socialist alike, since Smith and Bentham. The price paid to enter the Uffizi Gallery cannot be related, with any rationale, to the rapture to which an admirer of art may be moved by a few blobs of Botticelli's paint. Enjoyment is invaluable, it is its own priceless value. Men worry themselves over the economic value of things only after the joy, or as a substitute for the joy they are not getting.[4]

A complex of problems arises here. Enjoyment cannot be evaluated cardinally, that is, have a fixed price put on it which relates it precisely to the value of other things. But neither is an ordinal ranking plausible. No other person can convince the admirer of Botticelli that he gets *greater* pleasure from this painting, for emotive states in different individuals are incomparable; there is no arbiter who experiences the enjoyment of both persons. A second problem for an economic theory of price arises from the changeability of one person's enjoyment of the same object over time, according to his

[1] *Ego*, pp. 177–8, 207–8.   [2] Ibid., p. 179.   [3] Ibid., p. 182.
[4] Even the élitist Nietzsche communicated his disgust at the 'common man' being forced into the role of *homo economicus*: 'Shame, that there should be a price at which one is no longer a person, but becomes a screw' (*Morgenröte* 206).

mood, the state of his knowledge, and innumerable other unpredictable (chance) factors. The problem of how to quantify value, once it is accepted that its major index is that intangible and inconstant state we have categorized as 'enjoyment', seems insuperable. The Benthamite equation of market price with interest value is spurious, as both Marx and Stirner point out. Must economic theory hence turn in on itself, and accept that an unbridgeable chasm separates it from all questions of value? Must price theory limit itself to describing material intercourse as it *is* pursued, and forgo all interest in how a more total intercourse *could* be pursued?[1] Stirner's challenge is that economics must either mediate human interest or be scrapped. Liberal-rationalism, by focussing on positivist techniques of quantification, had launched economic science in precisely the wrong direction, effecting a repression of ethical questions.

Stirner's supreme economic value is enjoyment. He phrases the crux of his philosophy in terms of an alternative: 'not how one can acquire life, but how one can squander, enjoy it; or, not how one is to produce the true self in himself, but how one is to dissolve himself, to live himself out'.[2] Stirner exhorts: 'Consume yourself!' The command is directed wholly to the present moment; each moment is to be enjoyed in and for itself, so that with Goethe, in Faust's famous closing lines: 'to the moment I might say: Abide, you are so fair!' The slightest trace of the Puritan attachment of classical economics to *saving* is pleasure-destroying; moreover, in that it denies Stirner's existential 'I am — present', it denies the self and its unquantifiable logic of realization.

Stirner and Nietzsche choose the song and the dance respectively as the media providing the most complete possibilities of self-expression. In the dance, music and often poetry, the most refined of man's spiritual sublimations, are translated into the sensual. In the growing ecstasy of the performance the awakened body transcends its daily capability. It is here that the two souls in Goethe's breast,[3] the lusty earth-bound one, and its sublime brother which yearns for the heavens, are woven into one. Rare spiritual longing and intense corporeal eros infuse each other.

The metaphors of the dance and the song provide the clue to the key anarcho-psychological orientation which, drawing from

---

[1] The greatest practical advance made in the direction of taking more account of human interests in economic calculation was the adaptation of such techniques as cost-benefit analysis to notions of social cost and social benefit. Yet recognition that a planner must take account not only of the costs of building a motorway, but of the resulting despoilation of the environment, in no way eases the recurring problem: how to *quantify* the aesthetic cost of such a project.

[2] *Ego*, p. 225; see, in particular, my footnote.

[3] *Faust* I:1112–1121.

Schiller's 'aesthetic letters' of 1793–4, projects *play* as a fundamental component of satisfying behaviour. The predominant characteristic of play is that it is wholly immanent and self-contained, it encompasses its own course and meaning, it mediates no ulterior long-term purpose, and it is pursued in the present with no explicit hope of enjoyable after-effects.[1] The play ethic is counterposed against, on the one hand, rationalism, with its cold, prosaic dissection of living matter, and, on the other, utilitarian economics, with its dour teleological connections. In the language of utilitarianism, play is 'useless'.[2] Huizinga, following Plato in arguing that culture is born-of play, was to characterize the nineteenth century and its 'grotesque overestimation of the economic factor' with the telling metaphor: 'All Europe donned the boiler-suit'.[3]

In this view man is human not by virtue of his work and how *useful* he is, but by virtue of his play and how *superfluous* he is. It is his superfluity of energy which funds his play, and by means of which he creates his 'surplus product'—surplus to what is economically functional and necessary. Impulses surplus to the quanta required to provide for his economic needs are the source of his creativity, of the activities which fulfil him. Stirner's philosophy exhorts man to realize his abundance, to relish the exuberant playfulness, mischievousness, and curiosity for which he has plentiful energy.

The counterposition here of play against work does not carry the tone of carefree hedonism. Nietzsche defines *maturity* as 'having found again the seriousness one had as a child, at play'.[4] 'Serious play' is man's greatest achievement in sublimation: for Nietzsche it is supremely useful, as the principal creative means by which man learns to channel his surplus impulses, and thereby make himself 'interesting'. Freud elaborates this perspective. The psychoanalyst believes that the child uses his toys to represent the forces and

---

[1] J. Huizinga notes five characteristics of play (*Homo Ludens*, 1949, ch. 1). Apart from its self-contained nature he finds that play is always voluntary, it is a stepping out of 'real' life into a pretending, temporary sphere of activity, it can be repeated and usually is, and finally it creates order, a temporary, limited perfection.

[2] The germ of the idea was taken up by Veblen and developed in his theory of 'conspicuous consumption' (*The Theory of the Leisure Class*, 1899). He distinguishes useful consumption, conspicuous or ostentatious consumption, and conspicuous leisure. The latter two categories represent 'wasteful' activities (pp. 85, 97–101), in which life is not enhanced. Although Veblen does not discuss 'useless' activities which perform a positive psychological role, he stands out as one of the links between anarcho-psychology and modern theorists of leisure (e.g. Fromm, Riesman, Marcuse, Norman Brown, Mumford).

[3] *Homo Ludens*, ch. 11.

[4] *Jenseits* 94.

objects which dominate his world: he externalizes through his play the unconscious tensions which threaten to annihilate him, thereby managing to neutralize some of the terror which they induce by expressing them, and hence being able to test himself against their explicit form.[1] Play in this sense is a means of coping with anxiety through acting out the fantasy which provokes it. Play is satisfyingly serious in a way that work, divorced from imaginative associations, can never be.[2]

Stirner reinforces his case against *homo economicus* in his reply to Feuerbach's critique of *Der Einzige*. He develops his anti-rationalism:[3]

> Do you exist only when you think on yourself, and do you decay when you forget yourself; do you exist only through self-consciousness? Who would not forget himself every moment, who would not depart from himself a thousand times every hour? This self-forgetting, this self-losing is only a means of our satisfaction, of enjoyment of our world, our property, that is world-enjoyment.

Stirner's suggestion that man opens himself to ecstasy only when he 'loses himself', when his consciousness lapses, complements his earlier, immoralist stress on the need to transcend the bad conscience: when the child is fully absorbed in his play he does not bother to evaluate whether what he does is good or evil—he transcends both his self-consciousness and his superego in enjoyment. Play is self-justifying, and therefore obviates the need for a rationalization. At the opposite pole to clerical earnestness is the ideal of play, representing a seriousness which is uniquely personal and a gaiety which is abandoned.

Play, to go beyond Stirner, has another relevant quality: in what is complete, symmetrical, and closed, man seems to find a compelling harmony. The peculiar enchantment of the Euclidean theorem lies in its utter completeness; every step is precise and necessary, pointing unambiguously to the course of the proof, which in turn is simple, and thus all the more indelible. Analogously the hedonistic egoist wants each moment to be self-contained, self-determined, and closed—to be its own completeness. His attitude

---

[1] Freud: *Beyond the Pleasure Principle*, pp. 8–11. For examples, Melanie Klein: *The Psycho-Analysis of Children*, 1932, intro.

[2] Recent discoveries in the fields of molecular biology and linguistics support the hypothesis that man's highest function is his capacity for subjective simulation of his external environment. Play is the outward expression of this simulation (Jacques Monod: *Le Hasard et la nécessité*, 1970, ch. 8). This evidence favouring the defining image of *homo ludens* correspondingly devalues the image of man as the tool-making animal, or as *homo faber*.

[3] 'Recensenten Stirners', *Kleinere Schriften*, p. 355.

contrasts with that of *homo economicus*, whose attachment to future goals means that his experience is never closed, and never present. The numerous contrasts between the Stirnerian and liberal-rationalist philosophies emerge in full relief only when it is recognized what antithetical frames of mind, what antithetical tempos of being and structures of feeling, lie behind them. The tone of Stirner's orientation to life is gay and exuberant, playful and expansive; the tone of the utilitarian disposition is cautious and reserved, prudential and considered. Victorian morality, with its attitude that play is waste—wasted money, wasted time, wasted virtue—was the logical development of the liberal-rationalist tradition. What we are isolating here is an ontological dichotomy, one which can be characterized by juxtaposing two human types, on the one hand the bureaucratic accountant, ordering statistical facts, and on the other, Nietzsche's 'gay scientist', he who does all his thinking on morning walks in the Alps. The two experience different worlds: their perceptions, their interests, their emotional responses, share virtually nothing in common.

Hand in hand with the revaluation of property goes Stirner's endeavour to draw 'competition' back into the domain of the individual. He had learnt from Hegel that the first task of the philosopher was to make abstract concepts concrete through grounding them in experience. Stirner had a rare gift for accomplishing the third stage of Hegel's dialectical process, that of bringing concepts applicable to the object world beyond the individual, which have become dissociated from him, *back* into his own consciousness. He is one of the best examples of a philosopher who, again in Hegel's language, does not think 'abstractly'.[1] When he cannot reinterpret an abstraction, for example 'Man', in terms of the individual's living experience, he discards it.

'Things compete, whereas the individual asserts his competence', paraphrases Stirner's new economics.[2] The individual's unique force (*Kraft*) alone brings life and significance to labour;[3] satisfaction lies in the competence with which work is executed, and so the product's value to the maker, and indeed usually to the consumer, lies in the unique stamp that it bears.[4] Thus Stirner advocates a craftsman's morality; in urging men to follow their competence he emphasizes the need for each person to realize himself in the mastery of his craft.[5] The finest exemplification of this prominent, notably anarchist theme of the nineteenth-century was to come twenty years later with

---

[1] Hegel's article *Wer denkt abstrakt?*, included in Kaufmann: *Hegel* (pp. 460–5).
[2] *Ego*, pp. 171, 176.   [3] Ibid., pp. 183–4.
[4] Stirner elsewhere notes that alienation is an irremovable component of any creative process: 'as my own creatures they are already alienated from me after the act of creation' (ibid., p. 247).
[5] Ibid., pp. 102–3.

Wagner's musically rendered vision of the German artist-craftsman, *Die Meistersinger*, with his 'master-song'.

After the act of creation the subsidiary problem of exchange arises, the necessity for the individual to barter the products of his competence for a wider range of goods. Because the egoist is the only judge of his own worth there is no incentive for him to accept the State's valuation of his work. Stirner here appears to be advocating a meritocracy, in which the individual somehow asserts his own merit. But at this point *Der Einzige* is more convincing in its critique of a Benthamite or *laissez-faire* system than in providing a viable alternative.

We need to take care to distinguish Stirner, the practical guide to living in society here-and-now, from the Stirner who sketches the better social order of the future. In the former case his argument runs parallel with *laissez-faire* liberalism's defence of the individual, and his competence to do the best he can for himself. Marx accused Stirner of being a disguised utilitarian,[1] and indeed *Der Einzige* does appear to follow Bentham's utility theory half-way. By asserting that people ought to maximize their enjoyment Stirner presupposes a kind of pleasure principle. He makes one distinctively Benthamite statement:[2]

I *utilize* the world and men! . . . We have only one relation to each other, that of *usableness*, of utility, of use.

Moreover, his egoism recalls that of Adam Smith's comment:[3]

It is not from the benevolence of the butcher, the brewer or the baker, that we expect our dinner, but from their regard to their own interest. We address ourselves, not to their humanity, but to their self-love, and never talk to them of our own necessities, but of their advantages.

Both Stirner and the liberal-rationalists grant a central place in their respective schemas to some form of the pleasure principle. Any further similarities are secondary. Stirner dismisses the principle of the natural identity of interests, realized through the economic market, as a pure fiction; the surrogate principle of the artificial identification of interests through enforceable legislation, whether utilitarian or liberal, is regarded as likewise representing an arbitrary means of creating social cohesion. But the fundamental incompatibility between Stirner and liberal-rationalism is over the nature of the pleasure principle itself: for egoist philosophy there are no significant means of deriving the quantified indices necessary to the working of a rational economic model. Stirner's 'utility', founded

---

[1] *German Ideology*, pp. 448–60. [2] *Ego*, pp. 204–5.
[3] Adam Smith: *The Wealth of Nations*, vol. 1, p. 13.

upon the command 'Squander yourself!', cannot be used to generate a social principle: it is exclusively a-social in any terms but those of the small group. On the other hand, Bentham introduces egoism *within* the social system: he aims to unite the individual and society. Above all, and encompassing other distinctions, Stirner is concerned with questions of *being* and of *self*, with locating a centre to the individual's existence, sublimated from his passions, which qualitatively transcends biological descriptions of energy flow. Stirner's concept of utility is not that of Bentham; he holds to a joy-principle rather than to a pleasure-principle. The significant fact that he does not refer to getting *pleasure* out of life, but to getting *enjoyment*, illustrates the cardinal concern of the anarcho-psychological tradition with ontology. This concern is Hegelian. The case is opposite for Bentham, whose philosophical orientation virtually precludes a notion of the 'self'; the individual cannot be a phenomenon of *ontological* interest to the scientific mind which is intent on quantifying and correlating human satisfactions—the Benthamite passion to build a calculated system depends on an obliviousness to 'being', and an obliviousness to psychology as it has been characterized in this study. Thus although anarcho-psychology and liberal-rationalism start from a similar assumption about human motivation they soon develop into opposed social philosophies.[1]

Nietzsche too, in assessing knowledge in terms of its utility, had laid himself open to the charge of utilitarianism. But it is meaningless to define utilitarianism in terms of its focussing concern with 'utility': the decisive question is utility in terms of which goals. The values and goals which frame the Benthamite notion of utility are as remote from the Nietzschean Will-to-Power as from Stirner's 'interests'. Indeed, Nietzsche is at crucial odds with three central Benthamite concerns: quantification, useful work, and the notion of social and economic progress. He jots down in his notebook:[2]

> Utility and pleasure are *slave theories* of life: the 'blessing of work' is self-glorification of slaves.—Incapacity for leisure.

Stirner views the purely economic trade of utilitarian philosophy, and the endeavours of capitalist individualism, as constituting gross drudgeries. But a man must survive, and so it is necessary for him to play the economic game, at least for part of his day, with all the exploitative cunning at his call. Stirner's subversive advice, borrowing

---

1 This is not to deny that these traditions have in common a fundamental disagreement with the socialist assumption about the primacy of the social group. Stirner and Mill both make clear, for example, their contempt for the herding spirit—group action, group solidarity, and group security. But while they share individualist preferences in this context their concepts of the individual are radically divergent.

2 *Wille* 758.

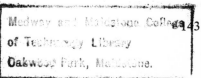

an image from Heine, is to *smuggle*, carry on free trade behind the back of the State.[1] Thieve, cheat, and deceive, he urges; these words frighten only those who affirm the laws of the State—Stirner does not accept the possibility of a 'social contract'. Once private property has been instituted so has theft, as the means to ownership. It is as foolish, Stirner adds, to expect the rich to give up their property (are they to be blamed for poverty? he asks), as to expect the State to raise the basic wage-level without its power being threatened.[2]

The discussion of work and its formative potential is closed with the point that too much time is spent on unenjoyable activity, on 'human labours'—those concerned with everyday necessity.[3] This argument is developed into a second, attacking the generative root of industrial society. Stirner describes the fragmentation enforced by the division of labour on the life of the worker. Industry selects which part of the labourer it needs to utilize, irrespective of his desire or his real talent. Here Stirner marches in step with the contemporaneously written *1844 Manuskripte* of Karl Marx. He refers to Adam Smith's discussion of pin-manufacture and the advantages of a division of labour:[4]

If a factory worker must tire himself to death twelve hours and more, he is cut off from becoming man. Every labour is to have the intent that the man be satisfied. Therefore he must become a *master* in it too, be able to perform it as a totality. He who in a pin-factory only puts on the heads, only draws the wire, works, as it were, mechanically, like a machine; he remains half-trained, does not become a master: his labour cannot *satisfy* him, it can only *fatigue* him. His labour is nothing by itself, has no object in itself, is nothing complete in itself; he labours only into another's hands, and is *used* (exploited) by this other. For this labourer in another's service there is no *enjoyment of a cultivated mind*, at most, crude amusements: *culture*, you see, is barred against him.

In Stirner's ideal social unit, the Union, the strategy of economic insurrection is no longer relevant; there socio-economic intercourse is carried out voluntarily, it is not bound by rules. However, Stirner does not devote much space to describing his ideal society. His achievement is not to draw up a comprehensive blueprint for how to live and what to do, but to uncover the non-abstract, living values in terms of which he conceives that human action at its best would be conducted. His work explores the possibilities of individual enjoy-

---

[1] *Ego*, p. 230.
[2] Ibid., pp. 163–4. The notion of property as theft is borrowed from Proudhon's *Qu'est-ce que la propriété?* (1840).
[3] Ibid., p. 178.   [4] Ibid., p. 102.

ment and fulfilment, and his maxims sketch the frame of mind most conducive to transforming life in society into the terms of these values. Stirner inaugurates the spirit in which human existence can be pursued egoistically. 'Egoist' and 'Union' are ideal-types, rough guides as to the direction in which individual and social life could become more gratifying. But it is unlikely that anyone other than a fanatic could embody them in a total sense, and this is their great weakness. Stirner paid a price for his own philosophy: it left him with the practical alternatives of translating his despised Adam Smith into German, or going to debtors' prison—he was, by the end, to have done both.

Marx and Engels have some grounds for levelling the charge of ideology at Stirner's economics. *Der Einzige* exhibits little understanding of the magnitude of the influence exerted by the forces of economic production over social structure, and the limitations that are thereby placed on patterns of individual behaviour. Stirner had not experienced the growing power of technology to determine the course of social development. Economic postulates bear the weakness of abstraction if they are not grounded in a detailed and systematic analysis such as that to which Marx devoted the later part of his life. Stirner's theory remains relevant mainly to those who live in the interstices of industrial society, or those few whose leisure hours are not contaminated by their work experience.

On the other hand Stirner's opening assumption has been borne out: he assumed that unless the fundamental categories of economics such as 'property' were to be redefined in a radically personal way the liberal-rationalist curse which had established economics as a scientific discipline cut off from human interests would proliferate. Economic models, whether in the tradition of Marshall, of modern neo-classical theory, of socialist theory, or even of Keynes, have failed to incorporate any meaningful index of individual benefit other than the original utilitarian one, successfully disqualified by both Marx and Stirner, the index of increasing income or an increasing flow of commodities. There has been no attempt to rethink the significance of 'property'. As Stirner would have put it, the State has won. Economics has not escaped from its self-created cage as positivist and ideological. Moreover, the onus is still on Marxist economics to prove that it too is not trapped in the same cage, that it can inspire and direct a better praxis than the Russian and Eastern European examples suggest.

Dostoevsky's critique of utilitarianism and socialism

Fyodor Dostoevsky stands out as a contributor to the anarcho-psychological perspective for a complex of reasons. His credentials as a pioneering *psychologist*, exploring similar territory to Stirner and Nietzsche, are indisputable. Nietzsche wrote: 'Dostoevsky, the only psychologist, incidentally, from whom I had something to learn'.[1] Freud acclaimed him as a creative genius only marginally less great than Shakespeare.[2] His work is directed by a pervasive interest in the unconscious patterns of human motivation.

One of Dostoevsky's key structural devices in his novels is to throw his characters into situations in which they are so involved, in passion or humiliation, that they do not reflect upon themselves, do not have time to arrange the face that they would wish the world to see. His ambition is to expose the deeper roots of the psyche by removing the character's conscience, and describing his less censored responses. Freud employs the analytical device of concentrating attention on neurosis in order to achieve precisely the same *psychological* goal.

We have included a second criterion in defining the psychologist: he evaluates human action in terms of its significance for the individual psyche. The *Notes from Underground* is unambiguously psychological in this sense; so are major sections of the novels, as illustrated by the intense absorption with which the central characters, with rare exceptions, pursue their individual salvation. The characters themselves provide the loci of coherence in the novels: no other structurings of reality recover from the demolition into chaos to which they are subjected. The paradigm is the underground man and his singularly anarchist politics. (We recall that any perspective which concentrates its interest on the individual bears implicit anarchist traits.)

But Dostoevsky also creates characters like Alyosha Karamazov who point beyond themselves, who are 'immune to egoism'. One of the recurring concerns of the other, Christian Dostoevsky is to show the destructive force of egoism. Through the character of Raskolnikov in *Crime and Punishment* he analyses the fall of a man who aspires to be 'extraordinary', and to have the will, the godlike confidence, the total lack of shame of a Napoleon. Raskolnikov gains salvation, antithetically, through his Christian compassion for the poor, the insulted, and the injured, through confession, and through a long period of self-effacing atonement.[3] In *The Possessed*, moreover, the critique of egoism is linked with a bitter critique of anarchist politics in both its individualist and terrorist forms.

It is not so much, finally, Dostoevsky's attachment to a mystical

---

[1] *Götzen-Dämmerung* ix:45.
[2] 'Dostoevsky and Parricide', *Collected Papers V*, p. 222.
[3] Raskolnikov does not provide an adequate test-case for rejecting the egoist as a viable human type. His Napoleonic pose represents an example of the Will-to-Power of which Nietzsche would not have approved: it bears too many of the traits of the slave morality.

ethic which divides him from Stirner and Nietzsche and their anarchism, as his recurring Christian devotion to the ideals of self-abnegation and compassion. Only the Shestovian Dostoevsky stands without qualification as a generative figure in the tradition we have named anarcho-psychology: for the rest his politics, and in association his ethics, moves in a highly intricate and not readily decipherable motion around an axis joining the anarchism of the underground world to the chauvinist conservatism of his late journalism.

Dostoevsky makes his explicit attack on the postulates of liberal-rationalism, which he identifies with the image of *homo economicus*, in the *Notes from Underground*, since accepted as one of the seminal texts in the existentialist tradition. He develops philosophical themes whose intensity and persistency—they recur in all his major novels—suggest that his entire work should be read in part as a reaction against this ideology, framing what he condemned as Western, bourgeois, industrial society. We have already considered the facet of his critique directed against rationalist-empiricist thought. But this is inseparable from the second facet, which we now examine, that directed against materialist utilitarianism and socialism of both utopian and materialist orientations.

The underground man is, in the first place, anti-Benthamite. He attacks Bentham's postulate (without mentioning or knowing of Bentham) that man acts according to his economic self-interest.[1] On the contrary, he argues, there is a force stronger than man's rational will which sometimes makes him act contrary to his advantage, against the useful, and even against the beautiful.[2] Freud might describe it as one aspect of the death instinct; Dostoevsky, however, places more positive value on man's ultimate weapon against order and stability—his whim, his caprice.[3] Independence, and the semblance of freedom, are valued above other types of interest. The underground man is optimistic enough to believe that whatever man might think he ought to want, he will never really desire a utilitarian society: the rebel in him will finally prevail, the one grain of freedom he would have to sacrifice to join a materially secure, planned society would prove too high a price.[4]

The Benthamite ambition to *quantify* pleasure necessitates differentiating its components, a process which inevitably leads in the direction of setting up 'pleasures' as supra-individual ends in

---

1 *Notes from Underground*, p. 106.
2 Ibid., pp. 104, 107.
3 Ibid., pp. 106–7.
4 *Summer Impressions*, pp. 85–6. Dostoevsky's optimism finds some historical support in Lewis Mumford's account of reactions against the 'megamachine' society of, for example, ancient Egypt (*The Myth of the Machine*, pp. 228–33).

themselves, separated from the actor. Dostoevsky's critique is directed primarily against this utilitarian habit, and against the consequent practice of consciously deciding useful goals and then setting instrumentally about realizing them. The *Notes from Underground* is fundamentally anti-teleological:[1]

> I agree that man is a creative animal, doomed to strive consciously toward a goal, engaged in full-time engineering, as it were, busy building himself roads that lead *somewhere*— *never mind where*. . . . But wait, . . . I wonder if he doesn't like chaos and destruction so much just because he's instinctively afraid of reaching the goal he's working for? . . . He loves the achieving, but does not particularly enjoy what he achieves.

The underground man, a nihilist in a nihilist world, observes his contemporaries striving to establish false goals where there are no naturally generated ones. While, like all men, they must continue to build roads, he argues that they should be conscious and honest enough to recognize that the goal itself is not an absolute, and probably not even very important. A strong attachment to the *telos* indicates that the spontaneous enjoyment the child once took in road-building has waned—his curiosity took him unproblematically along roads, which consequently defined themselves. A teleology directed to material ends has been substituted for the lust for adventure, variety, and play. Goals, *faute de mieux*, give a life shape and purpose; men become utilitarian out of fear of the alternative—the chaos of tangled or tepid desires, of rootlessness and boredom. At least it is possible on the level of judgment guided by criteria of instrumental rationality to believe that 'useful' activity is worthwhile; Dostoevsky interprets the modern wave of rationalism, empiricism, and/or socialism as the issue of this intellectual drive to establish worthwhile ends. Whilst in London in 1862 he visited the Crystal Palace, built largely of materials from the Great Exhibition of 1851. He saw in this first of industrial society's great exhibitions, showing the latest machines, factory processes, buildings, and so on, the chilling symbol of contemporary purpose, progress, and triumph —a 'colossal idea' signposting the technological paradise of the future, a terrifying 'achievement of perfection'.[2] Dostoevsky links this sterile world of science and technology with the archetypal emblems of a materialist-utilitarian culture: he observed in Paris that

---

[1] *Notes from Underground*, pp. 116–17. Cf. Nietzsche on *Tourists*: 'They climb mountains like animals, stupid and sweating; one has forgotten to tell them that there are beautiful views on the way up' (*Menschliches* II:ii:202). Again: 'Not every end is the goal. The end of a melody is not its goal' (Ibid. 204).

[2] *Summer Impressions*, pp. 58–60.

the ubiquitous drive for *money*, and in association, status, had destroyed the ideals of the revolution—real *fraternité* had become impossible in a bourgeois society in which the self-determined *I*, wedded to the cash-nexus, was opposed to nature and to the rest of mankind.[1]

The Crystal Palace is Dostoevsky's crowning symbol for the barrenness of industrial civilization. Virtually the whole Western world saw light, reason, and progress streaming in through its glass walls; he saw but the profile of a dark, satanic prison. In the Crystal Palace everything will be provided, man's every desire will be satisfied, he will be insulated from pain—but the more he becomes the automaton consumer the more he will also suffer from excruciating boredom. There he will become imaginatively imbecilic. Boredom will drive him to acts of the most vicious, gratuitous cruelty and sadism. The argument substantiates Nietzsche's genealogy of morals. The Crystal Palace is the supreme economic manifestation of the utilitarian, liberal-rationalist philosophy; and it is the bourgeois paradise. The ascetic morality manifest in the early phases of industrial society in the character-types of the capitalist and the rationalist social reformer prepared the ground for, on the one hand, bourgeois morality, and on the other, the chronic boredom of nihilism—both to be found side by side in the palace of glass.

Dostoevsky believed that the gods of rationalism and materialist utilitarianism had joined in conspiracy against all other ethical systems. There is a logic to this union. Reason finds its most effective application where a cluster of concepts is available which can be manipulated with mathematical precision. Any sphere of activity whose salient dimensions can be quantified falls under the iron grip of twice-two-equals-four. The accumulation of capital, or the acquisition of money, are endeavours *par excellence* which establish a quantifiable goal: hence they are directly amenable to maximization formulae. Significant steps can be taken here as in no other sphere of social action toward eliminating chance factors—hence positivizing the unknown.

There is a certain kinship of symmetry between reason and money. They both may bear a mesmeric power before which all other interests pale. Max Weber pointed out some historical links between the emergence of the Protestant ethic, in particular its emphasis on rational conduct, and the growth of capitalism. Moreover, there is an aesthetic congruency between the 'beauty cold and austere, capable of stern perfection' of reason,[2] and the magic and elegance with which money accumulates out of nothing, especially for the speculator who manipulates his financial interests through the Stock

[1] *Summer Impressions*, 'An Essay on the Bourgeois', pp. 70–87.
[2] Bertrand Russell on mathematics: *Philosophical Essays*, 1910, p. 73.

Exchange, and who thus is fully abstracted from the production process.[1]

Dostoevsky's attack on utilitarian teleology operates in two dimensions. Firstly, teleological thinking is repudiated *in toto*. The critique takes its point of departure from the conviction that the only worthwhile goal for human endeavour is the supra-phenomenal mystical noumenon: the unspecifiable which eludes conscious pursuit. Secondly, the critique raises specific objections to utilitarian ends, the style of life they determine, and the consequences of materialism. The utilitarian ethic is viewed as symptomatic of the worst degradation of man's spiritual qualities. The hope of an expanded consumption of matter is the surrogate for freedom of the spirit. This freedom is always clouded by uncertainty; and once the uncertain becomes unbearable the individual is driven to reduce its scale. (Both Nietzsche and Freud portray the individual most worthy of respect as he who is capable of enduring the greatest degree of uncertainty. The same is, in effect, true for Max Weber.) Dostoevsky accuses the liberal-rationalist of striving to fill in the spaces which are the trial of any man who lives by his inspiration with a series of infinitesimally close and predictable events, and thus reducing his life to banal, but comfortable, routine.

Dostoevsky backs his anti-utilitarianism with the claim that man can draw both insight into, and inspiration for, social action from the mystical. Alyosha Karamazov's particular experience, which he was always to remember in retrospect with 'someone visited my soul at that hour!', gave him strength to go out from the monastery into the world.[2]

The argument finds echoes in modern anthropology. Marcel Mauss, in his seminal *Essai sur le don* (1925), places a parallel emphasis on the non-utilitarian nature of economic exchange in primitive societies. The anthropology of Róheim and the more general cultural analyses of Mumford argue the same line. This tradition opposes the utilitarian assumption that the primitive chants as he sows seed because he believes that otherwise it will not grow, the assumption that his economic goal is primary, and his other activities are instrumental to it.[3] The planting and the cultivating are no less important than the finished product. Life is not conceived of as a linear progression directed to, and justified by, the achievement of a series of goals; it is a cycle in which ends cannot be isolated, one which cannot be dissected into a series of ends and

---

1 Cf. Oswald Spengler: 'Next of kin to thinking in money, however, is mathematics' (*The Decline of the West*, 1932, vol. 2, p. 482).

2 *The Brothers Karamazov*, p. 427.

3 Also I. C. Jarvie and J. Agassi: 'The problem of the rationality of magic', *Rationality*, ed. B. R. Wilson, 1970, ch. 8.

means. It is not our task to evaluate the degree to which this organicist perspective over-idealizes the past.

Freud gives support to the aspect of this tradition with which we are most concerned: he recognized that ritual acts are not essentially instrumental, but are motivated out of psychic need. They carry with them not a feeling of purpose, but one of compulsion. Nietzsche founded his rejection of causal thinking on a similar insight: indeed, his emphasis on the 'it' which initiates thought and action is singularly anti-utilitarian. Men rarely act rationally in the utilitarian sense of consciously planning the most efficient means of realizing a pre-determined goal: they are simply *driven* to act. This is not to assert that life does not usually obey an unconscious rationality, according to which action is directed to satisfying a self-preservative or homeostatic instinct.

A critique of utilitarian teleology and the empiricist, positivist view of progress simultaneously places some of the foundations of socialism under stress. Dostoevsky identifies socialism largely with social engineering, the pragmatic, materialist approach to improving the condition of man in society. The underground man rejects this prosaically atheist view of redemption: 'I don't accept as the crowning of my dreams a big building for the poor, with apartments leased for one thousand years and a dentist's sign outside in case of emergency.'[1] The credo suggested by this statement, taken with Dostoevsky's assertion that there are some truths which only the very poor can know,[2] mounts an unanswerable attack on all radical social action. The social reformer's goals have been deemed irrelevant, and even destructive of the human essence. A type of individualist fatalism is present in anarcho-psychological thought, and particularly in the work of Dostoevsky: it regards social conditions as no more appropriate for melioration than biological ones. The only object fit for ethical concern is the totality of the individual's life, and what is then significant is the manner in which he accepts his fate. The ultimate value of human dignity is reflected in how a man lives within the confines of his necessity: to regard as unjust the fact that some men gain vast riches would be to upset the balance of things — these men are compensated for their exclusion on earth from the kingdom of heaven.

We are again entangled in the net of the half-truth. Dostoevsky's portrayal of the unique depths of warmth and compassion to be found among people crippled by poverty is convincing. It gives a more piercing echo to Blake's parallel sentiments about the Clod and the Pebble. *Crime and Punishment*, in particular, generates imaginative substantiation for the proposition that much will be lost when

---

[1] *Notes from Underground*, p. 119.
[2] *The Brothers Karamazov*, p. 240.

poverty is ameliorated, when social life becomes more stable and secure. This has the status of truth. But the contrary truth is no less persuasive. Dostoevsky also shows the degradation of these people's lives, the hysteria and the misery bred of poverty and sickness. There is no pure resolution to lead us out of the impasse of such conflicting truths. We are left merely with Nietzsche's own peculiar dialectic: the axiom that every step forward is bought at a great price, that unreserved optimism about human progress is based on a delusion (or, at the most, represents one way in which an individual in an exuberant mood channels his goodwill). Pure optimism runs contrary to what it is possible to know about the human condition. No clear blueprint for action is available. At the best the individual can choose how to balance the conflicting truths, according to his own subjective criteria, and then, perhaps, act.

The underground man impeaches not only materialist socialism — communism, social democratism, syndicalism, and anarchist variants of these — but also Fourier, and by implication all the utopian or millenarian socialists. Shigalyov, the intellectual in *The Possessed*, is associated, as a 'fanatic lover of mankind', with Fourier, Cabet, and Proudhon.[1] Dostoevsky makes many references to Fourier's utopian community, the Phalanstery, but they are never detailed, and it is almost certain that he is one of the many who quoted Fourier without having read him. Nevertheless, Dostoevsky was right to associate him with the utopian vision of the harmonious community founded upon principles of order and symmetry. The Phalanstery is designed to nurture, with the help of a neo-Benthamite device, the calculus of passionate attraction,[2] the harmony which lies potentially at the root of human interaction. For Dostoevsky, Fourier is one of the industrious ant-hill engineers, busy, protected by the delusion that his goal, the well-ordered society, is the summation of all his desires. Man at his best is a system-breaker, an iconoclast seeking not only variety, but destruction; as in Stirner's vision he is an arch-criminal, but not necessarily the gratuitously cruel one, driven to bestiality by the boredom of living in a palace of glass. Dostoevsky is not only reacting against an untragic, naïve view of human capability and human satisfaction; he also accuses utopianism of providing an intellectual escape from involvement in concrete, living experience, whereby the conscience is salved through a painstaking elaboration of gigantic paper plans for human happiness.

If Dostoevsky had known Fourier's writing he would have

---

1 *The Devils*, p. 406 — using Magarshack's translation, but retaining Constance Garnett's more apposite title, *The Possessed*.

2 This discussion of Fourier's philosophy draws upon his *Oeuvres Complètes*, 1966–8, *Selections from the Works of Fourier* (trans. Julia Franklin) 1901 and Frank Manuel: *The Prophets of Paris*, 1962. In this instance, *Selections*, p. 66.

recognized a somewhat kindred spirit; the philosophy of this French utopian reveals an awesome imaginative range and force, sometimes manic and chaotic; often it demonstrates rare psychological insight. Fourier's life was rich in observation, of people of every age and type, of every trade and profession, and yet it was grey and undistinguished in itself. Thus, the seemingly paradoxical combination of a fertile and complex mind with an obsessive attachment to the utopian ideal of harmony, order, and symmetry is explicable as a compensation for a life which was at once dull and unstable. His philosophy magnifies this contrast: while he places great emphasis on the primary passion which he calls *papillonne*, the passion for change, alteration, and periodic variety, he sees it as only a part of a final, all-encompassing passion, Unityism or Harmonism.[1] There is a parallel significance in the fact that Dostoevsky too allowed himself a vision of utopia, not only in *The Dream of a Ridiculous Man*. Versilov, in *A Raw Youth*, relates his dream of a Golden Age, inspired by a Claude Lorraine painting, an Arcadian world of happiness and innocence.[2] Alongside the Dostoevsky who relished chaos and destruction is a more timid, hesitant figure, yearning for some absolute, womblike harmony; here is an instability of genius not structurally dissimilar to that of Fourier.

Dostoevsky presents his final, coherent view of politics and social organization in the fictional form of the legend of 'The Grand Inquisitor'.[3] Rationalist-empiricist habits of mind and the materialist-utilitarian ethic join forces in opposition to all that he considers to be valuable in the human condition. He poses a dichotomy between knowledge and liberty, between the flight, out of fear of the unbounded, into reason, and the capacity for the noumenal, for individual responsibility, for the caprice of the underground man. Knowledge is legitimated by political structure. Reason underpins the Grand Inquisitor's authoritarianism: once he has seen that men seek the tangible happiness of bread and miracles, and that they are afraid of the 'freedom' which the anarchist Christ offers, he applies his reason and his knowledge to satisfying their needs, indeed to maximizing their *happiness*—the emotional state diametrically opposite to that of freedom. At once the Inquisitor is the forgiving father, the scientific materialist, and the social engineer. He is the most compassionate, and honest, of politicians; he takes on great burdens of responsibility in order to protect his subjects from ethical doubt. But he also suppresses any attempt to expand their self-consciousness: he is the 'great simplifier', the shepherd to a flock of

---

[1] *Selections*, p. 61.
[2] *A Raw Youth*, pp. 461–3.
[3] All references for the remainder of this section are to ch. 5 of bk 5 of *The Brothers Karamazov*: 'The Grand Inquisitor.'

carefree children. Once the realm of the transcendental has been abandoned the politician is free to apply his equations: the greatest good is then calculable.

The underground man embodies the rejection of politics and its dictator. But Dostoevsky maintained his anarchism only momentarily. He himself impeaches Christ through the mouth of the Grand Inquisitor: 'It was pitiless of thee to value man so highly'. This Christ has no answer to the world of politics, of rational action, of knowledge. He is utterly Nietzschean in his intention not to pity, but to respect. At this point choice between the Nietzschean position and that of the Grand Inquisitor is purely subjective, depending on the degree of optimism with which human potentiality is viewed. Dostoevsky, for example, finally rejects his own Christ in favour of the Inquisitor's type of political compassion. To discover this we do not need to consider the conservative politics, the slavophilia, and the hope for a revitalized Russian Church proselytized in *The Diary of a Writer*: Dostoevsky transformed his Christ into Father Zossima, who pities more personally than the Grand Inquisitor, but who remains half an authoritarian figure.

Stirner, Nietzsche, and Dostoevsky, whether they articulate their views from the ethical standpoint of the egoist or that of the mystic, all develop a disdain for politics. Political affairs are regarded as banausic, fit at best for distracting banter: 'Who loses and who wins; who's in, who's out'—to recall the juxtaposing of love and politics towards the end of *King Lear*. But from here the ways part. The mystic, pictured from the egoist perspective, escapes from political reality into a world of religious abstraction; he should, however, be striving to transcend that reality in a politics of the self. He is truly apolitical. Shestov's atheist charge is that in the end the existentialism of the underground man is repressed, that Dostoevsky cannot face its nihilist implications.

On the other hand, for the mystic—here Dostoevsky—the egoist does not escape Thomas Mann's dictum: 'In our time the destiny of man presents its meaning in political terms'. His politics is the anarchism which brings moral and spiritual chaos, which legitimates self-destroying egoism, the modern vehicle for the Antichrist. Although the relationship of the egoist to practical politics is not satisfactorily resolved, as we have pointed out, he is not guilty of splitting the world into matter and spirit, and denying all ties with the former. His dichotomy is between experience which is realizable, and that which is dissociatedly abstract. Consequently, in principle, he is better able to cope consistently, from within his moral standpoint, with political realities than a Dostoevsky, who, incapable of incorporating their reality into his world-view, reacts to the extreme of joining the Grand Inquisitor, though in sadness.

The either-or posed by the confrontation of the anarchist Christ and the benevolently authoritarian Grand Inquisitor defines the key ethical question behind any choice to act politically. The issues at stake have never been more lucidly formulated, whether they emphasize such dichotomies as democracy/autocracy, self-determination/paternalism, *laissez-faire*/planned socialism, liberty/happiness, or such notions as 'false consciousness' and 'repressive tolerance'. Christ answers the Inquisitor with a kiss. He utters not one word in reply: his silence is emblematic of irrationalism. The kiss is the only answer, and yet it is no answer. It merely serves to emphasize the unbridgeable schism between the conflicting truths with which self-reflective man *in* society has to live.

Some notes towards a psychology of *homo economicus*

An adequate understanding of an area of the past which is for some reason considered to be of significance to the present, such as the development of capitalism is for us, would include a psychological analysis of unconscious forces of motivation. Thus, whilst the historian must investigate the technological and social preconditions of capitalism, such developments in Britain for example as the expropriation of the peasants from their own land and the expansion of colonial trade, he must also chart salient shifts in psychological needs. Moreover, a present which becomes interested in the psychological dimensions of its own problems will demand that history be written with a bias towards the logic of its psychological unfolding.

Psychology is like any other intellectual discipline in requiring some ordering principle. Weber, following Nietzsche, chose the historical development of Protestant religion as the framework from which to extrapolate psychological changes significant to the capitalist spirit. Scheler chose Nietzsche's category 'resentment' as the focussing lens for a phenomenological analysis of bourgeois society and its key psychological currents. More recently a genre of 'psycho-history' has evolved which grounds biographical study in Freudian principles.

We offer in this section a sketch of an alternative psycho-historical method, one which combines psychological biography with the setting up of Weberian ideal-types. It involves selecting character-types which embody nodal points of the social change under observation: men of the time, or, to employ Hegel's terminology, bearers of the *Zeitgeist*. Dostoevsky's recurring concern with the figure of *homo economicus* manifests itself in his fictional writings in the portrayal of a series of caricatures of this type's different vices. Thus the figures of the Rothschild and of the miserly, back-alley money-lender appear as the particular mediations of usurer traits. We choose, however, to illustrate our analytical technique by means of a third character-type, which Dostoevsky also identified with the emergence of capitalist-materialist society, and developed more fully: the gambler.

The aim of this section is to present an example of the type of historical analysis which an anarcho-psychological perspective makes possible, and to provide some evaluation of its usefulness. Dostoevsky's fictional analysis of the gambler joins Nietzsche's 'genealogy of morals' as the first detailed venture in applying the new psychology to social phenomena. It claims only to supplement, not to substitute for, a sociological analysis of *homo economicus*.

It is significant to the nature of anarcho-psychological thought, as we shall discuss in our conclusion, that none of its exponents, with the partial exception of Dostoevsky in his single work *Notes from Underground*, venture into a sustained systematic critique of the social and economic developments which they abhorred. The latter half of this section is devoted to applying one of their psychological insights, which characteristically eludes empirical specificity, as a critique of *homo economicus* drawing on concrete economic data in a fashion more typical of Marx's work. We justify this one excursion beyond the bounds of nineteenth-century anarcho-psychological practice on the grounds of the importance of determining whether this practice, in spite of its irrationalist preferences, might provide a basis for systematic non-positivist economic analysis.

Psychoanalysts have stressed the need to draw on studies of neuroses in making statements about 'normal', individual or social, behaviour, in the belief that neuroses are magnifications of determining traits present in all men. The assumption is that it is more fruitful to study a detailed film-negative when it is projected onto a large screen. Similarly, we search for insights into *homo economicus* by looking at his obsessions and compulsions, as they are expressed in the particular form of the gambler, again assuming that they provide the keys to the 'deep structure' of his character.

Dostoevsky's *Novelle*, *The Gambler* (1867), was written after a series of episodes in which the writer had reduced himself to poverty in the gaming houses of Europe.[1] He described the essence of his prospective gambler in a letter to Strakhov:[2]

> But the chief thing is that all his vitality, all his strength, his violent temper, his boldness—are spent on roulette. . . . He is a poet of sorts, but the point is that he is ashamed of his poetry, for deep down he feels how contemptible it is, though the fact there is risk ennobles him in his own eyes.

[1] David Magarshack: *Dostoevsky: A Life*, 1963, ch. 8.
[2] Quoted ibid., p. 297.

Dostoevsky recognizes a powerful drive in man to squander everything he possesses in one ecstatic experience of pure risk—in this case to focus all his talents, his ambitions, his emotions on one number on one roulette wheel at one moment in time. This can only destroy: creative passion finds its concentrated inversion and becomes a compulsive force for self-annihilation. Indeed, by contrast, an implicit value is placed on sublimation, on diffusing passion widely enough for its object attachments to bear its intensity. In the gambler the erotic drive, unleashed as dramatically and with as little diversion as in the Wagnerian *Liebestod*, is displaced onto the roulette wheel. In both types of sheer catharsis we witness the masochistic element of the urge to give all, without a touch of constraint, and thus to be wholly possessed, and dispossessed, which here amounts to the same. The state of ultimate trust is precariously close to being the one of ultimate self-disrespect, self-abandon close to being self-negation—in terms of a connection which recurs in the *Novelle*, the lover close to being the gambler.

The psychological state of the gambler in full motion is intoxication. 'Feeling as though I were delirious with fever', recalls Dostoevsky's hero, 'my whole body tingled with fire . . .'[1] Normal restraints imposed by the superego on instinctual energy yield; the exhilaration is intensified by daring the forbidden; an activated sense of guilt spices nervous excitement. Moreover, this rebel against his conscience is also a rebel against civilization: its order is impotent before the unleashed gambling passion. And the irrationalist Dostoevsky approves: he contrasts the gambler with the German *Vater*, whom he detests with his Protestant virtues of duty, frugality, and hard work.

The character of the gambler contains a strain of what was a perverse aspect of the alternative to ego-striving in *Crime and Punishment*: the impulse to deny the self, the case of someone deriving pleasure from humiliating himself.[2] The maintenance of a lucid sense of identity, of *ego*, is burdensome; it implies a series of responsibilities, a striving continuously to 'live up to' a certain self-image in the individual's own mind, and in the minds of his acquaintances. (The existentialist tradition would suggest that such a self-image is false, because it is forced.) A satisfying feeling of release follows the thrusting off of these burdens. The gambler acts out a personal assault on the core of the Protestant tradition, the beliefs in rational, frugal conduct and individual responsibility.

The play-drive in the case of the gambler is impelled by 'a terrible craving for risk',[3] and is funnelled into one outlet. The curiosity

[1] *The Gambler*, p. 129.
[2] *Crime and Punishment*, p. 298.
[3] *The Gambler*, p. 132.

which entices the child into secret gardens has ossified: what remains is the fetish of engineering one moment in which curiosity is to reach a fever pitch, then die. Curiosity, ambition, dream, and desire are dictated as if under a myopia of the psychic energy. Melanie Klein relates a case in which her teacher, Karl Abraham, cured a boy whose play-drive had been emasculated to the point where his only pleasure lay in philately: in clinical sessions he would ritually arrange, swap, and replace stamps.[1] The gambler is one of this boy's psychological twins. He has retired from a threatening world into one whose boundaries he can define. And yet he has institutionalized the very precariousness from which he seeks to escape.

For Dostoevsky, the gambler is Hyde to the mystic's Jekyll. The novelist is fascinated by this travesty of his mystical ideal. The gambler, like the mystic, knows that reason does not govern life. He detests the permanent and the material so much that he has to squander all that he possessed: he exorcizes these demons which threaten to possess him. The true mystic is indifferent to the material; he manifests none of this ambivalent love-hate for money. Twice-two-equals-four has more of a grip on the gambler; hence his fanatical rebellion, his turn to the game where the only recognizable skill is a 'mystical touch' which can intuit the roll of the ball. The gambler's success, too, is dependent on grace: however, it is the success which impels only greater failure next time. Dostoevsky himself, ever a man of clashing opposites, exhibits in his own gambling activities, and in his imaginative recreation of them, some symptoms of the mystic *manqué*.

The vision of the Midas touch, that everything can be had suddenly and for nothing, and this holds for capitalist and gambler alike, funnels drives in a way that can only shatter the pace of living in which experience is allowed to unfold in its own natural time. It is as if the delicate precision of a slow string quartet was interrupted by a frenzied and sustained crescendo. The self-destructiveness which permeates the gambler's character is highlighted in his incapacity to find any regenerative relationship to time. He differs from the capitalist, who suffers from a similar time-neurosis, in his compulsion to condense life's infinite number of dimensions of uncertainty into one experience: he has to cathart the unknown. We postpone discussion of how the capitalist copes with uncertainty.

Dostoevsky's critique is levelled from the standpoint of the mystical ethic. The mystic's search is also teleological, but of a different order. He waits, he observes, all his senses are finely tuned until the harmonies of the movement, the growth, and the decline of the objects around him, merge with his own inner rhythms:[2]

[1] Klein, op. cit., p. 125n.
[2] Rainer Maria Rilke: *Sonette an Orpheus*, I:ix.

Nur wer mit Toten vom Mohn	(Only she who tasted her own
ass, von dem ihren,	poppy-seed with the dead,
wird nicht den leisesten Ton	will not again lose the
wieder verlieren.	most fugitive tone.)

On the one hand gambling, for Dostoevsky, is indicative of a type of sensitivity, a vitality and poetry of spirit, especially when contrasted with the passionless boredom of bourgeois virtue. But, on the other hand, it is an opium which destroys its addict. (The Stock Exchange was to introduce the same ambivalent gambling qualities into economic life.) The first symptoms of debauchery are portrayed in the case of Dolguroky, the 'raw youth'. The hitherto frugal ascetic hires a coachman, eats seven-course meals, regularly visits the hairdresser, the French tailor, and so on, once he takes to gambling.[1] The superego, having lapsed at one level, abdicates at others. Dostoevsky implies that gambling is one last feverish defence against nihilistic roots. Salvation is not available to the gambler: he sustains surging passions for a while, but they are the substitutes in frustration for, rather than the mediators of, a 'more real' promise. By the end of the *Novelle* the gambler has become rationalistic in lieu of passion: he plays all day for small sums, he calculates, and inevitably he loses. Once his vitality is sapped he becomes the pathetic bearer of traits that he detests: his gambling is confirmed as a last act of revolt against vices which are deeply embedded in himself.

Just as Rousseau blamed contemporary society, and in particular its Parisian manifestation, for the corruption of man, Dostoevsky impeaches materialism, and in particular the money fetish, for the degradation of the spiritual. The gambler stands half-way between the mystic and the modern capitalist, sharing both worlds. He has moved towards the rational investor in living out the precise inversion of his values. But as long as the gambler's irrationalism saves him from the Midas curse, he remains but on the threshold of capitalism. He comes full of enthusiasm for a money game, but remains fearful of the consequences. Drawn by capitalism's promise, he rebels against its means. He is fascinated by the goose which lays golden eggs, yet suspects that if he holds the bird too long he will find nothing but cold flesh in his hands.

There are different types of gambler, corresponding to the relative weight attached to each of the three attractions of the game: adventure, winning, and skilful execution. Dostoevsky's roulette player is the most extreme example of the risk-seeking adventurer. He chooses a game which depends wholly on chance—skill is entirely absent. The irrationalist invents betting systems which disregard all laws of probability (the rational laws), and in his

[1] *A Raw Youth*, pp. 195, 276–9.

159

contrariness he even reverses his own system. He is interested in winning, but success leaves him unsatisfied, and he returns to the wheel. The compulsion lies in the delirious state of climactic risk. Ben Jonson's Volpone himself admitted to enjoying the gamble more than the gain. Blanche, a cheap French courtesan in the *Novelle*, understands the gambling syndrome. She exploits the gambler's lust for an ecstasy which for him is inversely related to time, and inevitably followed by disaster. Indeed, he is as masochistically drawn by the image she gives him of the catastrophic deluge, as by that of the preceding climax.

We now turn to consider, less speculatively, the place of the gambler in capitalism, and to enquire in what manner its functioning depends on exorbitant risk-taking. We are interested in whether the critique of *homo economicus* in terms of the psychology of his gambling traits has any relevance to the twentieth century. Our hypothesis is that although gambling, in forms playing a direct role in the economic system, has waned with the development of advanced industrial society, it has continued to provide a vital psychological undercurrent, influencing the emergence of new social and economic institutions. The case of gambling, which fulfils the function of an emotional release from the economic system, as conducted in marginal institutions such as casinos and bingo halls, is quite different.

Our main concern is the extraordinary extent to which economic life has been governed by the ambition to eliminate gamble and risk from its midst. The discussion hinges on the notion of *uncertainty*, which F. H. Knight distinguished from 'risk'. An action is risky if it leads to a set of possible outcomes, each occurring with a known probability; it is uncertain if its outcomes cannot be so predicted.[1] The gambler whom we have been discussing plays a game whose every outcome can be associated with a mathematical probability, yet he takes virtually no notice of this, and plunges into subjective uncertainty, applying the logic of his fancy. On the other hand, one of the major chapters in the history of capitalism's successful mutations has arguably been the mastering of uncertainty: suitable probability calculi have been devised which have progressively transferred 'uncertainty' into 'risk', which then can be minimized. A cursory glance at the proportion of its funds which a business enterprise today devotes to 'rationalizing' the basic processes of production and selling will illustrate this phenomenon. The trend towards 'specialization' derives from the need to employ the man of best judgment for each particular decision, he who will know which tools are available for quantifying the salient uncertainties. Computerized research, market surveys, and cost-benefit analyses have all added to the bag of 'rational tools'. Moreover, the drive to improve

[1] F. H. Knight: *Risk, Uncertainty, and Profit*, 1921, ch. 8.

the power of prediction has led to massive outlays on advertising; the producer now seeks not only to improve the efficiency of production and distribution, but to generate demand for his product; he creates a market rather than taps one—we have the phenomenon of 'manufacturing wants'.[1] In addition, expanding the size of a company, and merging with like companies, may confer monopolistic powers which help increase control over the future course of events.

At the government level this tendency has been equally pronounced. The hallmark of modern 'mixed capitalist' rationality is national accounting, developed to facilitate the planning for long-term, steady economic growth. Mathematical-economic tools are also applied to the associated goal of choosing investment priorities according to analyses of social benefit against social cost, thus reducing the possibility of a misallocation of resources (economic risk for governments is registered in terms of an inefficient use of resources). The case of central planning in France instanced the combination of business and government interests, co-operation eliminating particular uncertainties faced by both parties—in general, demand uncertainties for business, and supply uncertainties for government.[2]

The war against risk-taking has been the preserve, indeed the *raison d'être*, of the insurance company. The importance of the role which insurance has come to play in modern life is indicated by the fact that in 1960, in Britain, of the 8·3 per cent of personal disposable income which was saved, over half went into life assurance and pension funds (the remainder being distributed between housing and other forms of investment).[3] The notion of the commodity as a unit of exchange-value finds its purest expression in a fundamental axiom of insurance—every item has a replacement price. The ravages of hurricane, fire, even revolution in some cases, are quantifiable; the actuary, following a rigorous mathematical training, is the expert who can *rationally* assess the risk of virtually every earthly eventuality, and hence design a system for making money out of people's fears of 'chance' losses of property. The insurance company, in effect, gambles in *risk*. Even death has a replacement value; it is the norm today for a man to save during his working life in order to insure against ever-approaching death, through the agency named with disarming euphemism—*life assurance*. Life assurance gambles on the timing of certainty.[4]

However, the capitalist or mixed-capitalist economy is not so

---

[1] J. K. Galbraith: *The Affluent Society*, 1958, ch. 10.
[2] Andrew Shonfield: *Modern Capitalism*, 1965, ch. 7.
[3] George Clayton and W. T. Osborn: *Insurance Company Investment*, 1965 pp. 18, 21.
[4] In 1960, in Britain, life assurance companies accounted for £6,585m out of the total assets of £7,074m held by insurance companies—Ibid., p. 253.

simply open to the progressive elimination of uncertainty, if *efficiency* is to be considered one of its important goals. It is possible to reach the stage of 'over-insurance', in which diseconomies are introduced into the system. There is an incentive to deliberately lose or damage a fully insured durable good, after the glamour of novelty has faded. Moreover, in a second type of case, governments which tender for fighter aircraft on a 'cost-plus' basis, in order to bear the risk of the uncertain cost themselves, thereby reduce incentives to minimize the costs of production. (Knight articulated the often-voiced fear that within the framework of planned economic activity, where uncertainty plays a small or negligible role, managers will tend to 'play safe', with a resulting 'arrest of progress and vegetation of life'.)[1] As a consequence 'co-insurance' has evolved: the insurer pays some stated part or proportion of the loss, as for example with some motor car insurance—the claimant pays, say, the first fifty pounds of the cost of repairs.[2] Thus, within the economic system of profit maximization (ideally, maximum utilization of resources), it has proved necessary to maintain certain levels of risk.[3]

The Stock Exchange has provided the institutional means of diffusing risk in capital accumulation; although it is possible to insure against 'loss of profits',[4] insurance has played an insignificant role in hedging against uncertainty in capital formation and utilization. The Stock Exchange's function of shifting and spreading risk was originally second to its role as a capital market; however, this latter function is almost redundant today.

At the same time, this central institution for damping the risks of investment soon became the largest gambling casino in every country in which it was established. With the expansion of the European stock exchanges in the nineteenth century a new avenue for making money became available to every man with savings. In the 1830s and 1840s in Britain the investment mania for railway stock provided the first 'modern' example of mass gambling. The first two generations of the Industrial Revolution had accumulated funds to a level far outstripping the capacity of the outlets for investing or spending them. In the end the great splurge on railways

---

[1] Knight, op. cit., p. 361.

[2] Although it illustrates the point, this example is not altogether satisfactory. Insurance companies have no reason to be interested in an efficient allocation of resources in the economy as a whole. They are profit-maximizers, and by this criterion could offer full coverage by charging a higher premium. While 'co-insurance' is in the interest of the society, it is not necessarily in that of the insurance company.

[3] Moreover, Knight (op. cit., p. 369) also points out that from the standpoint of efficiency it is fairly clear that men work more interestedly and more effectively for an uncertain reward.

[4] Clayton and Osborn, op. cit., p. 12.

proved to be a gamble, with all its heedless and cavalier *élan*, which yielded only very moderate returns.[1] The landmark in the mass mobilization of credit in France, and hence the input impetus for capital accumulation, came in 1852 with the formation of the Société Générale de Crédit Mobilier. This bank, which by 1856 commanded combined capital to the value of one sixth of all assets quoted on the Bourse, also triggered off a speculation mania; previously untapped sources of middle-class saving flowed onto the investment market. Speculation was so wild at the inception of the Crédit Mobilier that the difference between its lowest quotation on the third day on which its shares had been officially sold on the Bourse, and its highest quotation on the following day, was 735 francs—the initial value per share being 1,100 francs.[2] This teething time in the development of large-scale capitalist finance was also the period of the first gold rushes in America and Australia.[3] It was as if a mass gambling hysteria seized this early generation, feeling its way tentatively, with impetuous thrusts and rebellious withdrawals, into the processes of modern capitalism. It was a time of youth, alternately carefree and intensely anxious; it was a time of exuberance, and a confidence which shrugged off the risk of squandering everything when there was the possibility of winning the omnipotence seen in economic fortune; the myths of the age were economic, and the institutionalized caution of middle age had not yet set in. In this genealogy, the last economic regression to youth came in the months preceding the 'Great Crash' in Wall Street in 1929.

Writing seven years after the Great Crash, Keynes argued that the 'best brains on Wall Street' had not furthered the proper social purpose of the Stock Exchange, which to his mind was to direct investment into the most profitable channels in terms of future yield.[4] He commented with acerbity on the irrationality which underpinned the working of stock markets, likening the activity of speculation to the game of musical chairs—the imperative is to be seated when the music stops.[5]

Moreover, life is not long enough;—human nature desires quick results, there is a peculiar zest in making money quickly,

---

[1] E. J. Hobsbawm: *The Age of Revolution*, 1962, pp. 64–5; E. J. Hobsbawm: *Industry and Empire*, 1969, pp. 118–19.

[2] Rondo E. Cameron: *France and the Economic Development of Europe, 1800–1914*, 1961, pp. 140–95.

[3] Marx regarded the gold rushes as introducing a new stage of development in bourgeois society (*Preface to the Critique of Political Economy*, included in *Selected Works*, p. 184).

[4] J. M. Keynes: *The General Theory of Employment, Interest and Money*, 1936, p. 159.

[5] Ibid., pp. 155–6, 157.

and remoter gains are discounted by the average man at a very high rate. The game of professional investment is intolerably boring and overexacting to anyone who is entirely exempt from the gambling instinct.

The proliferation of 'rationalizing' (in the Weberian sense) techniques, which we have sketched in these pages, has evolved psychologically as a reaction-formation against this gambling instinct upon which capitalism is dependent. This is not to deny the functionality of these techniques in terms of purely economic goals, but to argue that we must also take account of a second, equally important, pattern of causality: the motive force behind this 'rationalization' can be construed only partially in terms of the demands of economic efficiency and utility. There is simultaneously a primary psychological need, for a society as much as for its individual members, to establish a balance between the forces of order and chaos, between rationality/permanence and risk-seeking/transience.

When this balance breaks down social neurosis is imminent. In this respect, gambling and the drive to establish rationalistic teleologies, in their extreme forms, are complementary socio-cultural neuroses. The negation of a rationalistic teleology is the state of total chaos, its polar opposite. Taking *negation* to be the cancelling of a phenomenon by directly experiencing it, by living through its contradictions, rather than by merely dismissing it, then gambling stands as the socio-economic form of irrationalist rebellion against order available in Western, nineteenth-century industrial society. It was the gambler who, by taking up the values and the mechanics of the capitalist spirit, exposed some of the more prominent ways in which they masked forces blatantly destructive of the human essence. (An analogous counterbalancing in the reverse situation is also worth noting: the legitimation of rational goals is the means through which 'civilized order' might be imposed upon the frenzied anarchism of the gambler.)

Once the new vehicle that nineteenth-century capitalism had made available for the satisfaction of man's play-drive, his need to prove himself, to live dangerously, and to seek glory had become, in Weber's terminology, routinized and disenchanted, this crucial balance was lost; concomitantly grew the danger of too great a stability, indeed the danger of 'over-civilization'.[1] The 'captain of industry', who had combined the gambler's verve with sterner

---

[1] Freud, in his essay 'Thoughts for the Times on War and Death' (1915), describes the burdens that civilization places on its members, and the danger of socialization inhibiting their instincts too severely; these repressed instincts then break free at any opportunity for gratification (*Collected Papers* IV).

Protestant virtues, gave way to the bureaucrat.[1] Some of the turbulent social movements of this century can be read as attempts to live in the wake of this danger, and find new forms of passionate self-expression before the social repression of instinctual energy reaches crisis levels.[2]

Nevertheless, modern capitalism has so far managed to maintain workable equilibria. Just as a compensating reaction reduced 'over-insurance', so nationwide gambling disasters such as that of 1929, rather than inducing people to use money—now realized to have little substantial or permanent value—in a manner in keeping with its ephemerality, promoted the reaction of caution.[3]

We have outlined in this section some of the ways in which the gambling syndrome has played a prominent role in the institutional development and functioning of industrial society. We have not considered the phenomenal increase in *personal* gambling in, say, Britain in the last two decades. Detailed statistics indicating shifts of personal disposable income into the 'consumption' activities of 'playing the pools' and of bingo are not yet available.[4] Clearly our notes have provided only the outline for a historical study of the role of the gambling drive, and specific attempts to counter it, in the development of industrial society; our intention has been to indicate the usefulness of such an analysis. We have suggested that the critique of *homo economicus* in terms of his drive to gamble might still be relevant, not so much because this form of adventure is still prevalent, but more because it fulfils a necessary, if in its extreme form destructive, psychological function which has been progressively denied. One of the inferences to be drawn from these notes is that a society which is seen, by a growing proportion of its members, to be too rational, too well-planned, too bureaucratic, in short over-

1 It is illustrative of this transition that Huizinga's theory of play, with its bleak prognostications for a society which had abandoned the ludic principle, should be followed six years later by Morgenstern and von Neumann's *Theory of Games and Economic Behavior* (1944). Non-utilitarian, innovative play was thereby systematized into the 'theory of games', with ready application to the rationalization of problems of social, economic, and military strategy.

2 Erik Erikson stresses the use Hitler made of the prevalent scorn held by German youth for *Bürgerlichkeit*, for the well-ordered world of the 'mere citizen', the bourgeois (*Childhood and Society*, 1965, pp. 324–5). Similarly, a key component of the student unrest of the last decade has been its angry rebellion against the boredom of 'over-civilization'.

3 The West German reluctance in recent years to revalue the Deutschemark was rooted partly in an irrational fear traceable back to the savage inflation of the early twenties, which wiped out fortunes overnight.

4 This modern turn in gambling is in part an effect of affluence, and, in general, is not conducted with the desperate fanaticism of Dostoevksy's gambler. Nevertheless, it represents the search for some excitement to compensate for the chronic banality of much of modern life.

civilized, is going to experience to an increasing extent a return towards risky, more adventurous modes of social action, in the style of gambling.

The critique of the undialectical progress model

The Brothers Karamazov is epigraphed with the words:[1]

Verily, verily, I say unto you, Except a corn of wheat fall into the ground and die, it abideth alone: but if it die, it bringeth forth much fruit.

The theme that creation bears within itself its own destruction, and vice versa, is at the core of the anarcho-psychological position. It emanates from the conviction that the fall of man is irreparable. Such a recognition of original sin permits, at the best, the muted introspective optimism of St John, re-echoed in Goethe's 'Die and be reborn!', and taken up by Nietzsche and Dostoevsky. This optimism is that the dark forces which course in the substrata of human life can be overcome, if only momentarily, by facing them — in Nietzsche's language, by undergoing them. They may be transformed into an impetus for rebirth. An unambivalent notion of progress is precluded. The sense of the precariousness of human melioration is so acute that even the most utopian of the anarcho-psychologists, Dostoevsky, has the stranger who joins the perfectly harmonious community in which everyone is happy, in *The Dream of a Ridiculous Man*, inwardly driven to corrupt it.[2]

The notion of ambivalency frames the entire anarcho-psychological perspective. In the work of Nietzsche and Dostoevsky in particular, as later in that of Freud, love and hate, sadism and masochism, sanity and madness, projection and introjection, self-affirmation and self-denigration, lucidity and turbid silence, are respectively the reverse sides of the same thin coins. Christ is indicted by Nietzsche for bringing the 'good tidings', 'precisely that there are no longer any opposites'.[3]

In the specific context of economic life, consumption and destruction are correlates. The child gains as much pleasure, although of a different kind, from knocking down a house of playing cards, as he does from building it; we enjoy the eating of a sumptuous meal, as much as preparing it; it may even be the case that the planned obsolescence of durable commodities satisfies a need of the consumer to keep turning over his possessions, not only because he

---

1 John 12:24.
2 *The Dream of a Ridiculous Man* is included with *Notes from Underground*; p. 222 in particular.
3 *Antichrist* 32. The charge is, nevertheless, in itself unfair.

prefers novelty but because he gains satisfaction from exhausting objects as he uses them. Eating may be taken as a paradigm for the consumption process: enjoyment is the flame which lives off the matter it destroys. Again, the moment of rebirth is the moment of annihilation. *Wasting* is inherent in *consuming*, as is borne out by the German language, in which *verzehren* means either 'to consume' or 'to waste'.[1]

Anarcho-psychological theory emphasizes dichotomies between play and work, the superfluous and the necessary, and wasting or squandering and usefully consuming, in order to expose the inhibiting narrowness of liberal-rationalist categories. These categories deny the significance, in the sense both of value and actuality, of the former term in each of the dichotomies. The counter-claim is that gratifying human action defines itself conceptually as mediating the synthesis of each of these three pairs of opposites. The capitalist spirit is accordingly charged, in anticipation of a number of modern social critics, with wrecking the series of balances inherent in the processes of creation, or production, and consumption. To choose a domestic example, the plain and frugal meal of a family strongly endowed with the Protestant ethic embodies its own rigid stress on functionality: by guarding carefully against material wastage the family ensures emotional frugality—little wasted, little enjoyed, at least in an immediately hedonistic sense. The criticism is not directed at man's drive to keep himself adequately housed, clothed, and fed, but at a joyless, prosaic way of realizing this drive.

The ambivalencies at the centre of consumption and creation are particular cases of the dialectical nature of the human condition. For the remainder of this section Hegel, Dilthey, Nietzsche, Dostoevsky, Benjamin, and Adorno are taken as a collective representation of the dialectical critique of positivist habits of mind. On the question of liberal-rationalist methodology, anarcho-psychological and neo-Hegelian views run parallel. The critique hinges on the proposition that there exists a group of ultimately impenetrable, fundamental questions about human life, and that man is never more intensely and persistently interested than when he is seeking their answers. It is a truism that a question once answered loses most of its interest value; the dialectical perspective deepens the point, asserting that answerable questions are by their nature superficial, and evade pivotal issues. Man is abundantly interesting, implies this view, where his essence is opaque and interlaced with paradox. Moreover, it is precisely the precipitate of these paradoxes, the expression in consciousness of subliminal psychic conflicts—the dialectical ques-

---

1 The 'potlatch' celebration of the Kwakiutl Indians is a conspicuous example of the integration of consumption and waste in one ritual, which is of key social and religious significance to the community.

tions themselves—which form the molecular structure of a man's life. The dialectics of the Legend of the Grand Inquisitor, for example, haunted Dostoevsky; they run as a *leitmotif* through his works, which, in these terms, now read as a series of persistent, elliptical attempts to penetrate a few omnipresent paradoxes on ever new levels of differentiation.

This perspective, in contrast to, say, Piaget's psychology, is interested only in behaviour which is 'important' to the actor; that is, behaviour which is emotionally charged to the degree that it is either frequently recalled, reflected upon, or day-dreamed about, or causes anxiety such that memory of it is repressed—and if the memory ever returns to consciousness, it reawakens anxiety. Such behaviour, it is claimed, stimulates, and is stimulated by, emotional currents which are always criss-crossing; this behaviour and its emotional environment can be understood only through the employment of dialectical concepts. A corollary states that science which is less discriminating in the behaviour it chooses to investigate gains clarity and distinctness at the cost of confining itself to the trivial.

This view of life as being innately dialectical is the crucial point of departure for our psychology of *homo economicus*, for in his life-style is found its polar opposite. The economic model is a progress one, whether it is geared to the individual's acquisitive drive, or to a national pursuit of an increasing gross national product. It depends upon a positivistic attachment to a unique goal which can be worked towards without any necessary regression or contradiction developing. Unlike Hegel's progress model of history, which moves by stages, each containing its own logic of growth and decline, the economic model develops as the simple function of one money-variable over time, with a long-term trend which increases monotonically.

'Historical time' is a concept of critical importance for the Hegelian view; it takes on the erudite sense of time as phase, or cycle of significance in history, rather than a linear sequence of equivalent units. One year, such as 1789, may be more *significant* than an entire century, significant in the sense of Benjamin: 'History is the subject of a structure whose site is not homogeneous, empty time, but time filled by the presence of now'.[1] Moreover, the links between moments in history—the chronological term 'moment' is invested with a new and complex philosophical content—are so multi-dimensional as to prove impenetrable to value judgment.

It has become apparent that the dialectical and positivist minds are profoundly incompatible. The one reads the human condition as a net of unfolding contradictions, conflicting interactions, and even paradoxes, which can at the most be illuminated, never resolved.

[1] Benjamin, op. cit., p. 276.

Through thought, the universe of man comes to be understood as ever more complicated and problematical. The other views this condition as underpinned by a deep and universal structure of simple, logically connectible elements, in terms of which the meaning of its totality can be induced.

Nineteenth-century economic advancement vindicated its progress model, and bestowed on it the charisma of a self-fulfilling prophecy. Events over the last half-century have exposed the inadequacy of that same model as a representation of human possibility, and intimated the degree to which its goals incorporate distortions of human interest. Nevertheless, its force as ideology has proved resilient against its own deficiencies; today it still stands in the advanced industrial societies, if usually unstated, as the dominant conceptualization of social hope. It may be that the sophistication of any dialectical model, and the cautiousness with which it views possibilities for human progress, precludes wide transmissibility.

5 Conclusion

The formative period in the rise of anarcho-psychology, which had been initiated in 1844 with the publication of *Der Einzige*, came to a close in 1889 with Nietzsche's disintegration into madness. Our task has been merely to plot the genesis of the new philosophical perspective, but on the assumption that the past, because it is viewed under a searchlight directed from the present, provides immediate and relevant associations. We conclude by sketching what anarcho-psychology had achieved by 1889, mentioning some twentieth-century social theories which are in its debt, and assessing what has been the nature of *critique* from this perspective.

Anarcho-psychology transformed Feuerbach's materialist critique of theology and metaphysics into a psychological critique of ideology. It focussed on the individual psyche as the exclusive structuring of ultimate value, and isolated ideology as the primary social weapon for subjugating this unique entity to group norms and group practices. Ideology is a moral not an economic category: its roots lie in the history of religion and of man's struggle to reduce the burdens of original sin, not primarily in economic systems. Ideology establishes its own self-perpetuating vicious circle: by masking and distorting the individual's real interests it severs him from his own impulses towards enjoyment and realization, making him dependent *faute de mieux* on its impersonal hierarchy. In the wake of this psychological self-alienation, this repression of the unique Ego, this elimination of the category 'existence' in favour of essences, came the reactive emotions, hypocrisy, idealism, persecution, *homo economicus*, and, Nietzsche adds, culture. Anarcho-psychology conceptualized hope not in terms of economic progress, nor a more rational society, but in terms of the individual egoistically taking control of himself, liberating himself from the mists of ideology by

170

subjecting them to scrutiny, learning again how to play seriously, and how to exploit his own surplus energy for his own sake.

A critique of ideology which dismantles all but egocentric morality is quick to label objective or scientific knowledge as fictitious: just as there is no autonomous ethics, there is no knowledge independent of individual interests. In saying this, the anarcho-psychologists went further than Humean and Kantian epistemology and claimed that the pursuit of rationalist and positivist habits of mind has had two effects, both destructive of the human essence. First, this pursuit has worked in the service of moralistic ideologies, rationalizing distorted impulses as 'good', and at the same time has furthered the advance of technological-industrial society and its Crystal Palace. Second, it has cleared surrogate paths to knowledge, knowledge of a false, reduced self; while it thus gave man the semblance of control over himself and his environment, it turned him away from his true self, one whose logic is noumenal and dialectical, which can at best be viewed through a glass darkly.

The anarcho-psychological perspective tends towards irrationalism, and even undermines self-knowledge as ideology: even the structure which most intimately frames the private, noumenal ego is regarded as no more than a tentative, probationary convenience. Formal logic is replaced by paradoxical logic, that of Christ's anarchic reply to the Grand Inquisitor. At every turn the discussion controverts the liberal-rationalist assumption that the patterns of human behaviour are simple, that there is a certain economy of basic knowledge.

Anarcho-psychology confirms its individualist orientation in its social analysis, which it conducts in part as a comparison of different character-types. It focusses its critique of mid-nineteenth-century European society on the figure representative of the guiding aspirations and developments of the time: *homo economicus*. The figure of economic man serves both as the object of critique, as in the analysis of utilitarian and socialist philosophies, of the 'last man' and the 'gambler', and the negative against which to explicate a positive, as Stirner does in his redefinition of the economic categories of 'property' and 'possession'. Here are the first attempts at a psychological investigation of social and historical phenomena. *Homo economicus* is a figure of contemporary interest to us more than simply because he played a crucial historical role in the development of industrial society: just as the adult carries the imprint of his key childhood experiences, so mature industrial civilization carried traces of the psychic disposition which drove its formative phases.

Only in the decade after his breakdown in Turin were Nietzsche's hitherto neglected ideas to gain wide recognition; but, once the lid was opened, they immediately pervaded the centres of German culture, where for a time they exerted a dominant influence. The same period saw the renaissance of interest in Stirner. The decade of the 1890s was one of those widely considered to have created an 'intellectual revolution'—a period during which the inherited assumptions and prevalent structures of consciousness are revoked, and new ones emerge.[1] This decade was marked by a rapid intensification of imaginative activity on many diverse fronts; the mood of the time was one of experiment, change, and innovation. Hughes sums up this intellectual revolution as being characterized by a shift in interest from objectively verifiable phenomena to those which are subjective and only partly conscious:[2]

> Psychological process had replaced external reality as the most pressing topic for investigation. It was no longer what actually existed that seemed most important: it was what men thought existed. And what they felt on the unconscious level had become rather more interesting than what they had consciously rationalized.

The 1890s, however, are more accurately to be assessed as the decade in which the intellectual revolution which had already been pioneered, very much in isolation and generally without recognition, by such thinkers as Stirner, Dostoevsky, and Nietzsche, the anarcho-psychological revolution, took root over a wide spectrum of the radical consciousness of the time.[3] It inspired, in the words with which Hughes subtitles his chapter on this decade, 'the revolt against positivism', as it was emerging in literature and social theory.[4] By 1890, new ideas had germinated, owing to a complex of social and cultural factors which do not concern us here, to the point at which their growth had become self-supporting and could, to borrow a metaphor from economics, 'takeoff'.

[1] E.g. Talcott Parsons: *The Structure of Social Action*, 1968.
   H. Stuart Hughes: *Consciousness and Society*, 1967, in particular ch. 2.
[2] Hughes, op. cit., p. 66.
[3] There were a number of other influences at this time pointing in somewhat parallel directions; in the field of letters we should mention the significance of Paris, and, for example, the legacy of Baudelaire. We also note that the early work of Henri Bergson, whose irrationalist vitalism places him within these same philosophical bounds, cannot have been influenced by anarcho-psychology.
[4] In detailing the nature of this revolution and its central participants, Hughes understresses the role of socialist theory, and especially Marxism. Our own reappraisal of the decade is limited to the degree that the key change can be designated in terms of an awakening psychological consciousness. While to look at the literature of the time reinforces Hughes's emphasis, such a view is unbalanced—we note that a book titled *Consciousness and Society 1890–1930* does not mention class consciousness. An evaluation of the 1890s as a period in the development of socialist thought would stress *elaboration* and *consolidation*, rather than *revolution*.

To chart with confidence the influence of any body of ideas is impossible. We can at best note some of the areas in which its presence has been most acutely felt. The significance of anarcho-psychology after 1889 is no more marked than in the field of psycho-analysis and Freud's systematic elaboration of psychological insight. Its influence on sociological theory has necessarily proved more tenuous. But Simmel, Croce, and Sorel all confess their debt to Nietzsche. Pareto's late pessimism about the viability of democratic or socialist political systems, his scepticism about the possibility of systematic social science, presuppose the anarcho-psychological assault on liberal-rationalist theory. The case of Max Weber is more complex: but Weber is peculiarly akin to Nietzsche in his obsession with Kant's second question, What ought I to do? Both men achieve an unmatched deftness in writing about their central preoccupation, the problem of ultimate values.

We have pointed to the significance of anarcho-psychology for the existentialist tradition, in particular for Rilke, Heidegger, and Sartre. Shestov confessed that his mentors were Dostoevsky and Nietzsche. André Gide and Thomas Mann have been among a number of others in spelling out the debt that modern literature owes to these same two men.[1]

However, the question of influence is bound up with the more fundamental question of the nature of the anarcho-psychological *critique*. It was envisaged in planning this study that the intellectual forces would resolve themselves primarily into a direct dialectical conflict between anarcho-psychology and liberal-rationalism. In the period of genesis, 1840–90, this did not happen.

From the outset we recognized that three, not two, traditions were involved, and that the anarcho-psychological critique of liberal-rationalism would in part encompass, in part extend into, a critique of socialism. But the root of the problem as to what 'critique' in this study signifies does not lie here. For the argument did operate in terms of dialectical opposites in that anarcho-psychology portrayed socialist theory as an advanced development out of liberal-ration-alism, drawing its energy from the same materialist, positivist source. Nietzsche's analysis of the socialist emotion, compassion, as the ethical climax of the Christian-rationalist-democratic tradition exemplifies this dialectical model. (A similar habit of mind is em-ployed in reverse by Horkheimer and Adorno in their *Dialektik der Aufklärung* where Nietzsche is placed on a single path leading from the Enlightenment to modern fascism, as a key opponent of social-ism.) The one problem raised by this collapsing into one of two traditions, which from their own perspectives appear to be opposed,

[1] In particular, Gide's *Dostoïevsky* (1923) and Mann's 1948 essay, 'Nietzsches Philosophie im Lichte unserer Erfahrung' included in *Last Essays* (1959).

is revealed in the Dostoevskian defence of compassion. But the possibility that there might be a non-resentful type of compassion, one which could sustain a socialist ethic stripped of positivist-materialist tendencies, was taken up neither by the other anarcho-psychologists nor by followers of Marx; it remained the preserve of exponents of anarcho-syndicalism such as Proudhon.

The problem is rather this, that although the preconditions for a sustained and comprehensive debate between these dialectical opposites had been developed by 1890, the exchange did not fully take place until the twentieth century. The piers were fully constructed, but then left bridged by a merely tentative, flimsy structure. First, there was no liberal-rationalist reply to the anarcho-psychological thesis; the riposte came from Marx and Engels. Second, and crucially, the anarcho-psychological perspective did not itself come to firm grips with liberal-rationalism. The critique was initiated, fully implied, mounted through a series of barbed aphorisms, but, with the partial exception of Dostoevsky's *Notes from Underground*, never fully spelt out. The critique of socialism proved to be similarly intermittent.

The major explanation of this failure of execution is readily available. In the cases of Stirner and Nietzsche individualist, psychological anarchism is immediately incorporated into a mode of thinking which is personal, introspective, and which while often operating on alternative systems of belief and action does so only as a means of better grasping one dominant goal—the patterns of individual redemption. Stirner and Nietzsche are not primarily interested in critique as such, even as an objective exercise in using opposing theories against which to work out their own ideas. Their work is too egoistically compelled for them ever to employ the external world as more than the repository for a series of projections of their own psychological dilemmas. Their choice of phenomena from that world is governed by subjective criteria; objective social problems are of subordinate importance. Thus what stands most explicitly as critique in Nietzsche's late work is not a development from earlier interests but a return to two problems of enduring personal involvement for him, those of Wagner and of Christianity. *Der Antichrist*, to take one case, is not a response to a resuscitating public interest in the Christian religion; it is primarily a renewed attempt to resolve for himself the question of piety by a man who had lost his father, a Protestant pastor, at the age of four, who had himself been called 'the little pastor' at school, and who until middle-adolescence had wanted to follow in the footsteps of that father, whom he idealized.

However, the unashamedly subjective nature of the driving motive does not preclude the work of Stirner and Nietzsche from disclosing significant insights into the essence of European culture and society.

Thus, the thrust behind Stirner's work and its central concern with the concept of authority does derive from the author's own un-resolved and deeply personal conflict, but the resulting theory none the less contributes to the laying bare of a problem universal to mankind. This is not to deny the social factor: the issue of authority may be more acutely problematic for someone experiencing a highly paternalistic political system such as that to be found in nineteenth-century Prussia.

The nature of the critique levelled by Dostoevsky is not greatly different. *Notes from Underground* precedes the major novels. It provides his only concentrated attack on industrial civilization; thereafter he devotes himself to the more general ethical questions of what to do and how to live, choosing the more flexible medium of the novel.

The critique of Western capitalist society as a synthesis of ration-alist-positivist philosophy, technological progress, and the image of *homo economicus* remains only tentatively explicated until well into the twentieth century. The case for the critique is further strengthened after 1890, but still not realized, in the work of both Max Weber, with his sociology of the twin process of rationalization and disen-chantment, and Freud, with his psychological categories of the superego and over-civilization. When finally a sustained critique is levelled, by Horkheimer and Adorno in the *Dialektik der Aufklärung* (1944), it borrows from both Marxist and Freudian traditions, and partially implicates Nietzsche in the transition from the Enlighten-ment to fascism. It is also significant that Wilhelm Reich, who had earlier developed a more anarcho-psychological bias within the psychoanalytic movement, and accused Freud himself of being too rationalist, of driving sex into the head as D. H. Lawrence had put it, incorporated a Marxist social philosophy into his *Die Massen-psychologie des Faschimus* (1933).[1] However, the critiques presented since the Second World War have found less ambiguity in the relationships between the three social philosophies with which this study has been concerned.

Maybe it was only two world wars and the breakdown of European stability that made it possible for the Stirner-Nietzsche-Dostoevsky critique of rational-economic man to explode into the open, and into mass attitudes. This series of historical disasters, which undermined the nineteenth-century faith in human progress, provided the spark-ing condition for the liberal-rationalist riposte, and the association of irrationalist individualist philosophy with irrationalist mass move-ments. One example of the riposte was Bertrand Russell's attack on Nietzsche in his *History of Western Philosophy* (1946). A similarly inclined, but more historically comprehensive and systematic,

[1] W. Reich: *The Mass Psychology of Fascism*, 1946.

critique was levelled from an unambiguously socialist standpoint by Georg Lukács. His *Die Zerstörung der Vernunft* (1954) reproduces Marx's critique of Stirner as an updated assault on Nietzsche and his historical significance.

Maybe also the new levels of affluence which followed the Second World War provided a second condition, which finally made possible a sustained anarcho-psychological critique of rationalist *homo economicus*. Herbert Marcuse's *Eros and Civilization* (1955), whilst adapting some Marxist categories, develops a Freudian psychological orientation into an individualist anarchist affirmation of play, polymorphous perversity, joy, and self-expression as ultimate values. Marcuse's anarchist enthusiasms combine with a serious attempt to analyse the technological mechanics of advanced industrial society.

Two grave questions are raised by singling out Marcuse as a modern exponent of anarcho-psychology. First, it is probable that only Marcuse's background in the Marxist-oriented 'Frankfurt School' gave him the grounding and the interest to conduct social analysis which takes direct account of the laws of economic institutions. We are left with the suspicion that a pure devotee of anarcho-psychology would be constitutionally incapable of this.[1]

Secondly, serious doubts arise as to whether Marcuse's integration of Marxist economic analysis with anarcho-psychological values is in any significant sense successful. Indeed, the very indeterminateness of Marcuse's 'total argument' tends to confirm the sceptical hypothesis that a total social model synthesizing realistic economic analysis with ideals of individual fulfilment may not be possible in the context of advanced industrial society.

There have been other attempts, apart from Marcuse's, to advance with these tangled threads. The Freudian tradition through its delineation of anal-erotic character traits laid the ground for a psychological critique of *homo economicus* in terms of his infantile drive to play with money, to hoard and to invest 'filthy lucre'.[2] The critique was finally explicated by Norman Brown in his *Life against Death* (1959).

---

[1] The obvious example of an outstanding thinker who shares habits of mind with anarcho-psychology and who has avoided entering into sustained socio-economic analysis in any form is that of Heidegger: significantly, he has been the object of bitter attack from members of the Frankfurt School. Heidegger develops a dichotomy between meditative (*besinnliches*) and scientific (*wissenschaftliches*) thinking which he then uses to point out the inadequacy of the latter (e.g. 'Wissenschaft und Besinnung', *Vorträge und Aufsätze*, 1954).

[2] The key papers are: Freud: 'Character and Anal Erotism' (1908), *Collected Papers* II. Freud: 'On the Transformation of Instincts with special reference to Anal Erotism' (1916), ibid. Ernest Jones: 'Anal-Erotic Character Traits'

In the last five years the works of Marcuse and Brown have gained immense popularity throughout the Western world. This must indicate that they reach into the nerve fibre of both the severest anxieties and the profoundest hopes stirring beneath the skin of contemporary society. The same is the case for the works of R. D. Laing and Michel Foucault, who also employ psychological analysis in an anarchist repudiation of traditional definitions of rationality, of normality and madness.

The primary claim of this study has been as an essay in morals. Assessment of what has been achieved must be left to the reader. However, it is permissible to make some claims for what the work has achieved in the domain of intellectual history. The investigation has led, in spite of doubts about the true nature of the critique, to the spelling out of the central concerns of 'anarcho-psychology'. It has demonstrated the uniqueness and originality of what 'to think' signifies in this intellectual tradition, and shown the radical nature of the break from alternative models of social consciousness.

This study has also suggested some of the senses in which 'We have', as Hegel put it, 'in traversing the past only to do with what is *present*'. In this regard, that of relevancy, to the degree that the imaginative preoccupations of twentieth-century Europe have telescoped on to the individual, and interest has switched from the social realm to that of inner 'psychological man', we are all today heirs of the anarcho-psychological perspective, and its break-out from the Crystal Palace.

(1918), *Papers on Psycho-Analysis*, London, Tindall, 1948. Karl Abraham: 'Contributions to the Theory of the Anal Character' (1921), *Selected Papers*, London, Hogarth, 1927. Sandor Ferenczi also wrote several papers on this subject.

Bibliography

The method used to footnote the works of Stirner, Nietzsche, Dostoevsky, and Freud requires special explanation. Abbreviations used in the text are given below in parentheses.

STIRNER, MAX: *The Ego and His Own*, sel. and intro. JOHN CARROLL, London, Jonathan Cape, 1971 (*Ego*).

STIRNER, MAX: *The Ego and His Own*, trans. S. T. BYINGTON, London, Fifield, 1912 (*Ego* (1912)). Complete text.

STIRNER, MAX: *Kleinere Schriften*, ed. J. H. MACKAY, Treptow, Bernard Zack, 1914.

STIRNER, MAX: *Über Schulgesetze*, ed. ROLF ENGERT, Dresden, Verlag des dritten Reiches, 1920.

NIETZSCHE, FRIEDRICH: *Werke in drei Bänden*, ed. KARL SCHLECHTA, München, Hanser, 1954–6. Reference by the abbreviated title of the individual work and the section number of the excerpt.

English translations by WALTER KAUFMANN are used whenever available:

The Portable Nietzsche, New York, Viking Press, 1954 (includes *Zarathustra*, *Götzen-Dämmerung*, and *Antichrist*).

Beyond Good and Evil, New York, Random House, 1966 (*The Jenseits*).

On The Genealogy of Morals and *Ecce Homo*, New York, Random House, 1969 (*Genealogie*, *Ecce Homo*).

NIETZSCHE, FRIEDRICH: *The Will to Power*, ed. WALTER KAUFMANN, London, Weidenfeld & Nicolson, 1968 (*Wille*).

DOSTOEVSKY, FYODOR: *Crime and Punishment*, *The Idiot*, *The Devils*, and *The Brothers Karamazov* in the Penguin edition, translated by DAVID MAGARSHACK, 1951–8 (Harmondsworth and Baltimore). As neither the Garnett nor Magarshack translations have a decisive advantage, the more modern were chosen.

DOSTOEVSKY, FYODOR: *A Raw Youth*, trans. C. GARNETT, London, Heinemann, 1956.

DOSTOEVSKY, FYODOR: *The Gambler*, trans. J. COULSON, Harmondsworth and Baltimore, Penguin, 1966.

DOSTOEVSKY, FYODOR: *Notes from Underground*, trans. A. R. MACANDREW, New York, Signet, New American Library, 1961.

DOSTOEVSKY, FYODOR: *Summer Impressions*, trans. K. FITZLYON, London, John Calder, 1955.

FREUD, SIGMUND: Standard Edition of the *Complete Psychological Works*, 24 vols, ed. JAMES STRACHEY, London, Hogarth Press, 1953–66. Reference is to individual works, whenever available, published separately from the *Standard Edition* by the Hogarth Press.

FREUD, SIGMUND: *Collected Papers*, 5 vols, London, Hogarth Press, 1924–50.

FREUD, SIGMUND: *The Origins of Psycho-Analysis*, London, Imago Publishing, 1954.

ADORNO, THEODOR W.: *Minima Moralia*, Frankfurt, Suhrkamp, 1951.

ADORNO, THEODOR W.: 'Sociology and psychology', *New Left Review*, no. 46 (Nov.–Dec. 1967) and no. 47 (Jan.–Feb. 1968).

ALTHUSSER, LOUIS: *For Marx*, trans. B. BREWSTER, London, Allen Lane, 1969.

ANDLER, CHARLES: *Nietzsche, Sa Vie et sa pensée*, 6 vols, Paris, Bossard, 1928.

ANNENKOV, P. V.: *The Extraordinary Decade*, Chicago, Michigan University Press, 1968.

ARVON, HENRI: *Aux Sources de l'existentialisme: Max Stirner*, Paris, Presses Universitaires de France, 1954.

AVINERI, SHLOMO: *The Social and Political Thought of Karl Marx*, Cambridge and New York, Cambridge University Press, 1968.

BENJAMIN, WALTER: *Illuminationen*, Frankfurt, Suhrkamp, 1961.

BENTHAM, JEREMY: *An Introduction to the Principles of Morals and Legislation*, London, Oxford University Press, 1907.

BERDYAEV, NICHOLAS: *Dostoevsky*, New York, Meridian, World Publishing Co., 1957.

BERNARD, CLAUDE: *An Introduction to the Study of Experimental Medicine*, trans. H. C. GREENE, London, Abelard Schuman, 1927.

BERNOULLI, C. A.: *Franz Overbeck und Friedrich Nietzsche: eine Freundschaft*, 2 vols, Jena, Diederichs, 1908.

BOWLBY, JOHN: *Attachment*, Harmondsworth, Penguin, 1969.

BRAZILL, WILLIAM J.: *The Young Hegelians*, Newhaven, Yale University Press, 1970.

BROWN, NORMAN O.: *Life against Death*, London, Sphere, 1968 (First edition London, Routledge & Kegan Paul, 1959).

BUBER, MARTIN: *Between Man and Man*, trans. R. GREGOR SMITH, London, Fontana, 1961.

CAMERON, RONDO E.: *France and the Economic Development of Europe, 1800–1914*, Princeton University Press, 1961.

CAMUS, ALBERT: *L'Homme révolté*, Paris, Gallimard, 1951.

CLAYTON, GEORGE and OSBORN, W. T.: *Insurance Company Investment*, London, Allen & Unwin, 1965.

CONDORCET: *The Progress of the Human Mind*, trans. June Barraclough, London, Weidenfeld & Nicolson, 1955.

DAHRENDORF, RALF: *Essays in the Theory of Society*, London, Routledge & Kegan Paul, 1968.

BIBLIOGRAPHY

DANTO, ARTHUR C.: *Nietzsche as Philosopher*, New York, Macmillan, 1965.

DURKHEIM, ÉMILE: *Suicide*, trans. J. A. SPAULDING and G. SIMPSON, London, Routledge & Kegan Paul, 1952.

EHRENZWEIG, ANTON: *The Hidden Order of Art*, London, Paladin, 1970.

ELIADE, MIRCEA: *The Myth of the Eternal Return*, London, Routledge & Kegan Paul, 1955.

ERIKSON, ERIK H.: *Childhood and Society*, Harmondsworth, Penguin, 1965.

FAIRBAIRN, W. R. D.: *Psychoanalytic Studies of the Personality*, London, Tavistock, 1952.

FEUER, LUDWIG S.: 'Karl Marx and the promethean complex', *Encounter*, vol. 31, no. 6 (Dec. 1968).

FEUERBACH, LUDWIG: *The Essence of Christianity*, trans. GEORGE ELIOT, New York, Harper, 1957.

FOURIER, CHARLES: *Oeuvres complètes*, 12 vols, Paris, Éditions Anthropos, 1966–8.

FOURIER, CHARLES: *Selections from the Works of Fourier*, trans JULIA FRANKLIN, London, Swan Sonnenschein, 1901.

GALBRAITH, J. K.: *The Affluent Society*, London, Hamilton, 1958.

GIDE, A.: *Dostoïevsky*, Paris, Plon, 1923.

GIDE, A.: *L'Immoraliste*, Paris, Mercure, 1902.

GOFFMAN, ERVING: *Stigma*, Harmondsworth, Penguin, 1968.

GOMBRICH, E. H.: *Art and Illusion*, London, Phaidon Press, 3rd edition, 1968.

GOMBRICH, E. H.: *In Search of Cultural History*, London and New York, Oxford University Press, 1969.

GRODDECK, GEORG: *The Book of the It*, London, Vision Press, 1950.

HABERMAS, JÜRGEN: *Knowledge and Human Interests*, trans. J. J. SHAPIRO, London, Heinemann, 1972.

HABERMAS, JÜRGEN (ed.): *Friedrich Nietzsche. Erkenntnistheoretischen Schriften*, Frankfurt, Suhrkamp, 1968.

HALÉVY, ELIE: *The Growth of Philosophic Radicalism*, trans. MARY MORRIS, London, Faber, 1934.

HARTMANN, EDUARD VON: *Philosophie des Unbewussten*, Berlin, Duncker, 1869.

HEGEL, G. W. F.: *The Phenomenology of Mind*, trans. J. B. BAILLIE, London, Allen & Unwin, 1949.

HEGEL, G. W. F.: *The Philosophy of History*, trans. J. SIBREE, New York, Dover Books, 1956.

HEGEL, G. W. F.: *The Science of Logic*, trans. A. MILLER, London, Allen & Unwin, 1969.

HEIDEGGER, MARTIN: *Being and Time*, trans. J. MACQUARRIE and E. ROBINSON, London, SCM Press, 1962.

HEIDEGGER, MARTIN: *Nietzsche*, 2 vols, Pfullingen, Neske, 1961.

HELMS, HANS G.: *Die Ideologie der anonymen Gesellschaft*, Cologne, M. du Mont Schauberg, 1966.

HIMMELFARB, GERTRUDE: *Victorian Minds*, London, Weidenfeld & Nicolson, 1968.

HOBSBAWM, E. J.: *The Age of Revolution*, New York, Mentor, 1962.

HOBSBAWM, E. J.: *Industry and Empire*, Harmondsworth and Baltimore, Penguin, 1969.

HOLLINGDALE, R. J.: *Nietzsche: the Man and His Philosophy*, London, Routledge & Kegan Paul, and Baton Rouge, Louisiana State University Press, 1965.

HOOK, SIDNEY: *From Hegel to Marx*, New York, Humanities Press, 1950.

HORKHEIMER, MAX, and ADORNO, T. W.: *Dialektik der Aufklärung*, Frankfurt, Fisher, 1969 (First edition, 1944).

HUGHES, H. STUART: *Consciousness and Society*, London, MacGibbon and Kee, 1967.

HUIZINGA, J.: *Homo Ludens*, London, Routledge & Kegan Paul, 1949.

IVANOV, V.: *Freedom and the Tragic Life: a Study in Dostoevsky*, London, Harvill Press, 1952.

JARVIE, I. C. and AGASSI, J.: 'The Problem of the Rationality of Magic', in *Rationality*, ed. B. R. WILSON, Oxford, Blackwell, 1970.

JASPERS, KARL: *Nietzsche*, trans. C. F. WALLRAFF and F. J. SCHMITZ, Arizona University Press, 1965.

JOLL, JAMES: *The Anarchists*, London, Eyre & Spottiswoode, 1964.

JUNG, C. G.: *Collected Works*, eds. READ, FORHAM and ADLER, vol. 16 *The Practice of Psychotherapy*, trans. R. F. C. HULL, 2nd edn, London, Routledge & Kegan Paul, and New York, Bollingen Foundation, 1966.

JUNG, C. G.: *Psychological Types; or, The Psychology of Individuation*, trans. H. GODWIN BAYNES, London, Kegan Paul, 1923.

KAUFMANN, WALTER: *Hegel*, London, Weidenfeld & Nicolson, 1966.

KAUFMANN, WALTER: *Nietzsche, Philosopher, Psychologist, Antichrist*, Cleveland, Meridian, World Publishing Co., 1956.

KAUFMANN, WALTER (ed.): *Existentialism from Dostoevsky to Sartre*, Cleveland, Meridian, World Publishing Co., 1956.

KEYNES, JOHN MAYNARD: *The General Theory of Employment, Interest and Money*, London, Macmillan, 1936.

KLEIN, MELANIE: *The Psycho-Analysis of Children*, London, Hogarth Press, 1932.

KNIGHT, F. H.: *Risk, Uncertainty and Profit*, Boston, Houghton Mifflin, 1921.

KOESTLER, ARTHUR: 'Literature and the law of diminishing returns', *Encounter*, vol. 34, no. 5 (May 1970).

KOLAKOWSKI, LESZEK: 'Vom Sinn der Tradition', *Merkur*, vol. 23, no. 12 (Dec. 1969).

KUHN, THOMAS S.: *The Structure of Scientific Revolutions*, University of Chicago Press, 1970.

LANGER, SUSANNE K.: *Philosophy in a New Key*, Cambridge, Mass., Harvard University Press, 1957.

LEAVIS, F. R.: *Mill on Bentham and Coleridge*, London, Chatto & Windus, 1967.

LICHTHEIM, GEORGE: 'From Marx to Hegel', *TriQuarterly*, no. 12 (Spring 1968).

LICHTHEIM, GEORGE: *Marxism, An Historical and Critical Study*, London, Routledge & Kegan Paul, 1964.

LÖWITH, KARL: *From Hegel to Nietzsche*, trans. D. E. GREEN, London, Constable, 1965.

DE LUBAC, HENRI: *The Drama of Atheist Humanism*, New York, World Publishing Co., 1963

LUKÁCS, GEORG: *Die Zerstörung der Vernunft, Werke* vol. 9, Neuwied am Rhein, Luchterhand, 1962 (First edition 1954).

MACKAY, JOHN HENRY: *Max Stirner: sein Leben und sein Werk*, Berlin, Schuster & Loeffler, 1898.

MCLELLAN, DAVID: 'Marx and the missing link', *Encounter*, vol. 35, no. 5 (Nov. 1970).

MCLELLAN, DAVID: *The Young Hegelians and Karl Marx*, London, Macmillan, 1969.

MAGARSHACK, DAVID: *Dostoevsky: A Life*, London, Secker & Warburg, 1963.

MANN, THOMAS: *Last Essays*, trans. R. and C. WINSTON, New York, Knopf, 1959.

MANN, THOMAS: *Betrachtungen eines Unpolitischen*, Berlin, Fischer, 1918.

MANUEL, FRANK: *The Prophets of Paris*, Cambridge, Mass., Harvard University Press, 1962.

MARCUSE, HERBERT: *Eros and Civilization*, London, Sphere, 1968 (First edition Boston, Mass., Beacon Press, 1955).

MARCUSE, HERBERT: *Reason and Revolution*, London, Routledge & Kegan Paul, 1955.

MARX, KARL: *Capital*, trans. E. and C. PAUL, London, Dent, 1933.

MARX, KARL: *The Economic and Philosophic Manuscripts of 1844*, trans. M. MILLIGAN, ed. D. J. STRUIK, New York, International Publishing Company, 1965.

MARX, KARL, and ENGELS, FRIEDRICH: *The German Ideology*, trans. C. DUTT *et al.* (Russian edited), London, Lawrence & Wishart, 1965.

MARX, KARL, and ENGELS, FRIEDRICH: *The Holy Family*, Moscow, 1956.

MARX, KARL, and ENGELS, FRIEDRICH: *Selected Works* (Russian edited), London, Lawrence & Wishart, 1968.

MARX, KARL, and ENGELS, FRIEDRICH: *Werke*, 39 vols, Berlin, Dietz, 1956–.

MEAD, GEORGE HERBERT: *Mind, Self and Society*, Chicago University Press, 1967.

MIRSKY, D. S.: *A History of Russian Literature*, London, Routledge & Kegan Paul, 1949.

MONOD, JACQUES: *Le Hasard et la nécessité*, Paris, Seuil, 1970.

MORGENSTERN, O., and VON NEUMANN, J.: *Theory of Games and Economic Behavior*, Princeton University Press, 1944.

MUMFORD, LEWIS: *The Myth of the Machine*, London, Secker & Warburg, 1967.

OEHLER, MAX: *Nietzsches Bibliothek*, Weimar, 1942.

OEHLER, RICHARD: *Nietzsche-Register*, Stuttgart, Kröner, 1943.

PARSONS, TALCOTT: *The Structure of Social Action*, New York, Free Press, 1968.

PARSONS, TALCOTT (ed.): *Max Weber: The Theory of Social and Economic Organizations*, New York, Free Press, 1964.

PATERSON, R. W. K.: *The Nihilistic Egoist, Max Stirner*, London, Oxford University Press, 1971.

PLAMENATZ, JOHN: *Man and Society*, 2 vols, London, Longman, 1963.

POLLARD, SIDNEY: *The Idea of Progress*, London, New Thinker's Library, 1968.

REICH, W.: *The Mass Psychology of Fascism*, 3rd revised and enlarged edition, trans. T. P. WOLFE, New York, Orgone Institute Press, 1946.

RIEFF, PHILIP: *Freud: the Mind of the Moralist*, London, Gollancz, 1960.

RIEFF, PHILIP: *The Triumph of the Therapeutic: Uses of Faith after Freud*, London, Chatto & Windus, 1966.

RIESMAN, DAVID: *The Lonely Crowd*, Newhaven, Yale University Press, 1950.

ROAZEN, PAUL: *Freud: Political and Social Thought*, London, Hogarth Press, 1969.

RÓHEIM, GÉZÁ: *The Origin and Function of Culture*, New York, Nervous and Mental Diseases Monographs, 1943.

RUNCIMAN, W. G.: *Social Science and Political Theory*, Cambridge and New York, Cambridge University Press, 1963.

RUSSELL, BERTRAND: *Philosophical Essays*, London, Longman, 1910.

RUSSELL, JOHN: *Max Ernst*, London, Thames & Hudson, 1967.

SARTRE, JEAN-PAUL: *Being and Nothingness*, trans. H. E. BARNES, London, Methuen, 1969.

SCHELER, MAX: *Zur Phänomenologie und Theorie der Sympathiegefühle und von Liebe und Hass*, Halle, Niemeyer, 1913.

SHESTOV, LEV: *All Things are Possible*, London, McBride, 1920.

SHESTOV, LEV: *Anton Tcheckov And Other Essays*, trans. S. KOTELIANSKY and J. M. MURRAY, London, Maunsel, 1961.

SHESTOV, LEV: *Athens and Jerusalem*, ed. BERNARD MARTIN, Ohio University Press, 1968.

SHESTOV, LEV: 'Dostoevsky and Nietzsche: The Philosophy of Tragedy', included in *Essays in Russian Literature*, ed. S. E. ROBERTS, Ohio University Press, 1968.

SHESTOV, LEV: *In Job's Balances*, trans. C. COVENTRY and A. C. MACARTNEY, London, Dent, 1932.

SHONFIELD, ANDREW: *Modern Capitalism*, London, 1965, and New York, 1969, Oxford University Press.

SIMMEL, GEORG: *The Sociology of Georg Simmel*, ed. K. H. WOLFF, New York, Free Press, 1964.

SMILES, SAMUEL: *Self-Help*, London, Sphere, 1968.

SMITH, ADAM: *The Wealth of Nations*, London, Dent (Everyman), 1910.

SOREL, GEORGES: *Reflections on Violence*, New York, Collier, Macmillan, 1961.

SPENGLER, OSWALD: *The Decline of the West*, trans. C. F. ATKINSON, London, Allen & Unwin, 1932.

STEINER, GEORGE: *Tolstoy or Dostoevsky*, Harmondsworth, Penguin, 1967.

TAWNEY, R. H.: *Religion and the Rise of Capitalism*, London, Murray, 1926.

TERRAS, VICTOR: *The Young Dostoevsky (1846–1849)*, The Hague, Mouton, 1969.

THOMPSON, E. P.: *The Making of the English Working Class*, Harmondsworth, Penguin, 1968.

TUCKER, ROBERT: *Philosophy and Myth in Karl Marx*, Cambridge University Press, 1961.

VEBLEN, THORSTEIN: *The Theory of the Leisure Class*, New York, Macmillan, 1899.

WEBER, MAX: *From Max Weber: Essays in Sociology*, ed. H. H. GERTH and C. WRIGHT MILLS, London, Routledge & Kegan Paul, 1948.

WEBER, MAX: *The Methodology of the Social Sciences*, ed. E. A. SHILS and H. A. FINCH, Chicago, Free Press, 1949.

WEBER, MAX: *The Protestant Ethic and the Spirit of Capitalism*, London, Allen & Unwin, 1930.

WELLEK, RENÉ (ed.): *Dostoevsky*, Englewood Cliffs, Prentice-Hall, 1962.

WOODCOCK, GEORGE: *Anarchism*, Harmondsworth, Penguin, 1963.

Name index

Abraham, Karl, 158, 177
Adorno, T. W., 38, 107, 113, 167, 173, 175
Agassi, J., 150
Althusser, Louis, 61, 63–4, 66, 82
Annenkov, P. V., 30
Aristotle, 43, 104
Arvon, Henri, 19, 47, 58, 63
Avineri, Shlomo, 61, 65, 73, 78

Babbage, Charles, 9
Bacon, Francis, 107
Bakunin, Michael, 16, 19
Baudelaire, Charles, 95, 172
Bauer, Bruno, 18, 60, 63, 65
Bauer, Edgar, 67
Belinsky, V. G., 30
Benda, Julien, 23
Benjamin, Walter, 3, 167, 168
Bentham, Jeremy, 6–11, 13, 22, 26, 33, 36, 45, 51, 73, 81, 97, 98, 106, 107, 118, 137, 138, 142, 143, 147, 152
Berdyaev, Nicholas, 111
Bergson, Henri, 108, 172
Berkeley, George, 102
Bernard, Claude, 114–18
Bismarck, 47
Blake, William, 16, 151
Botticelli, Sandro, 137
Bowlby, John, 55–6
Brandes, George, 97
Brazill, W. J., 18, 32, 47, 105

Bruegel, Pieter, 119
Briggs, Asa, 13
Brown, Norman O., 60, 139, 176, 177
Buber, Martin, 55

Cabet, 152
Cameron, R. E., 163
Camus, Albert, 44, 53
Carroll, John, 15, 16, 25, 34, 36, 47, 48, 51, 52, 53, 99, 107, 138
Cervantes, Miguel de, 67
Clayton, G., 161, 162
Comte, Auguste, 12, 14, 81, 107, 118
Condillac, Etienne, 6
Condorcet, Marie-Jean, 6, 10, 12
Copernicus, 97
Croce, Benedetto, 173

Dahrendorf, Ralf, 49
Danto, Arthur C., 40, 102, 108, 132
Darwin, Charles, 11, 12, 71, 73, 97, 106, 111, 125
Demosthenes, 78
Descartes, René, 40, 106, 107, 120
Dickens, Charles, 33
Dilthey, Wilhelm, 4, 45, 167
Dostoevsky, Fyodor, 2, 14, 15, 16, 21, 30, 32, 42, 45, 61, 71, 79, 81, 101, 108, 111–18, 119, 120, 121, 122, 123, 130, 131, 132, 134, 136,

185

International Library of Sociology

Edited by
John Rex
University of Warwick

Founded by
Karl Mannheim

as The International Library of Sociology
and Social Reconstruction

*This Catalogue also contains other Social Science
series published by Routledge*

Routledge & Kegan Paul   London and Boston

68-74 Carter Lane London EC4V 5EL
9 Park Street Boston Mass 02108

Contents

● *Books so marked are available in paperback*
All books are in Metric Demy 8vo format (216 × 138mm approx.)

GENERAL SOCIOLOGY

Belshaw, Cyril. The Conditions of Social Performance. *An Exploratory Theory. 144 pp.*

Brown, Robert. Explanation in Social Science. *208 pp.*

● Rules and Laws in Sociology.

Cain, Maureen E. Society and the Policeman's Role. *About 300 pp.*

Gibson, Quentin. The Logic of Social Enquiry. *240 pp.*

Gurvitch, Georges. Sociology of Law. *Preface by Roscoe Pound. 264 pp.*

Homans, George C. Sentiments and Activities: *Essays in Social Science. 336 pp.*

Johnson, Harry M. Sociology: *a Systematic Introduction. Foreword by Robert K. Merton. 710 pp.*

Mannheim, Karl. Essays on Sociology and Social Psychology. *Edited by Paul Keckskemeti. With Editorial Note by Adolph Lowe. 344 pp.*

Systematic Sociology: *An Introduction to the Study of Society. Edited by J. S. Erös and Professor W. A. C. Stewart. 220 pp.*

Martindale, Don. The Nature and Types of Sociological Theory. *292 pp.*

● **Maus, Heinz.** A Short History of Sociology. *234 pp.*

Mey, Harald. Field-Theory. *A Study of its Application in the Social Sciences. 352 pp.*

Myrdal, Gunnar. Value in Social Theory: *A Collection of Essays on Methodology. Edited by Paul Streeten. 332 pp.*

Ogburn, William F., and **Nimkoff, Meyer F.** A Handbook of Sociology. *Preface by Karl Mannheim. 656 pp. 46 figures. 35 tables.*

Parsons, Talcott, and **Smelser, Neil J.** Economy and Society: *A Study in the Integration of Economic and Social Theory. 362 pp.*

● **Rex, John.** Key Problems of Sociological Theory. *220 pp.*

Urry, John. Reference Groups and the Theory of Revolution.

FOREIGN CLASSICS OF SOCIOLOGY

● **Durkheim, Emile.** Suicide. *A Study in Sociology. Edited and with an Introduction by George Simpson. 404 pp.*

Professional Ethics and Civic Morals. *Translated by Cornelia Brookfield. 288 pp.*

● **Gerth, H. H.,** and **Mills, C. Wright.** From Max Weber: *Essays in Sociology. 502 pp.*

Tönnies, Ferdinand. Community and Association. *(Gemeinschaft und Gesellschaft.) Translated and Supplemented by Charles P. Loomis. Foreword by Pitirim A. Sorokin. 334 pp.*

SOCIAL STRUCTURE

Andreski, Stanislav. Military Organization and Society. *Foreword by Professor A. R. Radcliffe-Brown. 226 pp. 1 folder.*

Coontz, Sydney H. Population Theories and the Economic Interpretation. *202 pp.*

Coser, Lewis. The Functions of Social Conflict. *204 pp.*

Dickie-Clark, H. F. Marginal Situation: *A Sociological Study of a Coloured Group. 240 pp. 11 tables.*

Glass, D. V. (Ed.). Social Mobility in Britain. *Contributions by J. Berent, T. Bottomore, R. C. Chambers, J. Floud, D. V. Glass, J. R. Hall, H. T. Himmelweit, R. K. Kelsall, F. M. Martin, C. A. Moser, R. Mukherjee, and W. Ziegel. 420 pp.*

Glaser, Barney, and **Strauss, Anselm L.** Status Passage. *A Formal Theory. 208 pp.*

Jones, Garth N. Planned Organizational Change: *An Exploratory Study Using an Empirical Approach. 268 pp.*

Kelsall, R. K. Higher Civil Servants in Britain: *From 1870 to the Present Day. 268 pp. 31 tables.*

König, René. The Community. *232 pp. Illustrated.*

● **Lawton, Denis.** Social Class, Language and Education. *192 pp.*

McLeish, John. The Theory of Social Change: *Four Views Considered. 128 pp.*

Marsh, David C. The Changing Social Structure of England and Wales, 1871-1961. *288 pp.*

Mouzelis, Nicos. Organization and Bureaucracy. *An Analysis of Modern Theories. 240 pp.*

Mulkay, M. J. Functionalism, Exchange and Theoretical Strategy. *272 pp.*

Ossowski, Stanislaw. Class Structure in the Social Consciousness. *210 pp.*

SOCIOLOGY AND POLITICS

Hertz, Frederick. Nationality in History and Politics: *A Psychology and Sociology of National Sentiment and Nationalism. 432 pp.*

Kornhauser, William. The Politics of Mass Society. *272 pp. 20 tables.*

Laidler, Harry W. History of Socialism. *Social-Economic Movements: An Historical and Comparative Survey of Socialism, Communism, Co-operation, Utopianism; and other Systems of Reform and Reconstruction. 992 pp.*

Mannheim, Karl. Freedom, Power and Democratic Planning. *Edited by Hans Gerth and Ernest K. Bramstedt. 424 pp.*

Mansur, Fatma. Process of Independence. *Foreword by A. H. Hanson. 208 pp.*

Martin, David A. Pacificism: *an Historical and Sociological Study. 262 pp.*

Myrdal, Gunnar. The Political Element in the Development of Economic Theory. *Translated from the German by Paul Streeten. 282 pp.*

Wootton, Graham. Workers, Unions and the State. *188 pp.*

FOREIGN AFFAIRS: THEIR SOCIAL, POLITICAL AND ECONOMIC FOUNDATIONS

Mayer, J. P. Political Thought in France from the Revolution to the Fifth Republic. *164 pp.*

CRIMINOLOGY

Ancel, Marc. Social Defence: *A Modern Approach to Criminal Problems. Foreword by Leon Radzinowicz. 240 pp.*

Cloward, Richard A., and **Ohlin, Lloyd E.** Delinquency and Opportunity: *A Theory of Delinquent Gangs. 248 pp.*

Downes, David M. The Delinquent Solution. *A Study in Subcultural Theory. 296 pp.*

Dunlop, A. B., and **McCabe, S.** Young Men in Detention Centres. *192 pp.*

Friedlander, Kate. The Psycho-Analytical Approach to Juvenile Delinquency: *Theory, Case Studies, Treatment. 320 pp.*

Glueck, Sheldon, and **Eleanor.** Family Environment and Delinquency. *With the statistical assistance of Rose W. Kneznek. 340 pp.*

Lopez-Rey, Manuel. Crime. *An Analytical Appraisal. 288 pp.*

Mannheim, Hermann. Comparative Criminology: *a Text Book. Two volumes. 442 pp. and 380 pp.*

Morris, Terence. The Criminal Area: *A Study in Social Ecology. Foreword by Hermann Mannheim. 232 pp. 25 tables. 4 maps.*

● **Taylor, Ian, Walton, Paul,** and **Young, Jock.** The New Criminology. *For a Social Theory of Deviance.*

SOCIAL PSYCHOLOGY

Bagley, Christopher. The Social Psychology of the Epileptic Child. *320 pp.*

Barbu, Zevedei. Problems of Historical Psychology. *248 pp.*

Blackburn, Julian. Psychology and the Social Pattern. *184 pp.*

● **Brittan, Arthur.** Meanings and Situations. *224 pp.*

● **Fleming, C. M.** Adolescence: Its Social Psychology. *With an Introduction to recent findings from the fields of Anthropology, Physiology, Medicine, Psychometrics and Sociometry. 288 pp.*

●   The Social Psychology of Education: *An Introduction and Guide to Its Study. 136 pp.*

Homans, George C. The Human Group. *Foreword by Bernard DeVoto. Introduction by Robert K. Merton. 526 pp.*

  Social Behaviour: *its Elementary Forms. 416 pp.*

Klein, Josephine. The Study of Groups. *226 pp. 31 figures. 5 tables.*

Linton, Ralph. The Cultural Background of Personality. *132 pp.*

Mayo, Elton. The Social Problems of an Industrial Civilization. *With an appendix on the Political Problem. 180 pp.*

Ottaway, A. K. C. Learning Through Group Experience. *176 pp.*

Ridder, J. C. de. The Personality of the Urban African in South Africa. *A Thematic Apperception Test Study. 196 pp. 12 plates.*

● **Rose, Arnold M.** (Ed.). Human Behaviour and Social Processes: *an Interactionist Approach. Contributions by Arnold M. Rose, Ralph H. Turner, Anselm Strauss, Everett C. Hughes, E. Franklin Frazier, Howard S. Becker, et al. 696 pp.*

Smelser, Neil J. Theory of Collective Behaviour. *448 pp.*
Stephenson, Geoffrey M. The Development of Conscience. *128 pp.*
Young, Kimball. Handbook of Social Psychology. *658 pp. 16 figures. 10 tables.*

SOCIOLOGY OF THE FAMILY

Banks, J. A. Prosperity and Parenthood: *A Study of Family Planning among The Victorian Middle Classes. 262 pp.*
Bell, Colin R. Middle Class Families: *Social and Geographical Mobility. 224 pp.*
Burton, Lindy. Vulnerable Children. *272 pp.*
Gavron, Hannah. The Captive Wife: *Conflicts of Household Mothers. 190 pp.*
George, Victor, and **Wilding, Paul.** Motherless Families. *220 pp.*
Klein, Josephine. Samples from English Cultures.
   1. Three Preliminary Studies and Aspects of Adult Life in England. *447 pp.*
   2. Child-Rearing Practices and Index. *247 pp.*
Klein, Viola. Britain's Married Women Workers. *180 pp.*
   The Feminine Character. *History of an Ideology. 244 pp.*
McWhinnie, Alexina M. Adopted Children. *How They Grow Up. 304 pp.*
Myrdal, Alva, and **Klein, Viola.** Women's Two Roles: *Home and Work. 238 pp. 27 tables.*
Parsons, Talcott, and **Bales, Robert F.** Family: Socialization and Interaction Process. *In collaboration with James Olds, Morris Zelditch and Philip E. Slater. 456 pp. 50 figures and tables.*

SOCIAL SERVICES

Bastide, Roger. The Sociology of Mental Disorder. *Translated from the French by Jean McNeil. 260 pp.*
Carlebach, Julius. Caring For Children in Trouble. *266 pp.*
Forder, R. A. (Ed.). Penelope Hall's Social Services of England and Wales. *352 pp.*
George, Victor. Foster Care. *Theory and Practice. 234 pp.*
   Social Security: *Beveridge and After. 258 pp.*
● **Goetschius, George W.** Working with Community Groups. *256 pp.*
Goetschius, George W., and **Tash, Joan.** Working with Unattached Youth. *416 pp.*
Hall, M. P., and **Howes, I. V.** The Church in Social Work. *A Study of Moral Welfare Work undertaken by the Church of England. 320 pp.*
Heywood, Jean S. Children in Care: *the Development of the Service for the Deprived Child. 264 pp.*
Hoenig, J., and **Hamilton, Marian W.** The De-Segration of the Mentally Ill. *284 pp.*
Jones, Kathleen. Mental Health and Social Policy, 1845-1959. *264 pp.*

King, Roy D., Raynes, Norma V., and **Tizard, Jack.** Patterns of Residential Care. *356 pp.*

Leigh, John. Young People and Leisure. *256 pp.*

Morris, Mary. Voluntary Work and the Welfare State. *300 pp.*

Morris, Pauline. Put Away: *A Sociological Study of Institutions for the Mentally Retarded. 364 pp.*

Nokes, P. L. The Professional Task in Welfare Practice. *152 pp.*

Timms, Noel. Psychiatric Social Work in Great Britain (1939-1962). *280 pp.*

● Social Casework: *Principles and Practice. 256 pp.*

Young, A. F., and **Ashton, E. T.** British Social Work in the Nineteenth Century. *288 pp.*

Young, A. F. Social Services in British Industry. *272 pp.*

SOCIOLOGY OF EDUCATION

Banks, Olive. Parity and Prestige in English Secondary Education: a Study in Educational Sociology. *272 pp.*

Bentwich, Joseph. Education in Israel. *224 pp. 8 pp. plates.*

● **Blyth, W. A. L.** English Primary Education. *A Sociological Description.*
   1. Schools. *232 pp.*
   2. Background. *168 pp.*

Collier, K. G. The Social Purposes of Education: *Personal and Social Values in Education. 268 pp.*

Dale, R. R., and **Griffith, S.** Down Stream: *Failure in the Grammar School. 108 pp.*

Dore, R. P. Education in Tokugawa Japan. *356 pp. 9 pp. plates*

Evans, K. M. Sociometry and Education. *158 pp.*

Foster, P. J. Education and Social Change in Ghana. *336 pp. 3 maps.*

Fraser, W. R. Education and Society in Modern France. *150 pp.*

Grace, Gerald R. Role Conflict and the Teacher. *About 200 pp.*

Hans, Nicholas. New Trends in Education in the Eighteenth Century. *278 pp. 19 tables.*

● Comparative Education: *A Study of Educational Factors and Traditions. 360 pp.*

Hargreaves, David. Interpersonal Relations and Education. *432 pp.*

● Social Relations in a Secondary School. *240 pp.*

Holmes, Brian. Problems in Education. *A Comparative Approach. 336 pp.*

King, Ronald. Values and Involvement in a Grammar School. *164 pp.*

School Organization and Pupil Involvement. *A Study of Secondary Schools.*

● **Mannheim, Karl,** and **Stewart, W. A. C.** An Introduction to the Sociology of Education. *206 pp.*

Morris, Raymond N. The Sixth Form and College Entrance. *231 pp.*

● **Musgrove, F.** Youth and the Social Order. *176 pp.*

● **Ottaway, A. K. C.** Education and Society: An Introduction to the Sociology of Education. *With an Introduction by W. O. Lester Smith. 212 pp.*

Peers, Robert. Adult Education: *A Comparative Study. 398 pp.*

Pritchard, D. G. Education and the Handicapped: *1760 to 1960. 258 pp.*
Richardson, Helen. Adolescent Girls in Approved Schools. *308 pp.*
Stratta, Erica. The Education of Borstal Boys. *A Study of their Educational Experiences prior to, and during Borstal Training. 256 pp.*

SOCIOLOGY OF CULTURE

Eppel, E. M., and M. Adolescents and Morality: *A Study of some Moral Values and Dilemmas of Working Adolescents in the Context of a changing Climate of Opinion. Foreword by W. J. H. Sprott. 268 pp. 39 tables.*
● **Fromm, Erich.** The Fear of Freedom. *286 pp.*
The Sane Society. *400 pp.*
Mannheim, Karl. Essays on the Sociology of Culture. *Edited by Ernst Mannheim in co-operation with Paul Kecskemeti. Editorial Note by Adolph Lowe. 280 pp.*
Weber, Alfred. Farewell to European History: *or The Conquest of Nihilism Translated from the German by R. F. C. Hull. 224 pp.*

SOCIOLOGY OF RELIGION

Argyle, Michael. Religious Behaviour. *224 pp. 8 figures. 41 tables.*
Nelson, G. K. Spiritualism and Society. *313 pp.*
Stark, Werner. The Sociology of Religion. *A Study of Christendom.*
Volume I. *Established Religion. 248 pp.*
Volume II. *Sectarian Religion. 368 pp.*
Volume III. *The Universal Church. 464 pp.*
Volume IV. *Types of Religious Man. 352 pp.*
Volume V. *Types of Religious Culture. 464 pp.*
Watt, W. Montgomery. Islam and the Integration of Society. *320 pp.*

SOCIOLOGY OF ART AND LITERATURE

Jarvie, Ian C. Towards a Sociology of the Cinema. *A Comparative Essay on the Structure and Functioning of a Major Entertainment Industry. 405 pp.*
Rust, Frances S. Dance in Society. *An Analysis of the Relationships between the Social Dance and Society in England from the Middle Ages to the Present Day. 256 pp. 8 pp. of plates.*
Schücking, L. L. The Sociology of Literary Taste. *112 pp.*

SOCIOLOGY OF KNOWLEDGE

Mannheim, Karl. Essays on the Sociology of Knowledge. *Edited by Paul Kecskemeti. Editorial Note by Adolph Lowe. 353 pp.*

Remmling, Gunter W. (Ed.). Towards the Sociology of Knowledge. *Origins and Development of a Sociological Thought Style.*

Stark, Werner. The Sociology of Knowledge: *An Essay in Aid of a Deeper Understanding of the History of Ideas. 384 pp.*

URBAN SOCIOLOGY

Ashworth, William. The Genesis of Modern British Town Planning: *A Study in Economic and Social History of the Nineteenth and Twentieth Centuries. 288 pp.*

Cullingworth, J. B. Housing Needs and Planning Policy: *A Restatement of the Problems of Housing Need and 'Overspill' in England and Wales. 232 pp. 44 tables. 8 maps.*

Dickinson, Robert E. City and Region: *A Geographical Interpretation. 608 pp. 125 figures.*

The West European City: *A Geographical Interpretation. 600 pp. 129 maps. 29 plates.*

● The City Region in Western Europe. *320 pp. Maps.*

Humphreys, Alexander J. New Dubliners: *Urbanization and the Irish Family. Foreword by George C. Homans. 304 pp.*

Jackson, Brian. Working Class Community: *Some General Notions raised by a Series of Studies in Northern England. 192 pp.*

Jennings, Hilda. Societies in the Making: *a Study of Development and Redevelopment within a County Borough. Foreword by D. A. Clark. 286 pp.*

● **Mann, P. H.** An Approach to Urban Sociology. *240 pp.*

Morris, R. N., and **Mogey, J.** The Sociology of Housing. *Studies at Berinsfield. 232 pp. 4 pp. plates.*

Rosser, C., and **Harris, C.** The Family and Social Change. *A Study of Family and Kinship in a South Wales Town. 352 pp. 8 maps.*

RURAL SOCIOLOGY

Chambers, R. J. H. Settlement Schemes in Tropical Africa: *A Selective Study. 268 pp.*

Haswell, M. R. The Economics of Development in Village India. *120 pp.*

Littlejohn, James. Westrigg: *the Sociology of a Cheviot Parish. 172 pp. 5 figures.*

Mayer, Adrian C. Peasants in the Pacific. *A Study of Fiji Indian Rural Society. 248 pp. 20 plates.*

Williams, W. M. The Sociology of an English Village: *Gosforth. 272 pp. 12 figures. 13 tables.*

SOCIOLOGY OF INDUSTRY AND DISTRIBUTION

Anderson, Nels. Work and Leisure. *280 pp.*
● **Blau, Peter M.,** and **Scott, W. Richard.** Formal Organizations: *a Comparative approach. Introduction and Additional Bibliography by J. H. Smith. 326 pp.*
Eldridge, J. E. T. Industrial Disputes. *Essays in the Sociology of Industrial Relations. 288 pp.*
Hetzler, Stanley. Applied Measures for Promoting Technological Growth. *352 pp.*
Technological Growth and Social Change. *Achieving Modernization. 269 pp.*
Hollowell, Peter G. The Lorry Driver. *272 pp.*
Jefferys, Margot, *with the assistance of Winifred Moss.* Mobility in the Labour Market: *Employment Changes in Battersea and Dagenham. Preface by Barbara Wootton. 186 pp. 51 tables.*
Millerson, Geoffrey. The Qualifying Associations: *a Study in Professionalization. 320 pp.*
Smelser, Neil J. Social Change in the Industrial Revolution: *An Application of Theory to the Lancashire Cotton Industry, 1770-1840. 468 pp. 12 figures. 14 tables.*
Williams, Gertrude. Recruitment to Skilled Trades. *240 pp.*
Young, A. F. Industrial Injuries Insurance: *an Examination of British Policy. 192 pp.*

DOCUMENTARY

Schlesinger, Rudolf (Ed.). Changing Attitudes in Soviet Russia.
2. The Nationalities Problem and Soviet Administration. *Selected Readings on the Development of Soviet Nationalities Policies. Introduced by the editor. Translated by W. W. Gottlieb. 324 pp.*

ANTHROPOLOGY

Ammar, Hamed. Growing up in an Egyptian Village: *Silwa, Province of Aswan. 336 pp.*
Brandel-Syrier, Mia. Reeftown Elite. *A Study of Social Mobility in a Modern African Community on the Reef. 376 pp.*
Crook, David, and **Isabel.** Revolution in a Chinese Village: *Ten Mile Inn. 230 pp. 8 plates. 1 map.*
Dickie-Clark, H. F. The Marginal Situation. *A Sociological Study of a Coloured Group. 236 pp.*
Dube, S. C. Indian Village. *Foreword by Morris Edward Opler. 276 pp. 4 plates.*
India's Changing Villages: *Human Factors in Community Development. 260 pp. 8 plates. 1 map.*

Firth, Raymond. Malay Fishermen. *Their Peasant Economy. 420 pp. 17 pp. plates.*

Gulliver, P. H. Social Control in an African Society: a Study of the Arusha, Agricultural Masai of Northern Tanganyika. *320 pp. 8 plates. 10 figures.*

Ishwaran, K. Shivapur. *A South Indian Village. 216 pp.*
Tradition and Economy in Village India: *An Interactionist Approach. Foreword by Conrad Arensburg. 176 pp.*

Jarvie, Ian C. The Revolution in Anthropology. *268 pp.*

Jarvie, Ian C., and **Agassi, Joseph.** Hong Kong. *A Society in Transition. 396 pp. Illustrated with plates and maps.*

Little, Kenneth L. Mende of Sierra Leone. *308 pp. and folder.*
Negroes in Britain. *With a New Introduction and Contemporary Study by Leonard Bloom. 320 pp.*

Lowie, Robert H. Social Organization. *494 pp.*

Mayer, Adrian C. Caste and Kinship in Central India: *A Village and its Region. 328 pp. 16 plates. 15 figures. 16 tables.*

Smith, Raymond T. The Negro Family in British Guiana: *Family Structure and Social Status in the Villages. With a Foreword by Meyer Fortes. 314 pp. 8 plates. 1 figure. 4 maps.*

SOCIOLOGY AND PHILOSOPHY

Barnsley, John H. The Social Reality of Ethics. *A Comparative Analysis of Moral Codes. 448 pp.*

Diesing, Paul. Patterns of Discovery in the Social Sciences. *362 pp.*

Douglas, Jack D. (Ed.). Understanding Everyday Life. *Toward the Reconstruction of Sociological Knowledge. Contributions by Alan F. Blum. Aaron W. Cicourel, Norman K. Denzin, Jack D. Douglas, John Heeren, Peter McHugh, Peter K. Manning, Melvin Power, Matthew Speier, Roy Turner, D. Lawrence Wieder, Thomas P. Wilson and Don H. Zimmerman. 370 pp.*

Jarvie, Ian C. Concepts and Society. *216 pp.*

Roche, Maurice. Phenomenology, Language and the Social Sciences. *About 400 pp.*

Sahay, Arun. Sociological Analysis.

Sklair, Leslie. The Sociology of Progress. *320 pp.*

International Library of Anthropology
General Editor Adam Kuper

Brown, Paula. The Chimbu. *A Study of Change in the New Guinea Highlands.*
Van Den Berghe, Pierre L. Power and Privilege at an African University.

International Library of Social Policy

General Editor Kathleen Jones

Holman, Robert. Trading in Children. *A Study of Private Fostering.*
Jones, Kathleen. History of the Mental Health Services. *428 pp.*
Thomas, J. E. The English Prison Officer since 1850: *A Study in Conflict. 258 pp.*

Primary Socialization, Language and Education

General Editor Basil Bernstein

Bernstein, Basil. Class, Codes and Control. *2 volumes.*
  1. *Theoretical Studies Towards a Sociology of Language. 254 pp.*
  2. *Applied Studies Towards a Sociology of Language. About 400 pp.*
Brandis, Walter, and **Henderson, Dorothy.** Social Class, Language and Communication. *288 pp.*
Cook-Gumperz, Jenny. Social Control and Socialization. *A Study of Class Differences in the Language of Maternal Control.*
Gahagan, D. M., and **G. A.** Talk Reform. *Exploration in Language for Infant School Children. 160 pp.*
Robinson, W. P., and **Rackstraw, Susan, D. A.** A Question of Answers. *2 volumes. 192 pp. and 180 pp.*
Turner, Geoffrey, J., and **Mohan, Bernard, A.** A Linguistic Description and Computer Programme for Children's Speech. *208 pp.*

Reports of the Institute of Community Studies

Cartwright, Ann. Human Relations and Hospital Care. *272 pp.*
  Parents and Family Planning Services. *306 pp.*
  Patients and their Doctors. *A Study of General Practice. 304 pp.*
● **Jackson, Brian.** Streaming: *an Education System in Miniature. 168 pp.*
Jackson, Brian, and **Marsden, Dennis.** Education and the Working Class: *Some General Themes raised by a Study of 88 Working-class Children in a Northern Industrial City. 268 pp. 2 folders.*
Marris, Peter. The Experience of Higher Education. *232 pp. 27 tables.*
Marris, Peter, and **Rein, Martin.** Dilemmas of Social Reform. *Poverty and Community Action in the United States. 256 pp.*
Marris, Peter, and **Somerset, Anthony.** African Businessmen. *A Study of Entrepreneurship and Development in Kenya. 256 pp.*
Mills, Richard. Young Outsiders: *a Study in Alternative Communities.*

Runciman, W. G. Relative Deprivation and Social Justice. *A Study of Attitudes to Social Inequality in Twentieth Century England. 352 pp.*

Townsend, Peter. The Family Life of Old People: *An Inquiry in East London. Foreword by J. H. Sheldon. 300 pp. 3 figures. 63 tables.*

Willmott, Peter. Adolescent Boys in East London. *230 pp.*
The Evolution of a Community: *a study of Dagenham after forty years. 168 pp. 2 maps.*

Willmott, Peter, and **Young, Michael.** Family and Class in a London Suburb. *202 pp. 47 tables.*

Young, Michael. Innovation and Research in Education. *192 pp.*

● **Young, Michael,** and **McGeeney, Patrick.** Learning Begins at Home. *A Study of a Junior School and its Parents. 128 pp.*

Young, Michael, and **Willmott, Peter.** Family and Kinship in East London. *Foreword by Richard M. Titmuss. 252 pp. 39 tables.*
The Symmetrical Family.

Reports of the Institute for Social Studies in Medical Care

Cartwright, Ann, Hockey, Lisbeth, and **Anderson, John L.** Life Before Death.

Dunnell, Karen, and **Cartwright, Ann.** Medicine Takers, Prescribers and Hoarders. *190 pp.*

Medicine, Illness and Society
General Editor   W. M. Williams

Robinson, David. The Process of Becoming Ill.

Stacey, Margaret. *et al.* Hospitals, Children and Their Families. *The Report of a Pilot Study. 202 pp.*

Monographs in Social Theory
General Editor   Arthur Brittan

Bauman, Zygmunt. Culture as Praxis.

Dixon, Keith. Sociological Theory. *Pretence and Possibility.*

Smith, Anthony D. The Concept of Social Change. *A Critique of the Functionalist Theory of Social Change.*

Routledge Social Science Journals

The British Journal of Sociology. *Edited by Terence P. Morris. Vol. 1, No. 1, March 1950 and Quarterly. Roy. 8vo. Back numbers available. An international journal with articles on all aspects of sociology.*

Economy and Society. *Vol. 1, No. 1. February 1972 and Quarterly. Metric Roy. 8vo. A journal for all social scientists covering sociology, philosophy, anthropology, economics and history. Back numbers available.*

Year Book of Social Policy in Britain, The. *Edited by Kathleen Jones. 1971. Published Annually.*

Printed in Great Britain by Lewis Reprints Limited
Brown Knight & Truscott Group, London and Tonbridge   1373